JULIAN V. STECHISHIN

A HISTORY
OF UKRAINIAN SETTLEMENT
IN CANADA

Translation by Isidore Goresky
Edited by David Lupul

UKRAINIAN SELF—RELIANCE LEAGUE OF CANADA
Saskatoon 1992

Julian V. Stechishin
1895-1971

© Ukrainian Self-Reliance League of Canada
Saskatoon 1992
Typesetting by *Multilingual on Whyte,* Edmonton
Printed in Canada by Trident Press Ltd., Winnipeg

Canadian Cataloguing in Publication Data

Stechishin, Julian V., 1895-1971
A History of Ukrainian Settlement in Canada

ISBN: 0-921545-00-2

1. Ukrainians in Canada - History

FOREWORD

The publication of Julian Stechishin's **History of Ukrainian Settlement in Canada** represents one of the major projects undertaken by the Ukrainian Self-Reliance League of Canada (USRL). The original volume in the Ukrainian language was published in 1971. This English text, also initiated by the USRL, was translated by Isidore Goresky and edited by David Lupul. It was prepared for publication in 1992 to commemorate the Centennial of Ukrainian Settlement in Canada.

ACKNOWLEDGEMENTS

Financial assistance for this publication from the SUS Foundation of the Ukrainian Self-Reliance League of Canada and the Ukrainian Canadian Foundation of Taras Shevchenko of the Ukrainian Canadian Congress is gratefully acknowledged.

Editorial assistance in the final preparation of this English text has been provided by the Publication Committee (1988-1992) as follows: Dr. Peter A. Kondra, Dr. Roman Yereniuk, Dr. Oleh Gerus, Geraldine Russin, Andrew Melnychuk, Yaroslaw Skrypnyk, Mary Tkachuk and Stefan Franko.

THE UKRAINIAN SELF-RELIANCE LEAGUE OF CANADA (USRL/CYC)

The USRL organization has its roots in the period of the first immigration from Ukraine to Canada from 1891-1914. These pioneer immigrants settled in the parkland areas of western Canada. To survive in the rugged, isolated farm environment and develop their family life, they relied on their own personal and heritage resources. On the one hand, they cleared the bush, built their homes and grew crops to feed their families. On the other hand, they also fostered their heritage language, arts and religion to satisfy their human needs. While establishing an economic, spiritual and social framework in the freedom of their new society, the pioneers also raised the national pride and consciousness of their community. They became known as nationalists or *Narodovtsi*. The trend toward assimilation of immigrants, popular at that time was, therefore, vigorously opposed.

A catalyst in the flowering of a Ukrainian national identity was the establishment, in the prairie provinces, of schools for training bilingual English/Ukrainian teachers. The first such school was founded in Winnipeg in 1906. The Ukrainian Teachers' Association of Canada was founded in Manitoba in 1907. The graduates of the bilingual schools became the educated leaders of the Ukrainian community in Canada. They led the movement which defined a Ukrainian national identity within the framework of Canadian democracy.

The first Ukrainian weekly newspaper, the *Ukrainian Voice*, was established by the immigrant leaders in 1910. Its purpose was to communicate with the Ukrainian community throughout the prairie settlements and to disseminate Ukrainian language and culture. It serves the community to this day in advocating the development of cultural heritage and material resources.

The self-reliant ideology of the Narodovtsi spurred the establishment of institutions which enhanced the retention and nurturing of Ukrainian traditions. Student residences, known as Institutes or *bursy*, were the first such institutions established. They included Petro Mohyla Institute in Saskatoon, 1916, with a branch in Winnipeg and Mykhailo Hrushevsky Institute in Edmonton, 1918, today St. John's Institute. In 1962, St. Vladimir Institute was founded in Toronto. The Institutes served as a home away from home for rural students pursuing higher education. The students were provided with inexpensive lodging, fellowship and opportunities to study Ukrainian language, history, literature, music and theatre arts. For the past 75 years, the Institutes have graduated several generations of leaders in the Canadian Ukrainian community.

The *Narodovtsi* leaders organized the autonomous Ukrainian Orthodox Church of Canada in 1918. Drawing on their spiritual heritage in Ukraine, they established a Seminary and organized hundreds of congregations throughout Canada. St. Andrew's College was established in Winnipeg in 1946 as the theological college of the Ukrainian Orthodox Church of Canada. It later moved to the campus of the University of Manitoba in 1964. The college affiliated with the University of Manitoba in 1981 and established the Centre for Ukrainian Canadian Studies.

From 1918 to 1927, the Ukrainian nationalist movement maintained its cohesion through the "Ukrainian Voice" newspaper, the church parishes and annual conventions. A need to unite community activities and institutions which would facilitate cultural development led to the founding of an umbrella organization. The Ukrainian Self-Reliance League of Canada was formally organized in Saskatoon in 1927 to meet this need. Initial organizations included: the Ukrainian Women's Association of Canada (CYK), actually initiated in 1926, the Canadian Ukrainian Youth Association (CYMK), 1931, and the men's section, later named the Ukrainian Self-Reliance Association of Canada(TYC). The USRL also includes the Institutes named above, the Ukrainian Museum of Canada, established in 1936, the Federation of Ukrainian National Homes and the SUS Foundation.

The ideology of the USRL was established in the early years of development. It is based on the principles of Self-Respect, Self—Help and Self—Reliance and signifies a pride in Ukrainian heritage coupled with independent thought and action. The USRL members participated fully in Canada's development while steadfastly maintaining their culture and traditions. The original mandate to coordinate and guide the development and dissemination of the Ukrainian heritage in Canada was strengthened by the formalization, in 1971, of Canada as a multicultural society.

Ukrainian nationalism and Canadian patriotism are complementary cornerstones of the USRL ideology. These guiding principles have helped to influence the re-kindling of democracy in the Ukrainian homeland. The ideals espoused by the early Ukrainian pioneer *Narodovtsi* of the Ukrainian Self-Reliance League of Canada have multiplied to nurture several generations in Canada. Having come full circle, the *Narodovtsi* leaders of today, in addition to participating fully in the development of multicultural Canada, are now also in a position to assist in the development of democratic freedom in Ukraine.

Contents

Translator's Notes

This translation was undertaken to acquaint the English-speaking world with the story of Ukrainian settlement in Canada, a field ably researched by the late Dr. V. J. Kaye and continued by the author of this history. The late Julian Stechishin's research added not only additional information on the early settlement of Ukrainians in Canada, but also sought to set that information in its proper perspective. This explains why he dealt with historical events, both in Ukraine and in Canada, preceding the period of mass immigration to Canada. The translation was an activity which extended over a period of six years owing to difficulties which followed the unfortunate death of the author in the midst of his research. Not only was there a delay in the production of materials, but I was also left without any clues in regard to many sources from which information had been obtained. Mrs. Savelia Stechishin's help during this period is gratefully acknowledged. Among others who aided me with advice and in my search for essential documents and early accounts of settlers and officials, sincere thanks are also due especially to Mr. John Hawrylko of Redwater, who read the translation and suggested many changes, and to my grandson, Mr. David Lupul, for editing it in its final form.

In transcribing names, a totally linguistic approach, as adopted by some writers, has been avoided because of the realization that the translation should appeal not only to the scholar, but also to the general reader. Following, is a list of letters as they were written in Austria-Hungary at the time of settlement, their pronunciation in English and the forms finally adopted to represent the pronunciation. Both the form of the name adopted and its Austrian equivalent are given in the index to give the reader some insight into the changes that must have taken place in these names. It must also be understood that the Austrian form of the name was not the original Ukrainian form according to the Cyrillic alphabet but an approximation of the pronunciation. For this reason, members of the same family often adopted different ways of writing the same name after they came to Canada.

Austrian Form	How Pronounced	Final Adoption
cz	ch	ch
sz	sh	sh
ch	as ch in Loch	kh
j	y	y
y	e	y
c	ts	ts
w	v at the beginning of a syllable	v at the beginning of a syllable
	w at the end of a syllable	w at the end of a syllable

(Because of the above use of y, it should be pronounced as e within a syllable and as y at the beginning or end of a syllable).

In closing I must pay tribute to my wife who has been understanding throughout and has made it possible for me to concentrate on the translation by undertaking many duties which would have naturally fallen to my lot.

Isidore Goresky

Foreword

The author of this history, the late Julian Stechishin, planned to write a well-documented history of Ukrainians in Canada with a critical interpretation of their socio-cultural development, including an account of church problems and denominational activities. He had witnessed many of the events included in this history and, in many cases, had participated in them. Having a particular interest in history, he zealously collected source materials about the life of Ukrainians in Canada and thoroughly researched these materials in his quest for historical truth. In his research he was always alert to the discovery of new historical information which sometimes reveals itself incidentally in the research process.

As an active community leader, Julian Stechishin visited Ukrainian colonies throughout Canada and had a wide circle of friends among Ukrainian pioneers. He met them on special occasions, recorded their experiences, and was particularly interested in collecting memoirs of former teachers and community leaders from the early period of Ukrainian settlement in Canada. In addition, he had accumulated a large collection of materials on the church question, in which he had a particular interest. This collection includes some rare documents. He also left an unfinished manuscript dealing with church history.

His unexpected death on February 24, 1971, caught Julian Stechishin in the busiest period of his life. He was thus not able to realize his dreams. He completed only a portion, the first volume, of his envisioned task. He had planned to expand some of the chapters of his written account by the addition of new materials, but was unable to do so in time. All of this rich source material, which he collected over the years, remains unexploited and awaits an editor. He has also left much in manuscript form which needs to be organized and edited.

I must add that Julian Stechishin was particularly grateful to Mr. Alexander Royick for his research and other services in 1969 dealing with the period prior to the beginning of mass immigration into Canada.

After Julian's death, it became my task to edit his manuscript, retype most of the chapters, check further certain sections, and fill gaps in others which the author had intended to finish before he became ill. It was also necessary to organize the bibliography and to locate suitable illustrations.

I am greatly thankful to everyone who aided me in bringing this task to completion. My gratitude is extended particularly to the Reverend Dr. Hryhory Udod for the author's biography, for editing the story with respect to both form and language, and for his constructive criticism. In this respect my thanks also is extended to Mr. Alexander Royick for his editorship of one of the chapters. For the preparation of maps of the Ukrainian settlement, I am grateful to Prof. A. Michalenko.

Savelia Stechishin

Julian Vasyliovych Stechishin

Julian Vasyliovych Stechishin was born on June 30, 1895, in the village of Hleshava, county of Terebowlia, in the Ukrainian province of Galicia* (then part of Austria). He was a member of a large family in which there were two children from his father's first marriage and seven from the second marriage. His father, Vasyl, was not a wealthy villager but, thanks to his native ability and his military service in the Austrian army, he could converse in five languages. As a result of this ability and because of the fact that he was literate, he was regarded with deep respect by his fellow villagers.

Beginning in 1890, Vasyl Stechishin became mayor of Hleshava and held this position until his tragic death during a fire in the village in 1900. Although he did not leave his family much in material possessions, he left them a much more valuable heritage which revealed itself in their thirst for knowledge, a burning desire for self-improvement, their keen sense of responsibility in public affairs, and a deep regard for the integrity of individuals as members of the human family.

After their father's death, responsibility for the children's future rested entirely upon their mother's shoulders. Julian attended elementary school in his native village but did not complete this phase of his education because he refused to attend a school with a Polish teacher. However, he overcame this deficiency by borrowing books from the library of the local priest, Father Petro Yezersky, from whom he also imbibed his ardent Ukrainian patriotism.

In 1910, fifteen-year-old Julian followed his older brothers, Myroslaw and Mykhailo, who had left for Canada somewhat earlier to seek a better destiny. For a year he studied the English language while working in a newspaper office where his brother was the editor. By 1911 he had made

---

*Galicia is the English name for the province which is known in Ukrainian as Halychyna. (Ed.)

such good progress in English that he began to attend the English School for Foreigners in Brandon. He continued in this school until 1915, when he obtained a teacher's diploma. He spent the next three years teaching in several schools in Manitoba and Saskatchewan but did not neglect his own education. After completing high school, he enrolled in the University of Saskatchewan in 1917 and obtained his B.A. in 1921. As a student he lived in the Petro Mohyla Institute in Saskatoon, where he took an active interest in student, civic, and religious activities. Coinciding with the period of his attendance at the university came the rebirth of the Ukrainian Orthodox Church in Canada, a religious movement in which Julian, his brother, Mykhailo, and others were active participants. While he was a student, Julian was often called to assume the duties of the rector of the P. Mohyla Institute, and was finally appointed to that position in 1921. During his regime, the Institute became a very progressive educational institution among Ukrainians in Canada. It became a hearthstone of Ukrainian national and Orthodox Christian education. To the Institute, under Julian's leadership, belongs the credit for broadcasting throughout Canada the conception of the rebirth of the Ukrainian Orthodox Church and the ideology of the Ukrainian Self-Reliance League. A large number of Ukrainian people of Canada were carried away by the appeal of this ideology.

In 1921, Julian Stechishin married a student of the Institute, Savelia Wawryniuk, who was not only a worthy helpmate but also a partner of his many and varied activities in the educational, civic, and religious fields. They had three children: Anatoly, Myron, and Zenia, all of whom were brought up to become good Ukrainian Canadian Christians.

Beginning of 1929, Julian enrolled in the Faculty of Law at the University of Saskatchewan and obtained his L.L.B. degree in 1931. After his graduation, he was again appointed to the rectorship of the Institute. In 1934, he began to practise law and continued in this career until his death. However, his law practice never absorbed all of his energy. His greatest aim in life was service to his people—a service which he performed in many fields: religious, civic, academic, and educational.

As a student, he was an active organizer of the "Kameniari" (Stonemasons) organization and associate editor of the student journal, *Kameniari*. He was the author of many educational and, more broadly, cultural articles pertaining to issues of concern to the Ukrainian community. He also revealed another of his many talents when he became the director of the church choir and a public chorus. In 1922, as a result of his teaching and directing, the first Holy Liturgy in the Ukrainian language was solemnized in the Ukrainian Orthodox Church in Saskatoon, where Julian was a cantor-director.

During the period of the organization of the Ukrainian Orthodox

Church, Julian wrote many articles in the press in its defence, delivered hundreds of lectures on many aspects of Ukrainian national and religious life, and directed the organization of national and education institutions. During the Second World War, he was prominent in the organization of the Ukrainian Canadian Committee. In the Saskatoon branch of that organization, he was president for many years and later became its honorary president.

His service among Ukrainians in the religious field was no less important. Beginning in 1921, he served for many years as secretary of the Ukrainian Orthodox Brotherhood, a position which carried with it the whole burden of organizing the Church and its parishes. From 1951, until his death, he remained a member of the Consistory of the Ukrainian Orthodox Church of Canada, defending constantly the basic principles underlying its existence and activities.

However, it is perhaps in the educational field that Julian Stechishin performed his greatest service to the Ukrainian public in Canada. A pioneering achievement was the preparation of his well-known *Ukrainian Grammar* for the use of English-speaking students, a book which has been widely accepted in high schools and higher educational institutions in Canada and the United States. Another outstanding historical production was the *Jubilee Volume of the Petro Mohyla Institute in Saskatoon*, the first history of its kind about Ukrainian organizational life in Canada.

His third accomplishment in the cultural field was this book, the *History of Ukrainians in Canada*, on which he laboured to the end of his life and for which he collected many basic source materials. Unfortunately, his sudden death on February 24, 1971, did not give him time to profit fully from these collected materials. Nevertheless, that which has been written will occupy an important place in the treasure-house of Ukrainian learning, both in Canada and abroad.

Summing up the great, self-sacrificing, and fruitful career of Julian Stechishin, Professor C. H. Andrusyshen said the following: "His life was a blessing to Ukrainians in this country." It is hardly possible to appraise more effectively the life and services of Julian Stechishin, author of this *History of Ukrainians in Canada*, than do the words of this learned academician and founder of the Department of Slavics at the University of Saskatchewan.

Very Rev. Dr. Hryhory Udod

1

An Overview of the History of the Ukrainian People

The Kievan Rus State

Ukrainians constituted one of the earliest Slavic peoples in eastern Europe and have continuously occupied the territory north of the Black Sea along the Dniester and Dnieper rivers. The ancient name of Ukraine was Rus (not Russia) and its capital was Kiev, the oldest city in eastern Europe. Kiev was a centre of trade between north and south,[1] as well as between western Europe and the Far East. It was a crossroads of trade routes extending from the Baltic to the Black Sea and further southward to Greece—or, as it was commonly referred to—"from Scandinavia to Byzantium". Kiev was also the trading centre between western Europe and the East, by way of the two rivers, Prypiat and Buh. In addition, a land route extended from western Europe across Ukraine to the Caspian Sea, India, and China.

The beginnings of the Rus state date back to antiquity. Historians estimate that it originated in the sixth century A.D. but to us it is more important that it developed virtually into an empire during the reign of Prince Oleh (879-914), a contemporary of King Alfred of England, who began the organization of the English state. Copies of written treaties between Rus and Byzantium, dating from 907 and 914, are still in existence. Prince Volodymyr the Great (972-1015) extended the boundaries of Rus to include all of the eastern Slavic tribes. To safeguard commerce, he extended his dominion even beyond these boundaries (see map of Rus in the tenth and eleventh centuries). Its territory stretched from the Black Sea in the south to the Baltic in the north, and from the Buh and Sian rivers in the west to the western channel of the Volga River in the east. The sources of the Volga and

Oka rivers were also under his dominion. The Rus state had the largest territory of any European state at that time.

In 988 Volodymyr the Great introduced Christianity into his realm from Byzantium, and married Anne, the sister of the Byzantine emperor, Basil II. He established close contact with the Byzantine Empire, which was then considered to be the most advanced state in the world. In assessing the results of the introduction of Christianity into Rus, the Ukrainian historian, Ivan Krypiakevych, draws the following conclusions:

> After the introduction of Christianity into Ukraine many Greek priests, teachers, merchants, and tradesmen followed. They remained in constant contact with Byzantium. Greek culture, of which Ukrainians had had some previous knowledge, now penetrated all parts of Rus very rapidly. Its religion and church rites were Greek, as were its schools, literature, and the arts. Beginning with this period, the so-called Byzantine style dominated architecture for centuries; painting and sculpture also retained their Greek influence. Byzantine culture occupied a dominant position as Constantinople still perpetuated the traditions of ancient Rome. Ukraine inherited its culture from a primary source, thus maintaining a close connection with the ancient world. Its civilization of that period was comparable to the contemporary German civilization and was certainly superior to that of the western Slavs, the Czechs, and the Poles.[2]

After the death of Volodymyr the Great, his son, Yaroslav the Wise (1019-1054), became the ruler of this vast principality. During his reign he consolidated his empire and heightened its glory. He introduced jurisprudence and codified customary laws into what is known as the *Ruska Pravda,* by which order was established in the courts and in government. The *Ruska Pravda* was in force not only during Yaroslav's reign but was retained as a source of law and court procedure for centuries afterward, even by the Lithuanians after they conquered a portion of Ukraine. Yaroslav's codification of the laws preceded that which occurred in England, where King John grudgingly conceded some civil rights and privileges during this same period, but only under compulsion from the barons led by Simon de Montfort (Magna Charta of 1215).

According to one chronicler, Yaroslav the Wise became famous because "he was diligent in his attention to books which he read by day and by night", and exerted much effort to spread literacy among his people. The Ukrainian historian, Hrushevsky, reports that Prince Yaroslav "maintained friendly relations and alliances with many crowned heads and became one of the most powerful rulers in Europe at that time."[3] Yaroslav married Ingigard, the daughter of the Swedish King Olaf; three of his sons married into ruling families in Germany. In 1044, one of his daughters, Elizabeth, married the Norwegian prince, Harold Haardrada, who later became king of Norway and tried to conquer England but was slain at the battle of Stamford Bridge in 1066. Another daughter, Anastasia, was married to Andrew, king of Hungary, in 1046. A third daughter, Anna, married Henry I, king of France, in 1051. The story of Anna is interesting because she became regent during her son's minority (the future Philip I), after the death of her husband in 1060. She was the first woman in French history to hold such a position and signed various documents as "Anna Raina". The historian Natalia Polonska-Vasylenko asserts that "on various documents her signature in Cyrillic-Slavonic or Latin can still be seen, but instead of signatures, her name is framed by the crosses of illiterate French barons, powerful vassals of the French throne."[4]

Yaroslav's son, Vsevolod I (1079-1093), maintained similar relations with the rulers of various European states. One of his daughters was married to the emperor of the Holy Roman Empire, Henry IV. His son, Volodymyr, known as Volodymyr Monomakh (1113-1125), married Gyda, the daughter of the English king, Harold II, who fought against William of Normandy and died in the battle of Hastings in 1066. Accordingly, Debrett's publication on British peerage, in its 1966 edition, lists the reigning queen, Elizabeth II, as a lineal descendant thirty-one times removed from Volodymyr Monomakh and Harold II.[5] These familial alliances of the Kievan princes with the crowned heads of Europe unquestionably attest to the power and importance of the Kievan state and the high cultural status of its ruling members.[6]

Decline of Rus

But the Kievan state did not endure for long, despite its power and a level of wealth which had Europe marvelling at its riches. Although the Kievan state was composed mainly of eastern Slavic tribes who could have been united by a shrewd and vigorous central government and a homogeneous culture—especially as they already adhered to a common church—such unity did not develop. The scattered tribes lived and developed under different geographical, economic, and ethnocultural conditions. For this reason, they shied away from central authority and supported local princes whenever weaknesses in central authority became apparent. During the period that Rus remained powerful and controlled trade along the Dnieper, from which all the tribes benefited, their ethnocultural tendencies to withdraw from the control of central authority remained weak. But when Asiatic hordes, such as the Cumans, subjugated the lower reaches of the Dnieper along the Black Sea and trade declined, with a corresponding decline in economic benefits, the tendency of these Slavic tribes to alienate themselves from the central government increased.[7]

Although Prince Yaroslav contributed to the alienation of these tribes —abetting the tendency to create new states which led to anarchy and the decline of Rus—most great states in Europe also had internal crises during this period. Byzantium was experiencing internal disorder; Germany was entering a period of disruption; and France was in the process of recovering from exhaustion as the result of struggles between various pretenders to the throne. Although the feudal system prevailed in France and Germany and vassals swore fealty to their lords, who also had papal sanction, the vassals still rebelled and waged war against their lords. But in Rus there was no feudal system. Since the princely inheritors did not swear allegiance to the Grand Prince of Kiev, they were morally but not legally bound to him. As a result, there was even less impediment to the fostering of rebellion by subject princes against the Grand Prince of Kiev than in the comparable situations elsewhere in Europe. In spite of this, Yaroslav the Wise still divided his empire among his sons as appanage princes, each of whom had only a moral obligation of fealty to the Grand Prince.

This system of dynastic succession soon proved to be very destructive because Rus was broken up into a number of small and weak principalities. Moreover, each prince sought the throne of the senior prince in Kiev. To reach that pedestal he had to embark on war in which he enlisted the aid of other dissatisfied princes or neighbours: Poles, Hungarians, Lithuanians, and even Asiatic hordes such as the Polovtsi. Also known as Kipchaks or Cumans, the Polovtsi were a Turkish nomadic tribe from Asia which broke into the Ukrainian steppe in the second half of the eleventh century, about 1061. As a nomadic tribe, their chief occupation was cattle raising and raiding for plunder. They made incessant attacks to plunder and devastate Rus territory, chiefly the dominions of Pereiaslav and Kiev, and to take people into captivity. Kievan princes, including Volodymyr Monomakh (1113-1125) and Mstyslav (1167-1169), attempted to unite the appanage princes against this horde and actually achieved peace for a period. The wars with the Polovtsi did nothing to strengthen the Kievan state and contributed to its collapse.

Origin of the Russian People

While the princes of southern Rus conducted their struggle against the Polovtsi and amongst themselves, another power, partly of their own lineage, was rising in the north. On the upper reaches of the Volga and the Oka rivers, in territory which was not Slavic but had been united with the Rus state by conquest, lived Finnish tribes: the Viesy, Mery, Muromy, and Mordoviany. According to Krypiakevych these people were "pagan with a primitive culture."[8] South-east of these Finnish tribes lived the eastern

Slavic tribes, the Viatychi and the Kryvychi, and north-east were the Sloveny. Advancing to the east among the Finns, the Slavs intermingled with them and introduced Christianity. As they accepted Christianity, the Finnish tribes lost their identity and gradually merged with the Slavs, creating "a new branch of Slavic-Rus lands: Suzdal, Volodymyr on the Kliasma, and much later Moscow, all of which constituted the future Muscovite nation."[9]

These Suzdalian or Muscovite people differed considerably from the Antian Slavs of Kiev, Pereiaslav, and the other Slavs who created the Rus state. They differed not only in their physical and spiritual qualities; they also differed in their concepts in regard to Christianity and the organization of the state. Though their territory was incorporated in Kievan Rus, the Muscovites always manifested a reluctance to accept the union and accepted dominion under the Khazars until the Rus princes destroyed the Khazar nation in 967. The Rus princes were forced to send expeditions repeatedly to curb the Muscovites. When the Polovtsi appeared on the steppes of southern Rus and the princes were compelled to wage war against them, the Muscovites adopted the Polovtsi as their closest allies.

A Suzdalian prince, Yuriy Dolgoruky, married a Polovtsian princess. When Kiev became exhausted by endless wars, Yuriy Dolgoruky captured the city and occupied the throne. After his death in 1157, however, the Kievans slaughtered all the Suzdalians whom Yuriy had appointed to direct the administration of the state because, according to Kostomariv, "the Kievans regarded Prince Yuriy as a foreign conqueror."[10]

Yuriy's son, Andrei Bogoliubsky, revealed his intentions more clearly. He resolved to build his state in the north and to conquer not only the neighbouring tribes but also Rus. Accordingly, he advanced on Kiev in 1169 and devastated it mercilessly. In describing this capture Krypiakevych reports as follows:

> "Andrei Bogoliubsky assaulted Kiev and devastated it savagely, pillaging all costly articles to remove them to the Muscovite realm. The assault and devastation were conceived and planned with the deliberate aim of destroying this ancient base of culture to gain an advantage for the northern Muscovite lands over the southern Ukrainian state. Following this event, Kiev never regained its former power."[11]

After destroying Kiev, Andrei returned to his capital, Volodymyr on the Kliasma, leaving his brother Hlib in Kiev. But Hlib did not last very long. As princely wars for the Kiev throne continued, the city passed from hand to hand, often with the help of Polovtsian forces. Appeals to the appanage princes to unite against the Polovtsi did not achieve much success because the Rus state was beginning to separate into three nations: in the north-east, into the Muscovite nation; in the north-west, into the Bielorussian nation; and in the south, it was becoming Ukrainian.

From the struggle against the Polovtsi, there remain two memorable accounts of this important period in the history of the Ukrainian nation:

(1)   In 1185, Prince Ihor of Novhorod-Siversky and his brother, Vsevolod, took the field in a campaign against the Polovtsi but their forces were routed and Ihor was taken prisoner. This battle was described by an eye-witness in a knightly-heroic epic poem known as the *Slovo o polku Ihora* (The tale of Ihor's host). It is considered a priceless and rare literary creation—a precious pearl and adornment not only of the princely era of Rus-Ukraine, but also a creation unequalled in the medieval poetry of European literature,[12] comparable to the French *Song of Roland* of the eleventh century, the German *Nibelungenlied* from the end of the twelfth century, and Chaucer's "Canterbury Tales" of the fourteenth century.[13] This heroic epic of Rus-Ukraine of the princely era was imitated both in Pskov and Suzdal and in this way the Muscovite story *Zadonshchyna* was also produced in the fourteenth and fifteenth centuries, but these imitations and variations are all inferior in quality.[14]

(2)   Ihor's campaign against the Polovtsi is also recorded in the Hypatian Chronicles where the word "Ukraina" instead of "Rus" is used for the first time. Some scholars conclude that the Ukrainian people already used the terms "Ukraina" or "Rus" synonymously to describe their land in the second half of the twelfth century, if not earlier.[15]

The Tartar Onslaught and the Perpetuation of the Traditions of Kievan Rus in Volhyn and Galicia

Although the Kievan principality declined, the tradition of Rus, or rather Rus-Ukraine, lived on in Galicia and Volhyn until 1340, or 170 years after Kiev was stormed and pillaged by Andrei Bogoliubsky in 1169. The prince of Halych, Yaroslaw Osmomysl (1152-1187), had expanded his principality into a powerful state, having extended its boundaries to the south-east into Podilia and Moldavia, as far as the mouth of the Danube.[16] At this point his successor founded the city of Little Halych (now known as Galatz). The prince of Volhyn, Roman the Great (1199-1205), united Volhyn with Galicia and acquired many other Ukrainian principalities while his son Danylo (1205-1264) became king in 1253 and added Kiev to his Galician-Volhynian state.

At the same time that Danylo was expanding and consolidating his state, a new enemy—the Tartars—appeared. They were a Mongolian horde under the command of Khan Batu, a grandson of the terrible Genghis Khan. In their campaign toward the west, the Tartar forces first destroyed the Polovtsian realm and then turned north to conquer the Suzdal-Muscovite lands before invading Ukraine in 1240. After conquering the principalities of Chernihiv and Pereiaslav, they stormed and savagely destroyed Kiev, Volodymyr, and Halych in turn, before proceeding west against Poland, Hungary, Serbia, and Bulgaria.

No matter how savage the Tartars were in their conquest of new territory and in crushing all opposition, they did not interfere in internal political or religious affairs after their conquest. It should also be pointed out that they did not destroy the Christian churches. They respected alien faiths, claiming that, "All faiths lead to God. As fingers on one hand are all equally useful to man, so are all faiths, even though they vary, equal in the sight of God."[17]

The Tartars were content if the princes of the territories they conquered continued to pay homage and accepted responsibility for collecting tribute from their own people. Beyond this, the princes could carry on their own affairs and even wage war among themselves or against their neighbours. In Danylo's case this meant war against Poles, Magyars, or Lithuanians. Thus King Danylo was still able to extend his principality from Kiev to the Wisla River and to conquer Bielorussian and Lithuanian tribes in the north, although he acknowledged the suzerainty of the Tartar Khan. Furthermore, after arranging a marriage in 1252 between his son, Roman, and Gertrude, the heiress to the Austrian throne, he dispatched Roman to Vienna with an army in an unsuccessful attempt to gain possession of the Austrian throne.[18] Another of his sons, Lev (1264-1301), added Transcarpathian Ukraine to his kingdom and thus extended its boundaries further than they had ever been in the history of the Galician-Volhynian state. Its boundaries "remained undisturbed for almost a hundred years,"[19] and it was "the most powerful nation of contemporary eastern Europe."[20]

But this state also ceased to exist. In the first half of the fourteenth century—actually in 1340—this dynasty which had produced such powerful rulers as Roman, Danylo, Lev, and Yuriy I, came to an abrupt end with the death of Yuriy II, who left no heirs. Weakened by the boyar oligarchy in their efforts to limit the king's power and harrassed by the neighbouring rulers of Poland, Hungary, and Lithuania who coveted the territory, their successors were unable to maintain themselves in power and the kingdom was dismembered. Transcarpathia remained with Hungary, Galicia was occupied by Poland, and Volhyn and the Dnieper lands became part of Lithuania.

The Significance and Characteristics of
the Galician-Volhynian State

Although the Galician-Volhynian state did not endure and was dismembered, it still played an important role in the history of the Ukrainian people. In the first place, it consisted of Ukrainian lands which had formerly been the core of the Kievan principality and, ethnically, the people inevitably had Ukrainian attributes.[21] Secondly, it inherited the highly developed Kievan cultural achievements, which continued to evolve and spread even after the fall of the Galician-Volhynian state. The Lithuanian conquerors even adopted the Ukrainian language as a state language and the *Ruska Pravda* became the foundation of their legal system. Using these laws as a point of departure, the Lithuanians later codified the "Lithuanian Statute", a new compilation of laws for the Lithuanian state.

Generally speaking, the Galician-Volhynian state followed naturally along the same path of development as the rest of the Ukrainian people, as it evolved on purely Ukrainian ethnic territory, was buttressed by the presence within it of people of a close national (ethnic) kinship, and was based on Kievan culture. On the other hand, within the Suzdalian, Volodymyrian, and Muscovite principalities there evolved and developed a quite different people who, according to Kostomariv, even had different physical and spiritual qualities. This development took place because the basis of support for these principalities was territory inhabited by people of other ethnic origins, except for one purely Slavic tribe of "Viatychi" which was completely absorbed in the creation of the Muscovite-Russian nation. Furthermore, these principalities were deliberately severed from southern Kievan culture and for many years were under the domination of the Tartars, with whom the people of these principalities intermarried very frequently.

This dissimilarity between the two peoples has also been recognized by Russian historians and students of Russian culture. For example, Kliuchevsky states, "We must acknowledge some admixture of Finnish blood in the formation of the anthropological type of the 'Great Russian' (as opposed to Little Russian or Ukrainian). Our Russian physiognomy does not reveal the usual Slavic features..."[22] He also admits that Finnish influence affected the Russian language. Platonov corroborates this information and Pokrovsky declares, "Great Russia has been erected on the skeletons of foreigners and in the bloodstreams of present day Great Russian flows eighty percent Finnish blood."[23] Still more clearly does the Russian writer Alexei Tolstoy characterize Muscovite-Russia in contrasting the mentality of the early Russian with that of the inhabitant of Kievan Rus (now Ukraine):

One Rus has its roots in universal or at least European culture. In this Rus, concepts of worth, honor, and liberty have the same connotation as in the West. But there is also another Rus, the Rus of the dark forests, the Rus of the Taiga, the animal Rus, the fanatical Rus, the Mongolian-Tartar Rus. This Rus adopted despotism and fanaticism as its ideal.... Kievan Rus was a part of Europe; Moscow remained a negation of Europe for a long time.[24]

Ukrainian Territory Under Poland and Lithuania

As noted earlier, Galicia came under Polish domination while Volhyn and the Dnieper lands were occupied by Lithuania. Lithuania emerged as a powerful state in the thirteenth century after wars with the Teutonic Order and the Galician-Volhynian kingdom. Under the leadership of able princes —Gedymin (1316-1341), Olgerd (1345-1377), Vitovt (1392-1430), and Svidrigaillo (1430-1435)—this comparatively youthful state grew in power and extent very rapidly. It expanded chiefly at the cost of Ukrainian *territory*, which had been devastated by the Tartars. By the end of the fourteenth century the Lithuanians had overpowered the Tartars and established themselves on the Black Sea and in Crimea, making the Tartars who had settled there vassals of the Lithuanian prince. They opened the commercial route to Byzantium once more and set free the steppe for a renewal of Ukrainian settlement.

Although the Lithuanians may be regarded as conquerors, one should remember that the Ukrainian nation offered almost no resistance to their occupation. The Lithuanians expelled the Tartars from Ukrainian territory and since Ukrainians had also sought to rid their lands of Tartars, they gladly supported the Lithuanians. But they had additional reasons for supporting them. The Lithuanians were closely associated with the Ukrainians. They had adopted Ukrainian culture, belonged to the Orthodox Church like the Ukrainians, and their aristocracy had even adopted the Bielorussian-Ukrainian language. Meeting with no opposition to their advance into this territory, they regarded the Ukrainians as allies rather than as conquered people. It is not surprising that the Lithuanians often declared in their official documents, "Ancient usages we do not disturb, nor do we innovate." As a consequence of this attitude of the Lithuanians

the Ukrainian nobility, descendants of princes and boyars, were on an equal basis with the Lithuanian nobility ... They retained their seats on the Great Prince's Council and in the central administration. In their own land they occupied almost all the important positions.[25]

The Lithuanians also retained the local language as the official language on Bielorussian and Ukrainian territory. They also did not disturb the economic organization, the judicial system, or other territorial customs.

"At first sight it would appear that the Lithuanian state was merely an extension of the ancient Ukrainian state."[26]

Two centuries under the rule of the Great Principality of Lithuania led to positive results in the development of the Ukrainian people. Although there were numerous handicaps to a complete evolution of their national-political development, it was still a fortunate period for the evolution of their cultural and national consciousness.

> Their attainments during this period under the Lithuanian great princes survived as a source of political capital on which future generations could draw. The development of Ukrainian political ideology cannot be understood without the tradition of statehood which the Dnieper provinces acquired in their relations with the Great Principality.[27]

Ukrainian Territory Under Poland

It should be understood that these acquisitions did not come to the Ukrainians like manna from heaven. The conditions for them had to be created, developed, supported, and finally, defended. Already in the second half of the fourteenth century the Tartar horde had splintered into several groups and the Tartars along the Black Sea and Crimea began to raid Ukraine in such numbers that the Ukrainians had to withdraw again from the steppe along a line through Cherkasy, Kaniv, Bratslav, and Vinnytsia. From another direction the Ukrainians were threatened by Poland which—in occupying Galicia—had begun to expand, and was now casting covetous eyes in the direction of Lithuania, and above all, toward the Ukrainian lands.

It is true that Poland did not set upon Lithuania by force of arms; she chose to proceed by diplomacy. When Yadviga became the Polish queen in 1382, the Polish nobles arranged her marriage to the Lithuanian Prince Yahailo in 1385. As a result of this marriage, Yahailo became king of Poland as well as Grand Prince of Lithuania. He united Lithuania with Poland, adopted the Roman Catholic faith, and immediately granted special privileges to Roman Catholic boyars (nobles).

By this act Yahailo humiliated all of his Lithuanian, Bielorussian, and Ukrainian princes and even provoked the resistance of his two brothers, Vitovt and Svidrigaillo, who were able to defend Orthodox interests and to maintain the independence of Lithuania for a time. But the Poles continued to extend their influence in Lithuania and persevered in their attempts to dominate both Lithuanian and Ukrainian territory. Taking advantage of the situation which arose from the united struggle of Poland and Lithuania against the Teutonic Order, Yahailo's descendant, Sigismund August, arranged a union of Lithuania and Poland in 1569 (known as the Union of

Lublin) in spite of the opposition of a large proportion of the Lithuanians, and almost all Bielorussians and Ukrainians. Under the terms of this union Lithuania itself retained much of its autonomy in the new Polish-Lithuanian state, but Ukrainian and Bielorussian territory suffered. Some Ukrainian lands came under Polish rule immediately and almost all the rest followed later as the result of Lithuanian weakness.

Even before the Union of Lublin, Polish kings had already begun to grant land to their nobles in Podilia, Pravoberezhna (Right Bank) Ukraine, and in Livoberezhna (Left Bank) Ukraine. After the Union of Lublin, Poland began to introduce its own laws and practices into Ukrainian territory. The first step was to deprive the Ukrainian nobility and gentry of their former positions in the state and to demote them to less important offices. In the larger cities of Ukraine they introduced what was known as the Magdeburg Charter; it granted special privileges to burghers of the Catholic faith. They did not forget the peasants in the villages where the large majority of the population lived. For them they introduced *panshchyna,* a variation of the feudal system, according to which peasants were deprived of their right to state courts, the right to own land, and their freedom of movement.

The Union of Berest

Not only did Poland launch an all-embracing attack on the political and economic life of the Ukrainian people; a still more systematic onslaught followed against the Orthodox Church, which the Poles persecuted more brutally than had ever been practised by the Tartar khans, Batu and Uzbek. As far back as 1412 King Yahailo, acting instinctively in accordance with Polish desires, deprived Orthodox adherents of their ancient cathedral in Peremyshl and transferred it to the Roman Catholics. At the same time, he ordered the destruction of the remains of Ukrainian nobles who had been buried underneath. Similar acts on numerous occasions were perpetrated on Ukrainian lands under Poland over a long period of time. When Poland occupied Bielorus and Ukraine after the Union of Lublin, she sought means to destroy the Orthodox Church on territory under her rule. Mistakenly or not, the Orthodox faith was synonymous with Ukrainian nationhood for the Ukrainians of that period. Whoever attacked their faith also attacked their nation. The Orthodox Church served to unite all classes, and was a bastion of national consciousness. What is more, the Poles knew that the Orthodox faith united Ukrainians with the remaining Lithuanians who had not yet adopted Roman Catholicism. Furthermore, it linked the Bielorussian people with the Ukrainians and, what was still more threatening, the church also provided a bond between the two nations and Orthodox Muscovy.

Recognizing that the Union of Lublin had been imposed on the Ukrainians against their will and that they were under no obligation to observe it, the Poles concluded logically that Ukrainians might ask for Moscow's help if circumstances warranted it, as Prince Hlynsky had already attempted in 1508. The Poles were therefore quite justified in fearing such a catastrophe. The Polish bishop Edward Likowsky, a well-known author on church history and relations between Ukrainians and Poles, conceded quite frankly that

> Poland could not rely upon Rus as long as there was a religious tie with Muscovy. The tie had to be broken as soon as possible. There was an immediate need as Russia had withdrawn its allegiance to the Constantinople patriarchate since a Russian patriarchate was created in 1589. Sooner or later, this patriarchate would embrace all the people of Rus and all Slavonic nations who still belonged to the Eastern church. This would include the *Rusyny* under Polish rule...[28]

Likowsky concluded that "political wisdom demanded that Rus be sundered from the Orthodox Church and thus severe its bonds with Moscow and Constantinople..."[29]

Ukrainian interests also demanded some solution because Ukrainian leaders could foresee that the despotic Muscovite princes, who had already entitled themselves princes of "All Rus", would want eventually to bring all of Ukraine under their dominion. If Poland had negotiated wisely, the Ukrainians could have been convinced to become her allies against Moscow. But Poland was not looking for allies, as the Poles were determined to crush Ukrainian resistance, compel them to accept Roman Catholicism, and assimilate them or use other means to break them away from Moscow. Inflamed with the spirit of Catholic messianism—the spirit of their special mission to establish "the true faith" in eastern Europe—the Poles under Jesuit leadership embarked on the destruction of Orthodoxy in their realm. They did not perceive that Orthodoxy, whether good or ill, was the soul of both the Bielorussian and the Ukrainian people. An attack on their soul would not attract them to Poland but rather thrust them toward Moscow, from which some had already sought aid.

Having already overcome a strong movement toward Protestantism in Poland, the Jesuits turned against Orthodoxy. They introduced their schools and colleges among Ukrainians and, being expert teachers and proselytizers, they convinced most of their students to embrace Catholicism, become Polonized, and prevail upon their families to join them. In a comparatively short time the Jesuits could boast of considerable success, since an impressive number of Bielorussian and Ukrainian noble families had embraced Catholicism and had become Polonized. They were, of course, lost to their own people.

But the Jesuits were not satisfied with the slow process of proselytizing princely and noble families. They wanted to divert the Ukrainian people from the Orthodox Church to which they adhered so stubbornly. Continuing their proselytizing activities among the nobility, they conceived for the Ukrainian masses a church union according to which the Eastern rite and married clergy would be retained, but by which the church would come under the jurisdiction of the Pope.[30]

The Poles knew well that the Orthodox Church governed itself through *sobory* (synods) and that all matters before a *sobor* were decided with the participation of the metropolitan, bishops, priests, and lay members. Because of this, they also knew that no *sobor* would support union with Rome. Therefore, the Poles resolved on the "shortest route"—convince the metropolitan and bishops of the merits of the union. They would then, in turn, prevail upon the priesthood and lay members to accept the union.

To the Poles, this "shortest route" appeared feasible and possible to accomplish. They knew that their king was very favorable to the union. Furthermore, all Orthodox bishops and the metropolitan were dependent on the Polish king because it had become the custom since the fifteenth century for the king alone to appoint both bishops and the metropolitan.[31] Since he appointed them,[32] he could also take steps to deprive them of their sees. They believed every bishop would bow to the wish of his sovereign for fear of losing his episcopate. However, to avoid any suspicion of "Polish coercion", it was necessary that some Orthodox bishops play a leading part in the union movement. Such a candidate was discovered in Kyrylo Terletsky, bishop of Polotsk*, an energetic, capable, and resolute personality. But time was short and he failed to achieve any success in spite of the fact that the king had made a promise to grant the bishops supporting the union the same privileges as the Roman Catholic bishops, including the right to seats in the Polish senate. The king and others interested in the union were becoming concerned about the delay when a fortuitous succession of events brought matters to a head.

With the death of Bishop Khrebtovych of Berest in 1593, the metropolitan lost his strongest supporter in opposition to the union. In his place, Ipatii Potii, a sober-minded, experienced, and determined individual, was appointed. Bishop Potii immediately joined the ranks of the proponents of the union. In cooperation with Bishop Terletsky, they succeeded in obtaining the signatures of all the Orthodox bishops to a declaration of union addressed to the Pope on June 12, 1595. Although Bishop Hedeon Balaban of Lviv and Bishop Mykhailo Kopystensky of Peremyshl repudiated their signatures by their subsequent actions, the two bishops, Potii and Terletsky,

---

* Terletsky was bishop of Lutsk and Ostroh. (Ed.)

left for Rome in the name of the whole Orthodox Church under Polish rule. In Rome they accepted the Catholic faith, acknowledged the primacy of the Pope, and placed their church under papal jurisdiction. From his side the Pope guaranteed the Uniates, as they were now called, their traditional Eastern Rite and married clergy.

The difficulty with the union was that all negotiations by Potii and Terletsky were carried on in secret without any knowledge on the part of the priesthood or lay people. They were carried on with the Poles—chiefly with the Polish Roman Catholic Bishop Matseyowski and the two Jesuits, Benedict Herbest and Petro Skarga. Most of them took place in Bishop Matseyowski's palace, in the course of which it earned the title "Centre of Union Affairs".

Having heard of these preparations for the union, Prince Konstantyn Ostrozky demanded that a *sobor* be assembled, but the Polish king would not grant his request. Only one other alternative was left to the prince. He circulated a letter to lay representatives and the priesthood to inform them that the bishops had

> treacherously reached an understanding among themselves and, having trans-
> muted themselves into sorcerers, they had betrayed their true faith, the Holy
> Eastern Church, deserted the patriarch to join the west, and secretly plotted
> together like Judas with the Jews to lead all God-fearing Christians to destruc-
> tion.[33]

Prince Ostrozky's letter appealed to all Orthodox adherents to rise in opposition to the union. This letter, which was printed and distributed to the whole Orthodox world, impressed both natives and foreigners. It impelled Bishop Balaban of Lviv to repudiate the union and to declare that his name was affixed to the bishops' declaration without his knowledge. Bishop Kopystensky of Peremyshl followed his example. On the other hand, the Polish king and the Jesuits became still more determined to establish the union.

In Constantinople the death of Patriarch Yeremiy was followed by a period of uncertainty during which the Greeks were unable to aid the Orthodox in Poland in their hour of need. Decisive action on the part of the Patriarch could have averted the union before the summoning of the *sobor* at Berest, at which time the union was proclaimed officially. It is true that the Patriarch did send his representative, Nicephorus, but the representative was arrested and detained in Wallachia at the request of the Polish government.

A request from Prince Ostrozky to the Polish king for permission to convene a *sobor* met with silence. Instead, the king published a "Universal" (decree) which announced that the "shepherds" of the Orthodox Church together with a substantial number of interested persons had agreed to a union with the Catholic Church and subjection to the Apostolic See".[34] Shortly thereafter, Bishops Potii and Terletsky journeyed to Rome at Royal expense to sign an agreement on December 23, 1595 which subjected the Orthodox Church to the papacy. In February 1596 Pope Clement VIII wrote a letter to the king of Poland thanking him for his efforts towards the successful conclusion of the union and asked him to continue extending aid and protection to the Uniates.

While this was in progress, anti-union agitation spread throughout Ukraine. The priesthood, church brotherhoods, gentry, and villagers simultaneously rose in opposition to the union and demanded that a church *sobor* be convened at which the union would not even be considered, as they wished to proceed with the trial and condemnation of the apostate bishops straight away. On the other hand, the bishops, with the aid of Polish arms, struggled to maintain the loyalty of the priesthood and lay people and appealed to their sense of obedience to the bishops' and the king's authority. Uniates also sought the convening of a *sobor*, as they needed to validate their action in some way. Accordingly, King Sigismund issued a proclamation on June 24, 1596 authorizing the calling of a *sobor*. Not long after, Metropolitan Rohoza also issued his declaration announcing that an "important *sobor*" would be held in Berest on October 6, 1596. In reality, this was to be a Uniate *sobor* in which only the priesthood and faithful of that church could take part. However, thanks to the resolute and energetic campaign of the Orthodox priesthood and lay people, the *sobor* at Berest became a *sobor* of the Ukrainian Orthodox Church in which all the people of Ukraine expressed their determination to struggle with all their power to annul the union, a creation foreign to the Ukrainian people.

In 1596, from October 6 to October 9, gathered the largest *sobor* that had ever been held by the Ukrainian Orthodox Church. It immediately split into two groups. In one group sat the representatives of the Polish government, the apostate bishops, their supporters, and representatives of the Roman Catholic Church. The second group consisted of representatives of the Ukrainian Orthodox priesthood headed by bishops Hedeon Balaban and Mykhailo Kopystensky, nine archimandrates (abbots), nearly two hundred priests, and numerous representatives from the Eastern Orthodox Church headed by Archdeacon Nicephorus, whom the Orthodox had managed to liberate from prison. In this group there was also a strong representation of laymen led by Prince Ostrozky. Among these were representatives of the Ukrainian nobility and gentry, members of the central and district Polish *seim* (parliament), and representatives of Ukrainian burghers and brotherhoods.

Thrice did the Orthodox *sobor* summon the metropolitan and the apostate bishops to appear and give reasons for their actions but the summons were ignored. Finally, on October 9 the *sobor* unanimously condemned the apostate bishops for treason against the Orthodox Church with the following declaration:

> The offended Holy Eastern Church commands us gathered in this Council that the metropolitan and the bishop-apostates be deprived of their hierarchical dignity, authority, episcopal titles, and spiritual status.[35]

At that same time the *sobor* resolved to send a delegation to the king to obtain his confirmation for its decision to deprive the apostate bishops of their authority and to request his consent for the election of new bishops by the *sobor*. Then they prepared a "Universal", a declaration to all Orthodox adherents, to inform them of the decisions of the *sobor* and to urge them to resist the union with all their power.

After celebrating mass in the Church of St. Mykolai in Berest on October 9, the Uniates, together with government representatives and those of the Catholic Church, caused a proclamation of the union to be read. At the same time they condemned as heretics the two bishops, as well as all archimandrites, hegumens, protopopes, and priests who remained faithful to the Orthodox Church, and directed that they be deprived of their positions in the church.

Obviously, King Sigismund, as a faithful follower of the Jesuits, did not accede to any of the requests of the Orthodox *sobor*. Instead, he issued a writ in which he deprived the priesthood of the Orthodox Church of all its rights and privileges. By this act the king embarked on the persecution of the Orthodox Church, which was now considered beyond the pale of the law. All rights and privileges formerly possessed by the Orthodox Church in the Polish state were now transferred to the Uniates. Accordingly, with the aid of Polish arms, the Uniates proceeded to seize all Orthodox churches, monasteries, schools, printing presses, and church lands. But this was to arouse the entire Ukrainian nation in defence of its church. In the beginning it was a peaceful struggle carried on in the Polish *seim* or local *seimy* and through volumes of polemical literature. Later, in answer to the armed oppression of Orthodoxy, the Ukrainian people responded with the armed strength of the *kozaky* or cossacks, who were becoming a powerful force.

The consequences of the Berest Union proved to be tragic not only to the Ukrainians but also to the Polish state. The union wrecked the unity of the Ukrainian people and the consequences of this breach can be felt to the present day. It also alienated the Ukrainian people from its leading class, the gentry, who soon enough landed in the Polish Catholic camp as they were scornful of the partial union and impatient to embrace Roman Catholicism, the state religion. The union, and particularly the means of its achievement, plunged the Ukrainian nation into an internecine struggle which ended with the weakened nation in the embrace of Moscow. Finally, the union was the main reason for the decline of the Polish state toward the end of the eighteenth century.

The Ukrainian Kozak Nation

After the Tartar attack on Ukraine in the middle of the thirteenth century the once large Ukrainian population along the Dnieper, though not totally eliminated, dwindled in size and became substantially smaller. This condition prevailed for a long time, even after the territory was annexed by Lithuania. The Crimean Tartars made annual inroads into Ukrainian territory, killing many of those who were left and driving away into bondage those who were younger and stronger. These attacks forced the population to settle near forested and swamp areas in the north or closer to the fortified towns of north-west Ukraine.

Since the Lithuanian state did not have the means to protect the extensive area of the Ukrainian steppe against Tartar inroads, all responsibility for defence rested with the local inhabitants. In these defensive activities of the Ukrainian people against the Tartars the famous *kozak* organization was born. In those days nature was bountiful in Ukraine and people could gain a livelihood with a minimum expenditure of labour. The rivers were teeming with fish, the forest and steppe abounded with animals, wild honey, and berries, and the soil was unusually productive. All this attracted the more daring members of the population to ignore Tartar danger and to venture into the distant steppe. Every spring, bands of these adventurous men journeyed into the steppe to remain there for the summer; these expeditions were known as *Ukhody*. Late in autumn they would return with large supplies of food. While remaining in the steppe they would hunt, fish, and collect wild honey, never leaving their weapons for a moment. In constant danger from Tartars and faced with continual warfare, the *kozaky* became hardened and grew in strength while developing those characteristics for which they became famous: valour, hardiness, and a love of liberty.

The word *kozak* is of Turkish origin. In the Polovtsian language it meant sentinel or guard but by the fifteenth century the Tartars used the term to denote light-armed cavalry who performed guard duty. Toward the end of the same century there are increasing references to Ukrainian *kozaky* at a time when the term was disappearing from use among the Tartars. The historian, Dmytro Doroshenko, states:

Having adopted from the Tartars their tactics in battle, the *kozaky* also appropriated their name. All references to Tartar *kozaky* disappear from common usage at the time Ukrainian *kozaky* began to achieve greater and greater prominence.[36]

The *kozaky* achieved fame in the first half of the sixteenth century for their chivalrous mode of life as well as their unremitting struggle with the Tartars. Young men from all ranks were attracted to their ranks as the concept of a *kozak* indicated the idealistic, daring, chivalrous, and freedom-loving individual. Among those who organized the dispersed groups into a chivalrous order the most prominent is Prince Dmytro Vyshnevetsky, known in song as Baida, who established the Zaporozhian (Beyond the rapids) Sich on the island of Khortytsia in the Dnieper River and thus began the organization of Ukrainian *kozaky*. At the beginning these *kozaky* continuously fought the Crimean Tartars and Turkey, often carrying on a foreign policy independent of Poland. However, when the threatening cloud of Polish repression and enforced church union advanced from the west, the *kozaky* resolutely turned against the Poles in defence of their people and their Orthodox faith.

The first anti-Polish uprisings, the campaigns of Christopher Kosinsky (1591-1593) and Severyn Nalyvaiko and Hryhory Loboda (1596), coincided chronologically with the period of preparation for the church union. However, while Kosinsky's rebellion had social motives, the main attacks of Nalyvaiko's *kozaky* were against supporters of the church union and their champions, the Poles. "At this time," writes Doroshenko, "toward the end of 1595 and the beginning of 1596, a desperate struggle was in progress over church union. Having returned from Bielorussia to Volhyn, Nalyvaiko mercilessly plundered the possessions of Kyrylo Terletsky, one of the main architects of the union. Other union supporters also suffered."[37]

Kozak power reached a high point at the beginning of the seventeenth century, during the regime of Hetman Petro Sahaidachny. The increase in *kozak* strength can be partially attributed to the fact that Poland was continuously engaged in a series of wars with its neighbours—Sweden, Muscovy, and Turkey—and was in need of *kozak* aid. Another contributing factor was the intensification of social and religious oppression by the Polish gentry, which aroused a deep resentment in the Ukrainians and drove them to join the *kozaky*. All those who could not bear the feudal yoke and the assault on their religious and national convictions fled into the steppe and swelled the *kozak* ranks. Undoubtedly, Hetman Sahaidachny was the most capable leader the *kozaky* had before Bohdan Khmelnytsky. They were a powerful force under his leadership because of his military prowess and his able statesmanship. Numerous sea expeditions against Turkey, especially the *kozak* capture of the Crimean city of Kaffa, brought Sahaidachny and his men great fame, particularly as Kaffa was a slave auction centre. The *kozaky* also served in the Polish-Muscovite war and it was only because of their aid in 1618 that the Polish Prince Wladislaw was able to besiege Moscow.

It was characteristic of the policy of Sahaidachny that while he consolidated the power of the *kozak* host and hardened his warriors in wars with foreign enemies of Poland, in his domestic policy he sought by legal means to achieve rights inherent to the Ukrainian people and to the Orthodox Church in the Polish state. Unfortunately, any hope for reform of urgent social and religious problems was useless as long as Sigismund III remained on the throne. Whenever a crisis threatened, the Polish government was always ready to agree to all *kozak* demands, among which the abolition of the church union was always most prominent. When the crisis passed, however, the king and his council always returned to their previous policy. Accordingly, in the later years of his life, Sahaidachny paid considerably less attention to the moods and humours of Warsaw but continued his resolute championship of Ukrainian rights by relying totally on *kozak* support.

As Uniate pressure became heavier on Ukrainian people in the west, where they bordered on Poland, the centre of Ukrainian national and religious life moved again to Kiev. Under the protection of *kozak* arms, the most capable Ukrainian leaders gathered in this new centre. Petro Sahaidachny was the first Ukrainian hetman to establish his capital in Kiev. Together with the whole Zaporozhian army, he enrolled in the ranks of the Kievan Bohoyavlensky Brotherhood, whose main purpose was the defence of the Orthodox Church. In 1615 this organization established a school which later developed into the Kiev Mohyla Academy, where the leading Ukrainian scholars of that period gathered. These scholars ably defended their faith and church against union, from the scholarly-theological standpoint, through the publication of large numbers of books by means of a newly established printing press in the Kievan Pecherska Lavra. In this way Sahaidachny combined *kozak* arms with Ukrainian intellect for the defensive effort.

But the greatest service of Sahaidachny to his people and the Orthodox Church, which can also be regarded as the crowning point of his career, was the revival of the Orthodox hierarchy in 1620. Following the abandonment of the Orthodox Church by its hierarchy, led by Metropolitan Rohoza, and the death of the two bishops who had remained faithful to the church, it was threatened with complete disorganization. Especially critical was the problem of a priesthood, since new priests could not be ordained. Sahaidachny conveniently took advantage of the presence in Ukraine of the Patriarch of Jerusalem to normalize relations within the Orthodox Church by arranging for the consecration of new bishops. Of course, it was dangerous for the Patriarch as a citizen of a foreign country to interfere in the internal affairs of Poland. Only when the Patriarch had the assurance of Sahaidachny that the *kozaky* would guarantee his safety did he consecrate the recommended candidates as bishops, with Job Boretsky as metropolitan. Thus the hierarchy of the Ukrainian Orthodox Church was revived in one of the most critical periods of the church's existence.

Obviously, the Poles not only refused to recognize the new Orthodox hierarchy but also declared all the members to be usurpers and outlawed them. But Poland was again compelled to seek *kozak* aid in a war with Turkey, and the *kozaky* consented to participate in the war only if their demand for the recognition of the Ukrainian Orthodox Church was granted —a demand to which the Polish government once again agreed. The *kozak* army saved the Poles from total destruction at the hands of the Turks in the battle of Khotyn in 1621, but after the war the Polish government forgot once more both the *kozak* sacrifices in the war and its own promises.

After Sahaidachny's death, the *kozaky* continued their struggle for their rights and for the legal recognition of the Ukrainian Orthodox Church. For ten years they struggled, without success, and it was only after King Sigismund's death in 1632 and the accession of Wladislaw to the throne that any concessions were made. The first concession recognized the *kozaky* as a separate class within the Polish state. In regard to the recognition of the Orthodox Church, the Polish *seim* effected a compromise: instead of abolishing the union as demanded by the *kozaky* and the mass of Ukrainian people, the *seim* recognized both churches, the Orthodox and the Uniate, as churches in the Polish state. It thus legalized the partition of the Ukrainian nation.

In the meantime, the existence of the Orthodox Church was secured and Petro Mohyla succeeded to the metropolitanate in Kiev. He had been Father Superior (archimandrite) of the Kievan Pecherska Lavra and now became head of his church at the time of its greatest achievements during the *kozak* period. But in spite of this improvement in the position of the Orthodox Church and a partial fulfillment of *kozak* demands, disaffection among the Ukrainian masses under Poland was never completely eliminated. The *kozaky,* especially those in Zaporozhia, continued to nourish their aspirations while the Polish government and the brutality of the Polish gentry and nobility kept their resentment alive on social, national, and religious grounds. The hardships of the *corvee,* or compulsory service to the landlord, the failure to pay *kozaky* for their service in war, and Catholic or Uniate repression of the Orthodox population and priesthood were the activators which impelled the stronger and more courageous elements among the people to enlist with the *kozaky,* whom they joined in armed uprisings in defence of their rights.

In 1637 a new *kozak* insurrection broke out under Pavliuk and in 1638 there was a still more menacing rebellion of *kozaky* and peasants under Hunia and Ostrianytsia. Both of these, as well as others, were mercilessly crushed by Polish armed forces in 1638. A large proportion of the *kozaky* under Ostrianytsia fled to the east across the Muscovite border, where they established a Ukrainian colony known as Slobidska Ukraina in the area where the city of Kharkiv was later established. According to Polish historians, a period of "golden peace" followed in Ukraine after 1638. In reality this was a calm before the storm.

One of the innumerable examples of the absence of any legal protection for the Ukrainian people in the Polish state, reflective of the autocratic and unprincipled behaviour of the Polish gentry, is the case of a Chyhyryn *kozak* lieutenant, Zenoviy Bohdan Khmelnytsky. He was well-educated, a good soldier, a competent landowner, and wholly loyal to the Polish crown, which he had faithfully served in wars against its enemies. Khmelnytsky administered his property peacefully from his farmstead until the Starosta of Subotiv, a Polish nobleman, unlawfully took possession of it. All of Khmelnytsky's attempts to bring the matter before the courts failed. An appeal to the king as the highest court was no less a failure; the king gave Khmelnytsky the advice that he could defend his rights among the Polish gentry by his sword alone.

Khmelnytsky escaped to Zaporozhia at the end of 1647. In Zaporozhia he enlisted the support of other discontented adherents and obtained control of the *sich* where the *kozaky* proclaimed him as hetman. Preparing for determined struggle with the Polish aristocracy, he established diplomatic relations with the Tartars, from whom he obtained military aid. Simultaneously, he sent agents throughout Ukraine to arouse the people to revolt.

The first battle of Khmelnytsky's *kozak* forces against the Polish troops took place on May 16, 1648, at Zhovti Vody (Yellow Waters) and ended with the total defeat of the Polish forces. Ten days later Khmelnytsky completely destroyed the main Polish forces in Ukraine near Korsun, where both Polish commanders were taken prisoners. When the news of this *kozak* triumph became known, all of Ukraine rose in their support. The people sought to obliterate all traces of Polish rule. They killed or drove out Polish administrators, burned down landowners' homesteads, and destroyed Polish churches. In a short time Ukraine was totally liberated from Polish rule. On August 23 of the same year a third battle was fought which once again ended with the total defeat of the Polish forces. The whole of Poland now lay open and undefended before Khmelnytsky. But Khmelnytsky had no intention of severing political bonds with Poland at this time. His purposes included only limiting the arbitrary power of the nobles, restoring *kozak* rights, and abolishing the church union. King Wladislaw died in the spring of 1648 during the most critical stage of the war. When Wladislaw's brother, Jan Kasimir, succeeded to the throne, Khmelnytsky stopped his advance on Warsaw and returned to Ukraine with his victorious army. Since he had supported Jan Kasimir's candidature for the crown in return for the latter's promise to grant everything which the *kozaky* were demanding, he wished to avoid further warfare.

Khmelnytsky's triumphal entrance into Kiev on Christmas Day 1648 and the brilliance and warmth of his reception by the Ukrainian population radically changed his attitude toward Poland. The Ukrainian nation welcomed Khmelnytsky as their liberator from Polish bondage and hailed him as a Ukrainian Moses. The clergy, at whose head were Metropolitan Sylvester Kosiv and Patriarch Paisios of Jerusalem, then visiting Kiev, hailed him as a defender of the Orthodox faith. But more significant for future relations between Poland and Ukraine were certain fundamental problems. The first of these was the Polish aristocracy's refusal to surrender their power in Ukraine. Opposing them were the masses of Ukrainian people who had no intention of returning to bondage under the same aristocracy. In addition, there was a more crucial problem: the keynote of Khmelnytsky's demands had always been the abolition of the church union. Since there was no likelihood that the Poles would ever agree to this demand, which was so important to the Ukrainians, further war could not be avoided.

In the spring of 1649 a Polish army again invaded Ukraine but its path was blocked once more by the hetman with a large army. The Poles were saved from total disaster only through the intervention of the Crimean khan, Khmelnytsky's ally. The war ended with the Treaty of Zboriv, but its terms were hardly satisfactory to any of the warring sides. According to this treaty, Ukraine obtained complete autonomy in three provinces: Kiev, Chernihiv, and Bratslav, and the Ukrainian army was to have a limit of 40,000 *kozaky*. The church union and Polish administrative powers were abolished within the limits of this territory. However, the peasants had to return to their feudal bondage, which included the *corvee*.

Though the brilliant *kozak* victories of 1648 did not bring the anticipated results, the Treaty of Zboriv gave the Ukrainian nation an opportunity to begin life anew. Considering former conditions in Ukraine, this treaty was a great step forward and Khmelnytsky proceeded to organize state institutions with his usual energy and innate ability. The whole country was divided into regiments *(polky)* and hundreds *(sotni)*, which served both military and civil purposes. *Kozak* administration and courts were set up in each unit. Schools were established and church life flourished. Simultaneously, the hetman state conducted a vigorous foreign policy by establishing diplomatic relations with such neighbouring countries as Muscovy, Turkey, Crimea, and Moldavia.

However, Poland was unwilling to accept a peace which would deprive her of sovereignty in Ukraine. In the spring of 1651, a large Polish army, recruited from almost every state of Catholic Europe, resumed hostilities. Engagements took place immediately after the Polish army crossed the Ukrainian border but the main battle was fought at Berestechko, in Volhyn, between June 28 and 30. Both sides wished to deliver a decisive blow at the enemy and regarded the campaign as a holy war for their faith. The Pope sent a special legate to the Polish king with his benediction for the success of the war in the interests of the Catholic Church, while the hetman received a visit from Metropolitan Joseph of Corinth who brought Khmelnytsky a sword blessed at the holy sepulchre in Jerusalem. He also brought blessings from the eastern patriarchs for defending the Orthodox Church.

Through the treachery of the Crimean khan, who also carried away Khmelnytsky as a prisoner, the *kozak* army was defeated, though the main *kozak* force was saved thanks to the strategic genius of Ivan Bohun, the deputy hetman. However, nearly 30,000 peasant insurgents perished on the field of battle. Fortunately for the *kozaky,* the Polish army also suffered such losses that it was unable to pursue them immediately. In the meantime, the hetman mobilized new forces and in October mustered a new and powerful army at Bila Tserkva against the Poles. This compelled the Poles to negotiate a peace, as a result of which the Treaty of Bila Tserkva was signed in October 1651. This treaty was even more unsatisfactory to both sides than that of Zboriv and was clearly only provisional in character.

Khmelnytsky and his supporters saw that Ukraine alone could not withstand Polish power, behind which the whole of Catholic Europe was aligned. It was evident that Ukraine must seek other allies in this supreme effort as Crimea and Turkey had proved very unreliable as allies. Though friendly to the *kozak* state, Sweden was too distant to be of much real help. The only possible ally for Ukraine was Muscovy, especially as its people were of the same faith. Understanding this, the hetman had instituted negotiations with the Muscovite government from the beginning of the struggle. These diplomatic negotiations received still more attention after the battle of Berestechko. As a result, the Muscovite *Zemsky Sobor* petitioned the czar to take Ukraine under its protection in the fall of 1653 and in January 1654 Ukraine became united with Muscovy through the Treaty of Pereiaslav.

Under the terms of this treaty Ukraine recognized the suzerainty of the czar but remained a state separate from Muscovy with its own socio-political organization, its own administration and army, its own financial system, and the right to carry on diplomatic relations with all other nations except Poland and Turkey. The *kozak* army was set at a maximum of 60,000 men and all *kozak* liberties and privileges were to remain in force.

The hetman was to be elected by a free vote according to established tradition and Muscovy was merely to be informed of the election.

It soon became evident that Muscovy had no intention of respecting the Pereiaslav Treaty and wished to subjugate Ukraine by exploiting its difficult situation. However, Ukraine had to continue its life and death struggle with Poland and Moscow's aid was a necessity. In answer to the Ukrainian-Muscovite alliance, Crimea had also joined Poland. This was the beginning of a bitter and prolonged struggle in which Poland eventually met with disastrous defeat. In desperation, the Poles offered the Polish crown to Muscovy as their reigning king, Jan Kasimir, was childless. Muscovy agreed to an armistice. As a precautionary measure, Khmelnytsky had concluded another anti-Polish alliance which included Ukraine, Sweden, Semyhorod (Transylvania), and Brandenburg. In this alliance Ukraine received recognition as an independent nation over the entire territory settled by Ukrainian people. Unfortunately, the unexpected death of the hetman on August 6, 1657 interrupted his plans and aspirations.

The Period of Great Ruin

With the death of Bohdan Khmelnytsky there followed a very disastrous period in Ukrainian history which is known to Ukrainians as *Velyka Ruina* (Great Ruin or Destruction). After the brief hetmanate of Bohdan's son Yuriy, the secretary-general of Khmelnytsky's administration, Ivan Vyhovsky, became hetman. He tried to follow the policies of Bohdan Khmelnytsky, but obstacles were placed in his way by Muscovy. Taking advantage of inconsistencies in the Treaty of Pereiaslav, the Muscovite government proceeded to limit the number of *kozak* troops and replaced them with Muscovite garrisons in the cities. Through czarist representatives in Ukraine *(voyevody)*, the Ukrainian population was incited to rebel against their own government to encourage conflict and anarchy. With Muscovite support, Colonel Martin Pushkar and his Poltava regiment mutinied; Otaman Sirko in Zaporozhia did the same. The hetman had to crush the mutineers by using his military forces.

Exhausted by the long war, Sweden began to seek peace with Poland, forcing Vyhovsky to find some other solution for Ukraine's problems. He concluded a treaty with Poland which was known as the Treaty of Hadiach. Under its terms Ukraine became a member of a federal state, together with Poland and Lithuania, as a separate principality under the name of Rus. The three nations were to be united only through the suzerainty of one person, the king. The church union was to be abolished in Ukrainian territory, and the Orthodox Church was to have equal rights and privileges with the Catholic Church in the whole kingdom.

Regarding the Treaty of Hadiach as a declaration of war, the Muscovite government dispatched an army of 100,000 men to invade Ukraine. This army was quickly routed by Vyhovsky near Konotop in 1659, but the victory did not strengthen Vyhovsky's position. Alliance with Poland was not popular with the Ukrainian nation and uprisings took place throughout Ukraine. Vyhovsky was forced to surrender the hetman's mace.

Yuriy Khmelnytsky succeeded to the hetmanate a second time. However, when his position as hetman was being confirmed, Moscow introduced so false an interpretation of the original Treaty of Pereiaslav that he followed Vyhovsky in abrogating the treaty and again joined Poland. Not long after, he again withdrew from the hetmanate and retired to a monastery. The next hetman, Pavlo Teteria, adhered to the Polish alliance. But Left Bank Ukraine chose a Muscovite supporter, Ivan Briukhovetsky, an action which divided Ukraine into two hostile sections. A ruthless civil war ensued, which was waged simultaneously with foreign wars on every side. Another contributing factor to the general disorder was the constant disaffection of peasant and common *kozak* masses as a result of their social and economic position. They were ready for insurrection at the summons of any adventurer at any time. To add still more to the horror of the situation for the Ukrainian people during this period of "Great Ruin", there were annual incursions by the Crimean Tartars for booty and slaves.

Difficult times prevailed in Left Bank Ukraine under Briukhovetsky. He sought every means to base his support on Moscow. His policies aroused such antagonism among the people that he was killed in a *kozak* uprising. The pro-Polish policies of Teteria on the Right Bank were no more successful. Under pressure from anti-Polish feeling, he gave up the hetmanate, crossed into Poland, and adopted the Catholic faith.

The hetman elected in Right Bank Ukraine in 1666 was Chyhyryn Colonel Petro Doroshenko, a staunch patriot and the most prominent figure in this period of disorder. He set as his first task the liberation of Right Bank Ukraine from the Poles and the union of the whole of Ukraine under one rule. Unfortunately, almost before Doroshenko had made any move in the desired direction, the Poles and the Muscovites, or Russians as they were beginning to be named, exhausted by the long war, signed the Treaty of Andrusiv in 1667. Under the terms of this treaty Left Bank Ukraine and the city of Kiev were awarded to Russia while Right Bank Ukraine reverted to Poland. Zaporozhia was to remain under the joint protection of both nations.

The Treaty of Andrusiv aroused the anger of the entire Ukrainian nation, and Doroshenko became the sole hope of all patriots. When Left Bank Ukraine responded to the treaty with massive uprisings in which Briukhovetsky lost his life, Doroshenko crossed into the territory with an army and united the whole of Ukraine under his rule. All too soon, however, Doroshenko had to return to Right Bank Ukraine to defend his capital from Polish attack. Taking advantage of his absence, the Russians invaded Left Bank Ukraine and forced the deputy-hetman Mnohohrishny to abandon Doroshenko and to accept their protection. Ukraine was again divided. In this difficult situation, Doroshenko requested and obtained help from Turkey. A large Turkish army advanced against the Poles in 1672 to force the Poles to surrender their claim to Ukraine once more.

In 1672 Left Bank Ukraine acquired an energetic and resolute hetman in the person of Ivan Samoilovych. He also hoped to unite Ukraine under his mace but he sought to do this under Russian protection. Since the alliance of Doroshenko and the Turks in Right Bank Ukraine threatened Moscow, and Turkish conduct in Right Bank Ukraine was arousing opposition there to both the Turks and Doroshenko, a united Russian-Ukrainian army under the command of Samoilovych invaded Right Bank Ukraine in 1674. The populace welcomed Samoilovych and the majority of *kozak* regiments joined his forces. However, when Turkish forces came to Doroshenko's aid, Samoilovych returned to Left Bank Ukraine. Unfortunately, the people who remained behind were subjected to harsh repression and many people abandoned their homes to move to Left Bank Ukraine. Much of Right Bank Ukraine became deserted. When many of his closest collaborators left him, Doroshenko relinquished his hetman's mace in favor of Samoilovych. Not long after, however, even Samoilovych was forced to abandon Right Bank Ukraine because of the superior forces of the Turks and Moscow's refusal to come to his aid. Evacuating the rest of the population across the Dnieper, he abandoned the desolate right bank territory to the Turkish forces. However, he never gave up hope that he would recover this territory some day and, during his fifteen years as hetman, he adamantly continued to pursue an anti-Polish policy.

Another catastrophic event for the Ukrainian people during Samoilovych's regime was the subjection of the Ukrainian Orthodox Church to the jurisdiction of the patriarch in Moscow. Though all events succeeding the Berest Union evolved in the direction of an eventual union with Moscow, the Ukrainian Church still remained under the jurisdiction of the patriarch of Constantinople for another thirty years. As proved by succeeding events, the consequences of subjection to the patriarch in Moscow meant disaster to the Ukrainians. In the first place, union with the Moscow church gave the Poles a pretext to extirpate Orthodoxy in their realm and to force Ukrainians to join the Uniates. Secondly, the Orthodox Church in Ukraine became an instrument of Russification and of spiritual control over the nation. Finally, it gave the Uniates the right to adopt the role of a Ukrainian national church and thus to sanction the religious division of Ukrainians into two groups, a division which has been cleverly manipulated by foreign elements until the present day.

Hetman Ivan Mazepa

The next hetman of exceptional ability after the death of Bohdan Khmelnytsky was Ivan Mazepa, who was elected to the hetmanate in Left Bank Ukraine after Samoilovych's downfall in 1687. The period of his administration is marked by internal stability and the creative force which infused all levels of national life. Toward the end of his regime, Hetman Mazepa attempted once more to release Ukraine from the deadly embrace of Moscow.

Mazepa was capable, well-educated, and distinguished both for his diplomatic skill and for his ability to attract able associates. Unfortunately for him and Ukraine, Peter I—a young, ambitious, and determined despot —occupied the Russian throne. At the outset, Mazepa adopted policies based on a close alliance with Moscow. Under his able administration, Ukraine slowly healed the wounds it had sustained in the period of the Great Ruin. His administration instituted the colonization of free lands, the restoration of destroyed towns and villages, and the establishment of new ones. Ukrainian scholarship also made much progress. Kiev Mohyla School became the Kievan Academy, whose annual enrollment rose to 2,000. The hetman himself endowed schools generously and also provided for other cultural needs, especially for the Orthodox Church. Though he continued to support the upper classes and maintained their privileges and education, he opposed the efforts of this group to exploit the rest of the population. In his foreign policy he sought to unite Right Bank Ukraine with the hetmanate and thus consistently followed an anti-Polish policy. He finally achieved his ambition in 1704, when all of Ukraine was united under his control.

Under Peter I the Russians were constantly fighting wars, beginning in the south against the Turks and Tartars in Crimea, and later in the north against the Swedes. While war was waged against the Turks and Tartars, Mazepa aided the czar quite readily as victory over the Turks yielded immense area for colonization and also access to the Black Sea. But when Peter I became entangled in a long exhausting war with Sweden, Mazepa and his supporters secretly but resolutely laid plans to hinder the czar's warlike aims, which brought no benefit to Ukraine, ruined it economically, and took the lives of masses of Ukrainian *kozaky*. Ukrainians became more and more restive with each succeeding year of the war and the hetman had to find some solution to the problem. As an experienced statesman he also concluded that Ukraine faced destruction no matter who won the war. A

Swedish victory would leave Ukraine prey to Poland, while a Russian victory would almost certainly end in Ukraine becoming a Russian province, as actually occurred.

In this situation, Mazepa opened negotiations with the Swedish king, Charles XII, and concluded a secret treaty through which Sweden guaranteed Ukrainian independence while Ukraine became Sweden's ally in its struggle with Moscow. In case of a Swedish advance on Moscow, Ukraine would form the right wing of the anti-Russian coalition. Unfortunately, the unexpected appearance of Charles in Ukraine as a result of his repulses on the direct road to Moscow brought the disaster of war to Ukraine. Mazepa was compelled to join Charles immediately with only a small force. The hetman capital, Baturyn, was captured by the Russians through treachery, and its inhabitants slaughtered. The subsequent Russian revenge on Mazepa's adherents, Peter's shrewd propaganda, and his lavish rewards to officers and *kozaky* who remained faithful to the czar had their effect. The Ukrainian nation failed to support Mazepa. The ensuing winter decimated the Swedish forces, and the combined Swedish and Ukrainian army suffered defeat in the decisive battle near Poltava on July 8, 1709. The defeat put an end to Sweden's role as a great power in Europe's political arena. For Ukraine it was also a tragedy which sealed the fate of Ukraine for centuries. Cruel repressions of Ukrainians followed not only for any avowed sympathy to Mazepa, but even for opposition to depredations of Russian emissaries. The czar even decreed that an anathema be pronounced against Mazepa once a year in every church to condemn him as an apostate of the Orthodox Church, a practice which continued annually until the Russian revolution of 1905. As a result of the Battle of Poltava, Russia emerged on the world's stage as a powerful empire.

Peter was determined to terminate the autonomy of Ukraine, but owing to the activities of emigrants abroad under the leadership of Hetman Philip Orlyk, he was discreet and secretive in his actions. After Mazepa's departure, Ivan Skoropadsky became hetman but his power was limited by the presence of an appointee of the czar, the resident-general, who had supervisory rights over the hetman. The resident-general was the real power in the administration of Ukraine. All wealth that could be squeezed out of Ukraine was utilized to wage the northern wars. Especially terrifying in its effect was the annual expatriation of thousands of Ukrainian *kozaky* and peasants to work on the canals of St. Petersburg (now Leningrad), where they died of cold, exhaustion, and hunger. The czarist capital veritably rose on the skeletons of its builders. To consolidate his power in Ukraine, Peter introduced the "cake and knout" policy, whereby he lavishly rewarded his adherents and inflicted cruel punishment on those who would not submit. Ukrainian scholars were enticed to Russia into high government or ecclesiastical positions. Accordingly, education in Ukraine fell into decline. He also seduced the *kozak* officer class by the distribution of rewards, orders, and estates, while those in opposition were crushed through exile and death. One noted defender of the rights of Ukraine, Pavlo Polubotok, was martyred in the Petropavlovsk fortress of St. Petersburg and died in this way. Simultaneously, Peter distributed Ukrainian estates to his Russian nobles, very often with attached peasants who then became serfs of their Russian masters. In some areas Russian landowners transferred their own peasant serfs from the north to cultivate lands which they had been awarded in Ukraine. Accordingly, Ukraine became settled by Russians, who further consolidated Russian influence. Eventually, this brought about a relentless Russification of all Ukrainian life with a prohibition of the publication of any books in the literary Ukrainian of that period.

Liquidation of the Hetmanate

Ukraine's misfortunes did not end with the death of Peter the Great in 1725. Although his successors on the czarist Russian throne often modified their policies in other state matters, there was no alleviation in their strategy toward Ukraine. Particularly prominent in the suppression of the rights and privileges of Ukrainians was Czarina Catherine II, who consummated the process of despotic centralization initiated by Peter I. During her reign, the hetmanate was abolished in 1764 when Kyrylo (Cyril) Rozumowsky "voluntarily" relinquished his authority on the request of the czarina and the election of a successor was forbidden. To replace the hetman, Catherine II appointed a Russian governor-general who was given secret instructions to extinguish tactfully but persistently all traces of Ukrainian autonomy. In 1775 the Zaporozhian Sich was also liquidated by czarist *ukase* (decree). Some of the *kozaky* managed to escape and were received under the protection of the Turkish sultan. They organized the Zadunaiska (Beyond the Danube) Sich on islands at the mouth of the Danube. In 1781 the old *kozak* administrative division of Ukraine was abolished. In 1783 Ukrainian peasants were bound to the land and the Russian system of serfdom introduced. The *kozak* army also became a victim of this policy. Some of the *kozaky* were turned into regular regiments of the Russian army while others were forced into serfdom. Ukrainian nobility were given the same privileges as Russian nobility and became the main support of the Russian regime in Ukraine.

The final blow to Ukrainian independence from the Russian government came in 1786, in the so-called secularization of church lands. For centuries monasteries in Ukraine had been the centres of cultural and educational life. Monastic lands, donated by princes and hetmans, were the foundation on which it was possible for the monasteries to continue their educational and cultural activities. Secularization not only abolished this independent activity of the monasteries, but also subjected the entire Orthodox Church to the czarist government. Accordingly, the church ceased to be a spiritual force of the Ukrainian people and the architect of their spiritual and cultural values. It was transformed into an instrument for their enslavement and Russification.

During Catherine's reign lavish grants of Ukrainian territory to favorites and court hangers-on continued as well as settlement on Ukrainian territory by foreigners. As Catherine was of German origin, she was particularly interested in settlement by German colonists, to whom she granted privileges. They were settled on the most productive areas expropriated in Zaporozhian territory from the *kozak* officer class. Under Catherine, Ukraine was finally incorporated into the Russian empire and ceased to be separate state organization.

The same fate awaited territory neighbouring on the hetmanate, which was known as Slobidska Ukraine. This area of Ukrainian territory had been part of the Muscovite state from ancient times. When religious oppression became rampant after the Berest Union, however, it began to be settled very quickly by Ukrainian fugitives from the area under Polish rule. To protect its southern borders from Tartar incursions the czarist government permitted *kozaky* to settle here with the same organization and privileges they enjoyed in the hetmanate. For a long period Slobidska Ukraine enjoyed a virtual autonomy with *kozak* rights and privileges. When Crimea was conquered in Catherine's reign and the danger from Tartars eliminated, the *kozak* system of state organization was also abolished in Slobidska Ukraine. Originally it was given the name *gubernia* (province) of Slobidska Ukraine, but this was later changed to *gubernia* of Kharkiv and its northern sections were annexed to the Russian *guberniyi* of Voronezh and Kursk.

The Fate of Right Bank Ukraine

Right Bank Ukraine belonged to Turkey from the period of the Great Ruin and for a long period was depopulated and desolate. On the basis of the Polish-Turkish treaty of 1714 this territory was again ceded to Poland and colonization of these lands proceeded rapidly. To these lands came the Polish magnates once more to entice settlers from Ukrainian territory in the north-west with the promise of various privileges and exemptions from the *corvee* for ten or fifteen years. Difficult conditions in the hetmanate also encouraged many to seek a brighter future in Right Bank Ukraine. As the population increased, however, the demands and exactions of the Polish gentry became more burdensome. Persecution of Orthodox adherents became more common and a steady pressure was exerted on the inhabitants to adopt the Uniate faith.

As an answer to Polish coercion, there was an intermittent series of uprisings of *Haidamaky* which reached their greatest dimension in 1734 and 1750. Particularly protracted and bloody was the Haidamak uprising of 1768, which was given the name of Koliivshchyna. The commanders of this insurrection were Maksym Zalizniak and Ivan Gonta, still glorified in the memory of Ukrainians. Unfortunately, the Haidamak uprising lacked the organization and the clearness of purpose of the former *kozak* revolts. Though the insurrections reached great dimensions, they always ended in defeat, after which the condition of the Ukrainian population became worse.

The unruliness of the Polish gentry and nobility progressively weakened Poland and their intolerance of other faiths gave Poland's neighbours a pretext to interfere in Poland's internal affairs. Towards the end of the eighteenth century—in 1772, 1793, and 1795—Poland was subjected to partitions on three occasions by its neighbours: Russia, Prussia, and Austria. In the second partition of 1793 all of Right Bank Ukraine was annexed to the Russian empire. But the Russian government left unchanged the socio-economic order which had existed under the Polish regime. Although serfdom had reached a limit in burdensome and oppressive exactions in Poland at the end of the eighteenth century, any expectation on the part of the Ukrainian peasantry for a change in conditions under the Russians was futile. The only change for the peasant was that he was free to return to the Orthodox faith but, considering that the peasant continued to be the property of Polish Catholic magnates, even this freedom had no practical significance.

Galicia was ceded to Austria in the first partition. Transcarpathia had been part of Hungary for many years and Bukovyna was also occupied by Austro-Hungarian authorities in 1774. These western Ukrainian lands had an especially difficult destiny. Separated from their Ukrainian homeland for centuries and subjected to the rule of foreigners of alien faith, they had to bear a very onerous national, social, and religious yoke for a long period. These territories came under Austria in a state of disorganization and ruin; the people were impoverished and culturally neglected. The upper layers of their society had been compelled to abandon their Orthodox faith and join Polish or Hungarian ranks. The state of spiritual darkness can be gauged from the fact that the Ukrainian inhabitants did not know that they were Uniates. Having discovered this condition, many reverted to the Orthodox faith of their fathers. That the church union was only a Polish device to fragment the Ukrainian nation is evident from the fact that Polish support for the Uniates extended only insofar as it undermined the Orthodox Church. In Poland itself the union was subjected to ridicule and oppression.

The Uniate priesthood in Galicia were subject to the *corvee* and other feudal exactions like other serfs, including punishment by flogging with a birch rod. Not until five years after the Austrian occupation did the Austrian government forbid the Polish landlords to exact feudal services from Uniate priests.

It was in the interest of the Austrian government to raise the material and cultural standards of the people in the newly annexed territory. But its meager achievements in this area were only a drop in the ocean in terms of the needs of the population. Serfdom and the *corvee,* which had burdened the people for centuries, was not abolished until 1848. Just as the Russian government, in annexing Right Bank Ukraine, assumed the role of a protector of Orthodoxy, the Austrian government, to justify its occupation of Galicia, took over from Poland its role as a protector of the church union. All else remained unchanged under both occupations; the Polish nobility remained unbridled and the burdens of serfdom, with its inevitable consequences for the Ukrainian population, continued to oppress the Ukrainian peasantry.

Ukrainian National Revival

The Ukrainian national revival began in Left Bank and Slobidska Ukraine, where the tradition of a Ukrainian state had existed for the longest period and where national consciousness had never been extinguished. Though they had lost self-government, there were still many vestiges of Ukraine's former status as a separate state. The *kozak* class remained a separate class of society which meant that one-third of the population was exempt from the demands of serfdom. The courts also retained vestiges of Ukrainian law though the courts themselves were Russian. All administrative positions, from the governor to the village secretary, were filled by Ukrainians. Most importantly, Left Bank Ukraine retained an upper class of old *kozak* officials, now a gentry who cultivated the Ukrainian language and traditions in their daily life. This class proved to be important in the resurgence of Ukrainian nationalism as Catherine II raised *kozak* officials to an equal rank with Russian nobility (*dvorianstvo*). In order to prove their descent from *kozak* officials, many began to study the Ukrainian past in searching for their ancestry. Proof of ancestry of a *kozak* official was often necessary as a means for him to escape the compulsory services of serfdom. This research later formed the basis of Ukrainian historical studies and also provided information to submit to the Russian government in support of the claims of the Ukrainian nation to their rights under the terms of the Treaty of Pereiaslav.

Another influence in arousing national consciousness was the Ukrainian philosopher of the eighteenth century, Hryhorii Skovoroda (1722-1794). Through his teachings he influenced the revival of modern Ukrainian literature. The first literary production written in the modern Ukrainian language, the *Aeneid,* was produced by Ivan Kotliarevsky (1769-1838). With his drama, *Natalka Poltavka,* he is also regarded as the father of Ukrainian drama and the later development of the Ukrainian theatre. At the beginning of the nineteenth century there also appeared *Istoriia Rusov* (History of Rus), a highly patriotic work which reveals the perpetual aspirations of the Ukrainians for an independent state. This production influenced a whole group of authors of the Ukrainian revival of the nineteenth century. Especially important was its impact on the creativity of the great poetic genius and creator of modern Ukrainian thought, Taras Hryhorovych Shevchenko (1814-1861), and on the idealistic aims of the Kyrylo Metodiivske Bratstvo (Brotherhood of Saints Cyril and Methodius), the first Ukrainian political society.

The centre of this Ukrainian revival at the beginning of the nineteenth century became Kharkiv, the capital of Slobidska Ukraine. The first university was established here with the support of the gentry and merchant class. Around this university were grouped the following scientific and cultural leaders: Hryhorii Kvitka Osnovianenko, Petro Hulak Artemovsky, Levko Borykowsky, Mykola Kostomariv, and many others. The first journals also appeared here: *Ukraiinsky Viestnyk, Kharkivsky Demokrat,* and *Ukraiinsky Zhurnal.*

The French Revolution and the Napoleonic wars were favorable to the further development of the Ukrainian revival. A part of Ukrainian society even hoped for the creation of a Ukrainian state with the help of Napoleon but the majority still supported Russia. When Napoleon was marching on Moscow, Czar Alexander even gave permission for the formation of *kozak* regiments in Ukraine. After fifteen such regiments were rapidly organized, the government became so apprehensive that they were disbanded without ever being used against Napoleon.

In the period following Napoleon's defeat, a very severe reaction known as *Arakcheyevshchyna* set in. Revolutionary movements among the people, especially among army officers, grew in protest against this reaction, finally culminating in the Decembrist Rebellion of 1825. The southern branch of the Decembrists, led by Sergei Apostol, a descendant of Hetman Danylo Apostol, had definite national aims. The climax in the activities of this southern group was reached in the mutiny of the Chernihiv regiment in Vasylkiv.

Czar Alexander died childless and was succeeded by Nicholas I. The new czar crushed the rebellion ruthlessly, hanging five of its leaders, condemning hundreds to flogging, and exiling over a hundred to Siberia for life. In 1830, not long after the Decembrist rebellion, there was a Polish uprising in Warsaw which was also suppressed by Russian troops. However, it had beneficial results for the Ukrainian population in Right Bank Ukraine. As mentioned earlier, this territory had retained the Polish administrative system, which included Polish serfdom. After the rebellion the Russian government imposed changes which limited the despotic power of the Polish gentry. Moreover, the government confiscated the estates of those who had taken part in the rebellion and the estates became state property. At the same time the Polish language was forbidden in state institutions and all vestiges of church union were obliterated. Also quite important was the establishment of the St. Volodymyr University in Kiev in 1834. In the second half of the nineteenth century and the beginning of this century it became the centre of another Ukrainian revival.

Nicholas I's reign (1825-1855) was marked by a suppression of all manifestations of liberalism. Disturbed by the Decembrist and Polish uprisings, the czar feared free expression whether in speech or in print. Notwithstanding all the restrictions, the Ukrainian national movement grew steadily. In the beginning its centre was St. Petersburg, the capital of the Russian Empire, where Mykola Hohol (Gogol) also began writing. He was a descendant of a colonel (Ostap Hohol) of the *kozak* army in the Khmelnytsky period. In his novels Hohol made Ukraine known to the whole world, emphasizing particularly the heroic struggle of the *kozaky* for their freedom and for the Orthodox faith. The creativity of Hohol had tremendous impact on the growth of the national consciousness of the Russianized Ukrainian gentry. In St. Petersburg, Taras Shevchenko's poetic genius first began to unfold. In his *Kobzar,* Shevchenko gave to Ukrainian literature its greatest poetry and simultaneously provided Ukrainian people with a program for their liberation from national bondage. His poetry aroused enthusiasm throughout Ukraine among all classes of the population. True national revival began under the influence of his poetry in such distant areas of Ukraine as Bukovyna and Transcarpathia.

At the same time Shevchenko and a group of Ukrainian intelligentsia in Kiev formed the Kyrylo Metodiivske Bratstvo in 1846. Its main platform was the creation of a free Ukrainian republic within a federation of all Slavonic peoples based on the teaching of the Holy Evangelists. The brotherhood was betrayed to the police and its members were sentenced to varying periods of imprisonment. Because of his inflamatory, anticzarist, revolutionary poems, Shevchenko was condemned to exile as a private in the Russian army with an additional sentence forbidding him to paint or write in exile.

This setback to the Kyrylo Metodiivske Bratstvo was a great blow to the Ukrainian revival in Russian Ukraine. But Russian defeat in the Crimean War (1853-1855) aroused a new wave of revolutionary sentiment in the entire Russian Empire and Ukrainian cultural life began to flourish again. Many of the members of the brotherhood returned from exile to St. Petersburg, where Shevchenko also journeyed when his period of exile was terminated (after the death of Nicholas I). Ukrainian life began to revive. *Hromady* (societies) were organized, schools were established, cultural-educational activities became more numerous, and the publication of books increased. On February 19, 1861, serfdom was abolished in the Russian empire and a series of reforms designed to improve the condition of the people followed in succeeding years. But the Polish insurrection of 1863 and the violence of the Russian revolutionaries again brought a government reaction in which Ukrainian hopes also suffered. Russian chauvinists became obsessed with the nightmare of Ukrainian separatism, an obsession which grew out of sentiments which were best expressed by the contemporary minister of the Russian government, Valuyev, who asserted that "The Ukrainian language does not exist, has never existed, and must not exist." Simultaneously, many leaders who were active in Ukrainian organizations were again arrested and exiled. Following these events in Russian Ukraine, Ukrainian national life found a centre in the Austrian province of Galicia, where conditions were more favorable for Ukrainian cultural development.

Western Ukrainian Lands

When Galicia was annexed by Austria after the first partition of Poland in 1772, the inhabitants, as the result of long years of Polish oppression, were in a state of abject poverty and cultural deprivation. The upper classes of the nation had become Polonized long before and had adopted Roman Catholicism. The brotherhoods had been liquidated after the church union and education was in total decline. Above all, serfdom crushed the people like a heavy millstone, a condition from which even the clergy were not immune. The hierarchy of the Uniate Church were either Poles or Polonized Ukrainians whose language and culture had become Polish. Under Austria the Poles remained in authority. The government, wealth, administrative posts, and the Uniate Church were all under their control.

For its own interests, the Austrian government decided to help the Uniate Church be restored to new life. In this process the educational level of the clergy was raised, Uniate priests were put on an equal basis with the Roman Catholic clergy, and the Uniate Church was officially renamed the Greek Catholic Church. The action of the government was galling to the Poles, who thwarted Ukrainians wherever possible.

True national awakening took place in Galicia with the appearance of the so-called *"Ruska Triitsia"* (Ruthenian Trinity) consisting of Markian Shashkevych, Ivan Vahylevych, and Yakiv Holovatsky. Influenced by the literary revival in eastern Ukraine, these three students from a theological seminary published in 1838 an almanac, *Rusalka Dnistrova* (Dniester Water-Fairy), in the Ukrainian vernacular of their day. It is true that this publication was seized and banned by the Uniate hierarchy because of its anti-Polish sentiments but this did not arrest the national revival in Galicia.

One of the results of the European revolution of 1848, which also reached Galicia, was the final abolition of serfdom, bringing to an end the Ukrainian spiritual and physical dependence on the Polish landlord. On May 2 the first Ukrainian political organization, Holovna Ruska Rada (Central Ruthenian Council), was founded in Lviv. Its manifesto declared that Galicia was a member of the greater Ukrainian nation and demanded that the Austrian government divide Galicia into Polish and Ukrainian sectors and to include Transcarpathia in the Ukrainian sector.

But the "Spring of Nations" was of short duration. After suppressing the revolutionary movements with the help of the Russian army of Nicholas I, the Austrian government abolished the constitution and re-established absolute government. The entire administration again fell into the hands of the Poles.

In their despair, many Ukrainians in Galicia turned to their powerful neighbour, Russia, for salvation, in the same way as many of their predecessors had done under Khmelnytsky. In this way, the first Muscophile or Russophile movement in Galicia was born, which was to bring Ukrainians much tragedy in the First World War.

In 1860 a new constitution was adopted in Austria-Hungary. Galicia, as well as other provinces of the empire, became autonomous and was granted its own Diet. But the Poles continued to obstruct Ukrainian efforts to improve their lot by constitutional means. The Polish majority in the Galician Seim (Diet) rejected even the most modest and legitimate proposals of the Ukrainians. At the same time they intensified the already existing apprehension of the Austrian government in regard to Muscophilism, though they supported it locally to weaken the Ukrainian movement.

As a reaction against Muscophilism there arose in the 1860s a so-called *narodovetsky* (populist) movement among Ukrainians, which was enthusiastically supported by eastern Ukrainian leaders. This movement played a large part in arousing national consciousness from its apathy and despair. It performed its greatest service in the cultural-educational field. As all printing in the Ukrainian language was forbidden in eastern Ukraine, writers often published their works in Galicia, usually with the financial aid of benefactors from eastern Ukraine. In 1868 the populists founded the Prosvita Society in Galicia; it was to play a very important part in stimulating Ukrainian national consciousness and particularly in raising their educational and cultural level. Aroused by deterioration in the political field, the populists gradually became more involved in political activities by founding in Galicia the Narodna Rada (National Council), which had the same basic aims as the Holovna Ruska Rada.

In 1891 the Ukrainian Radical Party was organized in Galicia. The most prominent positions in this party were held by Ivan Franko, an outstanding poet, writer, and scholar, and Mykhailo Pavlyk, a leading political and community activist. This was really the first political party of its kind in Galicia. On economic and social questions its platform was based on socialism but on the national question it was the first party in the modern history of Ukraine to issue a call for complete Ukrainian independence. Its policies were also adopted in eastern Ukraine, where its greatest support came from the Revolutionary Ukrainian Party.

Though the national and political consciousness of the Ukrainian people increased, their economic condition grew steadily worse. The poverty of the peasants reached its lowest limits. The concentration of the village population on a limited land area, the lack of any manufacturing industry, and the concentration of vast estates in the hands of a small group of Polish landlords brought the peasants to most abject destitution. There was no hope of improvement through reform and for many Ukrainian villages in Galicia there was only one solution; they had to return to labour on the estates of those landlords from whom their parents had been liberated when serfdom had been abolished. In this way began the formation of a class of landless villagers, the village proletariat, whose demands for their rights became increasingly urgent. Masses of these people left their homes for seasonal work in Prussia. In a relatively short time another possibility emerged for the peasant to improve his lot. He could emigrate to far away lands beyond the ocean: first Brazil, then the United States, and Canada.

The First Great War interrupted in Galicia both the Ukrainian struggle for national and political rights, and their search for a better destiny by emigrating across the ocean. Almost identical were the fortunes of other parts of western Ukraine, Bukovyna and Transcarpathia. Most of the Ukrainian immigrants to Canada between 1891 and 1914, when immigration ceased owing to the outbreak of war, arrived from western Ukraine where economic conditions were most unfavorable and from where it was comparatively less difficult to obtain permission to emigrate than from eastern Ukraine, which was still under Russian rule.

Independent Ukrainian Statehood

The first Russian revolution, which broke out in 1905 after Russian defeat in the Russo-Japanese War, did not bring any fundamental change in the lives of Ukrainians or those of other people in the Russian Empire. It is true that a constitution was adopted in which the state Duma (parliament) and the guarantee of civil liberties were included, but reactionary measures which followed the suppression of the uprisings terminated any concessions which had been made. On the other hand, the revolution of February 1917, which erupted as the result of difficult conditions created by the long and exhausting war (1914-1918), brought basic changes to the nationalities of the empire. Immediately after its outbreak the Ukrainians in Kiev formed Ukrainska Tsentralna Rada (Ukrainian Central Council) as the central representative body of the Ukrainian people. Mykhailo Hrushevsky, a famous historian, was elected to head this body. On the appeal of the Rada the whole of Ukraine awoke to the necessity of creating new life in the state. There followed army, peasant, labour, and professional mass congresses which unanimously declared their support of the Rada and demanded the restoration of autonomous rights to Ukraine from the Russian Provisional Government on the basis of the Treaty of Pereiaslav.

Unfortunately, democratic government in Russia lasted only for eight weeks, after which the Bolsheviks usurped power through treachery and force. After seizing power in Russia, the Bolsheviks immediately invaded Ukraine for they realized that, without it, world revolution was doomed to failure and Bolshevik rule in Russia itself was threatened. For Russia's existence, Ukrainian grain, coal, and steel were a necessity, like air itself.

In this situation, the Ukrainian Central Council proclaimed its fourth universal declaration. It declared that Ukraine was a free, sovereign state, an independent nation of Ukrainian people, and appealed to all its citizens to come to their government's defence against Bolshevik Russian invasion. Simultaneously, the Ukrainian government signed the Berest peace treaty with the Central Powers on February 9, 1918. Great and glorious perspectives of state organization appeared to await the Ukrainian nation. Unfortunately, the Germans, who had been invited into Ukraine as allies in the war against "Red Moscow", very soon began to behave like an ordinary occupationary force whose main task was to obtain Ukrainian grain to feed their own hungry people and their army. To facilitate their plans, the Germans encouraged a plot to overthrow the Ukrainian government. Hetman Pavlo Skoropadsky's regime succeeded that of the democratic Rada. During the short period of this regime, the hetman did much to establish state organization and he might have accomplished more had he not been hampered by the German army command.

Following the defeat of Germany in November 1918, the hetman announced a federation with Russia, which he felt the Entente powers would want to rebuild. This act immediately provoked an uprising of the Ukrainian people, under the leadership of a great national figure in the Ukrainian struggle for independence, Simon Petliura, now a national hero. All of Ukraine was liberated from the German army very shortly and the Ukrainian National Republic was proclaimed once more. Bolshevik Russia, no longer bound by the terms of the Berest treaty, invaded Ukraine soon after. For the next four years Ukraine waged a difficult and unequal war, not only with the Bolshevik and "White" Russian armies, but also with Poland, which had invaded Galicia after the disintegration of Austria-Hungary. The most momentous episode of this period was the proclamation on January 22, 1919 of the union of all Ukrainian territory into one united Ukrainian state. Unfortunately, this union was never fully realized.

Abandoned by the victorious Entente powers, surrounded by enemies on all sides, decimated by typhus without medical help of any kind, the ragged and hungry army of the Ukrainian National Republic fought to the end. Weakened remnants of the army crossed borders to the west without surrendering, to live as emigres, while others continued the struggle in guerilla bands. Eastern Ukraine was occupied by Russia while Poland, with Entente aid, was able to retain Galicia and Volhyn. Romania seized Bessarabia and Bukovyna, and Transcarpathia went to Czecho-Slovakia. However, the great national revolution and the four year struggle of the Ukrainian people were not all lost. The Bolsheviks had to recognize the existence of Ukraine as a separate state and nation in the formation of a Ukrainian Soviet Socialist Republic within the Soviet Union. Ukraine was even admitted to the United Nations Assembly as a separate independent state after the Second World War.

During 1921-22 millions succumbed to a terrible famine which followed the revolution. This famine was really the first effort of Bolshevik Russia to break the resistance of the Ukrainians against Bolshevik usurpation of their territory. Nevertheless, Ukrainians again revived in the comparatively more liberal atmosphere ushered in during the period of the New Economic Policy (NEP), which was instituted by the Russian government between 1922 and 1928 to relieve the difficult economic situation. Under these conditions, the Ukrainian Orthodox Church revived and expanded its activities, becoming a true spiritual force in the nation. Ukraine achieved prominence in scholarship, education, and other kindred fields. But new oppressive tactics were brought in by Moscow after 1928 which soon destroyed these achievements. The first step of the Soviet government was the liquidation, or exile with a slower death, of large numbers of the Ukrainian intelligentsia. The attack then proceeded against the Ukrainian

Orthodox Church. Finally, it concluded with the utilization of mass terror against the foundation of the nation, its *selianstvo* (village peasant farmers). As a consequence of forced collectivization of these village farmers and another artificial famine in 1932-33, over seven million Ukrainians died of starvation. The mass terror of the 1930s, known as the *yezhovshchyna,* was a fitting climax to all acts of violence and completed the ruin of Ukraine on the eve of the Second World War.

Ukrainian territory under Poland between the two wars found itself in somewhat different circumstances. Though Polish terror was often prevalent and the Ukrainians were subjected to national and religious oppression, the Poles were still sensitive to world opinion. Of special importance is the fact that emigration from Poland was permitted. As a result, 68,000 Ukrainians, chiefly former members of Ukrainian armies or anti-Polish resistance movements, landed in Canada between 1923 and 1939. However, the resistance of the Ukrainian population against their conquerors never ceased in areas occupied by Poland. Revolutionary activities were continued under the leadership of the Ukrainska Viiskova Orhanizatsiia (Ukrainian Army Organization) and later by the Orhanizatsiia Ukrainskykh Natsionalistiw (Organization of Ukrainian Nationalists). The constitutional struggle was maintained by the various political parties which were permitted in the Polish state.

On September 1, 1939, the Second World War broke out with the German invasion of Poland. The Soviet army, on the basis of an agreement signed between Russia and Germany, crossed the eastern border of Poland on September 17 to occupy Ukrainian territory under Polish rule. This area was proclaimed part of the Ukrainian Soviet Socialist Republic. In the summer of 1940 the Soviet army also occupied Bessarabia and Bukovyna, an act which brought almost all Ukrainian lands under one dominion, the Soviet Union.

On June 22, 1941, the most frightening war known to mankind was unleashed in Ukraine with Hitler's attack on the Soviet Union. In this war Ukrainians lost ten million people—including dead and wounded, and those martyred in prisoner of war camps or in Siberian exile. A large element simply disappeared without any trace. Hundreds of towns and villages were destroyed by both armies and over two million Ukrainian youth were deported to forced labour in Germany, many of whom died of hunger, exhausting labour, or from Allied bombs.

In the beginning Ukrainians welcomed the Germans as liberators but it soon became evident that the Germans were as remorseless in their hostility to Ukrainians as were the Russians. In a short time partisan bands opposing the Germans appeared everywhere. Beginning in 1942 there appeared the UPA, Ukrainska Povstanska Armiia (Ukrainian Insurgent Army), which carried on the fight against the Germans. After the German defeat, UPA prolonged the struggle against Bolshevik forces until 1950.

The end of the war found hundreds of thousands of Ukrainians in western Europe who did not want to return to Russian Bolshevik bondage. Over 38,000 of these refugees arrived in Canada between the end of the war and 1961. This component of Ukrainian immigration to Canada was mainly composed of educated individuals whose arrival strengthened very markedly the earlier Ukrainian settlement in Canada.

The difficult historical path of the Ukrainian nation was not ended with its complete emancipation from national, social, and religious bondage, which even the less fortunate nations of Asia and Africa have accomplished. Recovering from wounds inflicted during the Second World War and the succeeding period of Stalinist terror, the Ukrainian nation continues its efforts for full liberation and to attain rights of self-government as guaranteed in the constitution of the Ukrainian Soviet Socialist Republic. Ukrainians refuse to remain a colony of the Russian-Bolshevik empire—the only empire now left on our planet in the twentieth century.

2

Historiography

Sources About Ukrainians in Canada

Many people whose lives might be considered a source of historical study
often fail to leave any written records. While building a new life under un-
familiar conditions and experiencing new problems, they lack the time to
record daily occurrences. Besides, they are seldom consciously aware that
they are creators of events which have historical significance. This was also
largely true of the first Ukrainians who arrived in Canada. Initially, they
found themselves in a strange and foreign land, without a knowledge of the
language of its inhabitants, and without any material possessions for the
start of a new life. Although their immediate task was to earn enough
money to support themselves and their families (who had either accompanied them to Canada or had been left in their native village), they still
found time and energy to describe their environment and experiences to
their relatives or friends at home. They did not yet have their own Ukrainian newspapers in Canada and even in the United States they were without a
newspaper during the years 1891 to 1895*. But in their personal correspondence the first Ukrainian immigrants in Canada left researchers and
historians a wealth of source materials, without which it would be impossible to write a history of Ukrainians in Canada. A large proportion of these
materials were also preserved in the Ukrainian press published in the

---

* Stechishin is slightly in error here, as a Ukrainian language newspaper called *Svoboda* began
publishing in Jersey City, N. J. in September 1893. The first Ukrainian newspaper in the
United States was *Ameryka*, published by Father Ivan Voliansky in Shenanadoah, Pa., between 1886 and 1890. (Ed.)

Austro-Hungarian and Russian Empires before the first newspapers were published in Canada and the United States. In this respect the first Ukrainian settlers differed from other immigrants. Though they were not always aware that their actions had historical significance, they still recorded everything they saw and heard around them, what they heard from others, or what others had experienced. Almost as soon as Ukrainians began to reach Canada, especially when they began arriving in larger groups, it was their good fortune that either their leaders or others among them began to write about the experiences of the settlers almost as soon as they could buy their first writing paper and had a post office established in their area. This certainly became true when they began to receive the first copies of *Svoboda* from the United States, or one of the newspapers from their homeland, and, much later, the first Ukrainian publications in Canada.

Among the first accounts was that of Dr. Osyp Oleskiw. Even prior to his visit to Canada in the summer of 1895 under the auspices of the "Prosvita" Society, he wrote about Canada in the brochure *Vilni Zemli* (Free Lands), published in Lviv by the same society in July 1895. Following this, he visited Canada himself to make an on the spot investigation of possibilities for settlement and returned to Galicia. Upon his return, he published in December 1895 a second brochure, entitled *O emigratsii* (About emigration).[1] In this publication he described the small Ukrainian settlements about which there was information, namely: Edna, Neudorf, and Winnipeg. Furthermore, he listed by name almost every Ukrainian immigrant in Canada. These brochures are the first authoritative sources of historical materials dealing with Ukrainian immigration to Canada.

One year later an American Ukrainian, Dionisey Salley, a bookseller from New York visited Canada on his own and described very accurately the life of Ukrainians in both Alberta and Winnipeg in a five-part series in the American weekly *Svoboda*.[2]

In the same year (1896), Dr. Oleskiw, already in ill health and resting in the health resort at Carlsbad, wrote his third book, *Khliborobstvo za okeanom, a pereselencha emigratsiia* (Agriculture beyond the ocean and transplanted emigrants) which he published at his own expense in the press of the Basilian Fathers in Zhovkva. In this Polish-language booklet of forty-eight pages, Oleskiw stressed the necessity for establishing an efficient emigration and colonization bureau in Galicia to plan emigration intelligently and conscientiously. As an authoritative source for research in Ukrainian-Canadian history, this pamphlet should also be popularized and included in any study of Oleskiw's publications.[3]

Probably the most fortunate event to befall the early Ukrainian immigrants was the arrival in 1897 of Father Nestor Dmytriw from the United States. Not only was he the first Ukrainian Greek Catholic priest in Canada but he was also editor of *Svoboda*. He was sent to Canada by the American organization, the Ruthenian (Ukrainian) National Union, to bring moral support to the new Ukrainian immigrants and to provide them with religious services. Father Dmytriw wrote a detailed account of his Canadian visit in a brochure entitled *Kanadiiska Rus* (Canadian Rus) as well as in other articles and contributions to *Svoboda*. This brochure and other articles have become mandatory sources for all primary research into the early period of Ukrainian immigration to Canada.[4]

In the same year (1897), Kropotkin, the famous Russian revolutionary, arrived in Canada and also visited the Ukrainian settlements. An account of his visit was translated from the English language to Ukrainian and published in *Svoboda* by Father Pawlo Tymkevych.[5]

Valuable information about Ukrainians in Canada can be found in articles contributed to *Svoboda* by Father Pavlo Tymkevych during 1898 and 1899. As the second Greek Catholic priest to visit Canada, he was concerned not only about religious and national matters but also about the economic condition of both labourers and farmers. His articles relating to the history of these settlements also occupy a prominent place among historical accounts of this period.

It would also be an act of negligence to omit Kyrylo (Cyril) Genik-Berezowsky, who was a director of the Canadian Department of Immigration responsible for directing Ukrainian immigrants to settlement areas in Canada. He often visited Ukrainian colonies in the company of Father Dmytriw.* Genik wrote many articles to *Svoboda*, signing them simply as "Correspondent of *Svoboda*". His official pronouncements with regard to Ukrainian immigration, as well as his warnings and advice, also comprise valuable material for the study of Ukrainian settlement in Canada.

In addition to the contributions of these eminent Ukrainians, immigrant labourers and farmers also wrote letters and articles to *Svoboda*. It should be remembered that with the beginning of mass immigration in 1896, largely as a result of Oleskiw's efforts, there were settlers of above-average financial means as well as some with formal education on the first few steamships which arrived in Canada. It should, therefore, not surprise us that there should appear correspondents to *Svoboda* everywhere—in farming communities, in every city, in mining towns, and even on "extra-gangs" (labourers recruited for the building and repair of the railroad). Between 1896 and 1906, over 150 correspondents from Canada have been identified,

---

* Actually, Genik was not a director, only an officer of the Immigration Branch of the Department of Interior. As an immigration agent, he supervised the immigration of Ukrainians and other nationalities into Western Canada. Genik visited colonies with Dmytriw only during 1897-98, for in 1898 Dmytriw returned to the United States. (Ed.)

among whom were the following: Antin Sawka, Vasyl Ksionzhyk, Teodosy Wachna, Ivan Bodrug, Ivan Negrych, Nykola Gavinchuk, Taras Ferley, Yurko, Ivan and Vasyl Syrotiuk, Ivan Danylchuk, Hryhor Kraykiwsky, Alexander Zhylych, Alexander Karpets, Yosafat Dziobko, Ivan Kun, Ivan Rzesniowsky, Apolinarii Novak, Myroslaw Stechishin, Vasyl Romaniuk, Vasyl Holovatsky, Mykhailo Gowda, Toma Tomashevsky, Ivan Drohomoretsky, Sava Chernetsky, Orest Zherebko, Dmytro Solianych, Teodor Stefanyk, Vasyl Kudryk, Yosef Sikorsky, Rev. Andrew Vilchynsky, Osyp Bubniak, Hr. Begar, Pavlo Onyschuk, Yordan Lastiwka, Vasyl Standryk, Mykhailo Pryhrotsky, Nykola Palahniuk, Warwara Katerynych, Anna Chernetska, Petro Woycenko, Ivan Nimchuk, Mykola Babych, Yurko Machula, Anastaziewsky, N. Nadia, and many others. Some of the above wrote under various *noms de plume* and pseudonyms.

Their correspondence encompassed the entire range of activities in their communities, especially their religious, cultural and economic problems. In addition to the articles in *Svoboda*, there were novels, stories, essays, poems, translations from other languages, and other samples of literature of that period. By no means a small number of these correspondents achieved prominence as leading personalities, becoming publicists, poets, editors, civic, and religious leaders.

Ten years after the inauguration of mass emigration to Canada under Oleskiw, the Lviv Prosvita Society, which had sent Dr. Oleskiw to Canada ten years earlier, now decided that someone else should be sent to investigate conditions of settlement in Canada and the United States. In consultation with the Shevchenko Scientific Society, they chose Dr. Julian Bachynsky to make this study. Bachynsky reached the United States in August 1905. After visiting all the main Ukrainian settlements in the United States, he arrived in Canada in June 1906. During his four month visit[6] in Canada, he was hosted in Ukrainian communities from Montreal to Vancouver and collected the necessary information on the life of Ukrainians in Canada for future publication. As a result of this journey, he published in Lviv in 1914 a very authoritative and exhaustive study based on documentary evidence about Ukrainians in the United States.[7]

A similar publication was projected for Canada and the type had already been set when the First World War broke out. The enterprise was postponed until the end of the war but, for some unknown reason, the book was never published. Not only were the plates lost but even the manuscript disappeared. Some authors, including M. Marunchak in his *History of Ukrainians in Canada*, assume that the plates were lost as the result of wartime conditions. However, judging from an article first published by Bachynsky in *Dilo*, which was reproduced in *Svoboda*,[8] both plates and manuscript could have been lost not only because of wartime conditions but also because the book's appearance was not welcomed by some sources. Bachynsky himself wrote a brochure on its loss sixteen years later, entitling it *Yak ya vydavav "Ukraiinsku emigratsiiu"* (How I published "Ukrainian emigration").[9] In it he blames the executive of the Prosvita Society, claiming that, without his approval, they collected all unbound volumes from the bookbinding section and sold them to a Jewish merchant for wrapping paper in the bazaar. He termed the action of the Prosvita group barbaric and culturally criminal. Needless to say, the loss of his manuscript was a cruel misfortune for the history of Ukrainians in Canada.

In the same year (1906), probably at the urging of Bachynsky, Osyp Megas, then editor of *Kanadiisky Farmer*, also broached the subject of a history of Ukrainians in Canada. He appealed to the readers of his newspaper to send him photographs and information which he could use in publishing "The History of Canadian Rus". And indeed, in the next year, there appeared a forty-six page brochure entitled *Western Canada* with valuable information including statistical data and a map about Ukrainian settlements in Manitoba, Saskatchewan, Alberta, and British Columbia. It is curious that this brochure was authorized by Frank Oliver, the Minister of the Interior. Though the book omits the name of the author, there is no doubt that the author was Osyp Megas or someone under his supervision. Whoever was the author, this was the first book written by a Ukrainian-Canadian writer.

In the next two years there appeared in Kiev two brochures about Ukrainians in Canada and the United States. The first, *Pro Kanadu—Yaka tse zemlia i yak u nii zhyvut ludy* (About Canada—The country and its people), did not include the name of any author but was published in 1908 by the Kievan Prosvita Society. This was a forty-seven page publication, most of which was devoted to the history of Canada. It included only one small chapter of seven pages with very scanty information about Canadian Ukrainians. The second publication, a somewhat larger brochure, was published in 1909 by the same society under the title *Ukrayintsi u Amerytsi* (Ukrainians in America). The author of this work was V. Korolov. Before writing his brochure, he had appealed to Ukrainians through the columns of *Svoboda* to send him all materials and information to Kiev.

Unfortunately, no copy of this work is available and we do not know how much of the information in this book was devoted to Ukrainians in Canada. There is also some doubt about its date of publication being 1909. In the first brochure, published in 1909 by the same Prosvita Society, there is the following information: "If any reader desires more information about the life of our people in Canada, he should read *Ukrainians in America* by V. Korolov, published by the Prosvita Society in Kiev."[10] This note could indicate that Korolov's book was published earlier than the brochure *About Canada—The country and its people.* Either there is some error of Korolov's brochure of 1909 is a second edition.

During the First World War, in 1916, there appeared another forty-page brochure, *Ukrainians in America,* published by the Union for the Freedom of Ukraine. The author of this work was Orest Kyrylenko, in all probability a *nom de plume* of Orest Zherebko, who had left Winnipeg in 1913 to continue his education in Galicia. He was caught in Europe by the outbreak of war and finally landed in Vienna, from where he returned to Winnipeg in 1916 with the help of Ukrainians in Canada. In this booklet the author discusses in turn such matters as religion, politics, schools, press, and assimilation, pointing out the principal shortcomings of Ukrainian society in Canada.

Apart from all these attempts of Ukrainian writers to depict the life of Ukrainians in Canada, the Canadian Department of Immigration and Colonization in 1916 engaged J. S. Woodsworth, a Methodist minister, to pursue research into Ukrainian settlement in Manitoba, Saskatchewan, and Alberta. With the help of Wasyl Swystun, who was also engaged for this purpose, he prepared a very objective study. At present it is considered to be a very valuable primary source about Ukrainian settlement in western Canada and has been used as a reference in all research about Ukrainians in this country.[11]

Eventually, as the lives of Ukrainians became normalized following the First Great War and when more native intellectual leaders appeared, the project of writing a history again became prominent in the minds of Canadian Ukrainians.

For example, at a meeting of the Board of Directors of the Petro Mohyla Institute in Saskatoon in 1920, a decision was made to engage Wasyl Swystun and Julian Stechishin to tour Ukrainian settlements both for the purpose of collecting funds for the Institute and tabulating information about the first Ukrainian pioneers in Canada, especially about the beginnings of organized life. Although both of them set out to visit communities with that purpose, they were compelled by circumstances to limit themselves to the most pressing objective in that period, the collection of funds. For the time being, the gathering of historical materials assumed a secondary role.

Two years later, at the Sixth National Convention of the Petro Mohyla Institute in Saskatoon, December 27 and 28, 1922, the matter of a history and the collection of source materials was again proposed in the presence of a speaker from Europe, Dr. Osyp Nazaruk. Following this discussion, the convention passed a resolution directing the Petro Mohyla Institute to establish an art gallery and to undertake the collection of all other materials of cultural or historical significance. The resolution is as follows:

This convention resolves that, after the debts of the Institute have been liquidated, special attention should be directed to the collection of all Ukrainian
newspapers in Canada, United States, Brazil, Zeleny Klyn (Eastern Siberia), as
well as those of other emigrant groups, including references from the foreign
press about Ukrainian matters; furthermore that there be established a gallery
of paintings and scenes which, in the first place, would depict more important
events in Ukrainian history from ancient to modern times, as well as accounts
of individual phases of Ukrainian life, in addition that there be established a
Ukrainian museum in the Institute with a division for early editions, printed
materials, manuscripts, and biographies of Canadians; that in the museum
there be historical accounts of each settlement in Canada, money samples,
photographs of the lives of Ukrainians in Canada, former weapons, and a
natural museum.[12]

Eventually, the Petro Mohyla Institute in Saskatoon established a very
valuable library, where the Ukrainian Women's Association later located
their ethnographic museum, but it fell far short of what was intended in
these extremely idealistic resolutions. On the other hand, Nazaruk contributed a good deal to the history of Canadian Ukrainians by his accounts
of his journey through Canada.[13]

In 1927 another work appeared, entitled *Tserkov Ukraintsiv v Kanadi*
(The Ukrainian Church in Canada), written by Father Panteleymon
Bozhyk. Three years later, it was re-published as *Istoriia Ukrainskoii
Emigratsii v Kanadi za chas vid 1890 do 1930 r.* (A History of Ukrainian
Emigration in Canada). Bozhyk, a former priest of the Russian Orthodox
Church, had switched to the Greek Catholic Church under Bishop Nykyta
Budka's jurisdiction. Though much of Bozhyk's account is biased, it
brought many new events to light. Although the title under which the book
was initially released indicates an exclusively religious orientation, it actually relates many other events from the life of Ukrainians in Canada, and thus
the title of the 1930 edition is a more appropriate description of the book's
contents than was the earlier one.[14]

A wealth of interesting, primary source material about Ukrainians can
also be found in *Beyond the Ocean* by Lev Yasenchuk.[15] Yasenchuk travelled to Canada and the United States as a representative of the Ridna
Shkola Association in Galicia, an organization devoted to the promotion of
Ukrainian schools. Having journeyed through all of Canada, he described
Ukrainian settlements, their organizations, and the leading personalities
whom he had met. His observations with regard to cultural and educational
life as well as religious relations, both in Canada and the United States,
were recorded very objectively.

To the historical literature regarding Ukrainian life in Canada, one
could also add a work in English, *The Ukrainian Canadians* by Charles H.

Young.[16] He was commissioned by the National Committee on Mental Health with the Department of Immigration to investigate thoroughly the life of Ukrainian settlers in the three western provinces of Canada. The author visited Ukrainian districts in Manitoba, Saskatchewan, and Alberta, collected a wealth of material about every activity in their lives, and reported his findings objectively and exhaustively in his book.

The Ukrainian question in Canada was often dealt with by Ukrainian authors even when their books were written primarily about Canada. We discover this to be the case, for instance, in the brochure of the Kievan Prosvita Society published in 1908 and, subsequently, by Zygmunt Bychynsky, a Protestant minister, who wrote the *History of Canada* in 1928[17] in which he included a chapter of thirteen pages on the history of Ukrainians in Canada.

The story of the arrival of Ukrainians in Canada aroused the interest of Professor Ivan Bobersky, who travelled to Canada and the United States in 1920 as a representative of the Ukrainian Citizens' Committee in Lviv to appeal for aid to the homeland. After completing his assigned task, he remained in Canada for several years. When it came to his attention that Ivan Pylypiw (Pylypiwsky)* and Wasyl Eleniak were regarded as the first Ukrainians to arrive in Canada, he interviewed them and recorded their story. His interview with Eleniak was published in the almanac of the newspaper, *Providnyk,* in 1933; that with Pylypiw appeared in the almanac of *Kanadiisky Farmer* in 1937. The information submitted by Bobersky about these two early settlers became an authoritative source for the history of Ukrainians in Canada.

---

* Ivan Pylypiw's original surname was Pylypiwsky, but he shortened it to Pylypow when he came to Canada (but it was pronounced by Ukrainians as Pylypiw and thus we refer to it as such). The use of the letter "o" in the name, pronounced as the letter "i" in Ukrainian, is probably a result of the influence of the Old Slavonic orthography of that period. (Ed.)

3

Were Ukrainians in Canada Before 1891?

Although Ukrainians are among the most recent arrivals in Canada, numerically they are fourth in the list of national groups, after the Anglo-Saxons, French, and Germans. In the prairie provinces the Ukrainians numerically are third; Anglo-Saxons and Germans are the two most numerous groups and the French are fourth.[1]

When did the Ukrainians first come to Canada? It is generally believed that immigration in large numbers began with the arrival of Ivan Pylypiw and Wasyl Eleniak in 1891. However, this does not mean that no Ukrainians could have come to Canada prior to that date.[2] With the adverse living conditions which were chronic in Ukraine, within both the Austro-Hungarian and Russian empires, it is possible that some Ukrainians might have arrived earlier, either across the Pacific or Atlantic oceans, and there is some documentary evidence as well as oral tradition to support this view.

Ukrainians on the West Coast of Canada?

We must first turn our attention to the northwest coast of the North American continent since, according to Dr. Mykhailo Huculak, "ships direct from the Black Sea coast of Ukraine brought people and provisions to the Russian fortification, Fort Ross", even during the first half of the nineteenth century.[3] As early as 1724 Peter I, the Russian Czar, had ordered Vitus Bering, a Dane who had distinguished himself in the Russian naval service, to explore the northern area of the Pacific Ocean to determine whether Asia and North America were joined at any point. With a crew of forty-four men, Bering crossed the strait between Chukotsk Peninsula and Alaska in 1728 and discovered that the two continents were entirely separated by water.[4] In 1741 a second expedition under Bering, consisting of two vessels and six hundred men, started from Petropavlovsk in Kamchatka. After discovering the Aleutian Islands, Bering explored the southern coast of Alaska, reaching a point near Mt. St. Elias. Ill with scurvy, Bering wrecked his ship on the way back on one of the Commander Islands three hundred miles from Petropavlovsk where he died, together with a large number of his men. Only a tragic remnant of the expedition reached Petropavlovsk, but it arrived with a large quantity of seal, otter, and beaver skins, which encouraged other expeditions in later years in spite of the dangers.

In the years that followed, the Russians became very active in the fur trade among the Aleuts and, since there were no rival countries involved in this area before 1775, soon gained complete control of the territory, formally calling it Russian America. With the occupation of Unalaska and the Kodiak islands in 1784, Kodiak became the capital and remained an important centre of population and trade until the end of the century. Early in the nineteenth century, it declined in importance, ceding first place to the island of Baranov, closer to the mainland. On the site of the Sitka settlement, which the natives had destroyed earlier, the Russians built a new capital in 1804, called New Archangelsk. It grew very rapidly and a ship building industry was developed which served Russia until 1860. A lumber mill, a wood factory, and a magnetic observatory were also built and, for a time, there even existed a seminary for the training of priests.[5]

From New Archangelsk the Russians continued to explore North America's west coast, especially what is now British Columbia, and had plans to occupy Vancouver Island. But for some reason they occupied Bodega Bay in California instead, founding Fort Ross, slightly north of San Francisco. Plans to establish themselves in Hawaii[6] were curtailed after the Napoleonic Wars, as the Spaniards, the English, and the Americans began to exert pressure on Russia's advance posts, forcing a diplomatic retreat. In 1824 Russia's consular office in Philadelphia arranged a treaty with the United States in which Russia agreed to surrender her claims to all territory from Bodega Bay north to the fifty-fourth parallel[7], retaining only Alaska and the Aleutian Islands. In 1841, as a corollary to this agreement, Russia sold Fort Ross to the United States. In this fort, according to Russian sources, there were sometimes as many as eight hundred people. Nevertheless, disputes with the sailors of the above-mentioned countries continued and to avoid further friction after the Crimean War, Russia agreed to sell Alaska and the Aleutian Islands to the United States for $7,200,000.

For Ukrainians these events are important because they took place after the battle of Poltava in 1709, which saw the defeat of the Ukrainian hetman, Mazepa. A period of merciless oppression followed, resulting in the exile of Ukrainian *kozaky* and civilians who served as convict labourers in the farthest corners of Siberia. This oppression lasted until the destruction of the Zaporozhian Sich in 1775, when a large contingent of *kozaky* were exiled beyond the Amur River in the east. Some of these *kozaky,* traditionally restless and venturesome, may have played an important role in the above events. Ukrainians, then, could well have formed part of the crews of the ships of Bering's first and second expeditions. They could have taken part in the exploration of Alaska and the whole western coast of the North American continent, as did Yuriy Lysiansky (1773-1837), and could have laboured in the shipbuilding yards, the foundry, the lumber mill, and the wood-working shops in Kodiak and Archangelsk. They might even have been involved in missionary activities from Alaska to California. Undoubtedly, they could also have been in Fort Ross as "Russian" soldiers, defending the fort but also busying themselves in horticulture, fruit and grain-growing, and shipbuilding.

In his monograph on *Ahapius Honcharenko*[8], Wasyl Luciw, using Polish sources in the U.S.A., notes that there were 20,000 Ukrainians in California and Alaska in 1865, although he himself questions the figure. Nevertheless, the same number was used by Honcharenko himself in an article written before 1894, entitled "The *Kozak* Country in North America, or Alaska", published in *Narod,* a newspaper published in Kolomyia, Galicia. Later his article was quoted in the American newspaper *Svoboda.*[9] Summarizing the general tenor of this article in the *U.N.A. Commemorative Book,* Luka Myshuha, the editor of *Svoboda,* comments:

> Honcharenko writes that the route from Kamchatka to the Kuril Islands was well known to the *kozaky* and from the latter they sailed on their *baydaky* (boats) all the way to Astoria in Oregon and San Diego and Mendocino in California. However, Russia joined the English in driving these fearless seamen with their *baydaky* back to Kamchatka. In 1724 Russia equipped an expedition with a German, Captain Bering in charge, to search for new lands, but his guides were Kamchatka seamen—*kozaky.* It was very convenient for them as they knew these areas. While Bering rested, *kozak* Chernykhiv with others continued the search for islands and discovered them. On these settled the relatives of the free Kamchatka inhabitants and the islands were named the Aleutians. When the governor of Alaska asked the inhabitants to identify themselves, they informed him that they were *kozaky.* After Russia sold Alaska to the United States in 1867, the czar issued an *ukaz* that all *kozaky* return to Kamchatka. However, they ignored the order and remained in Alaska, about twenty thousand of them living on the islands of Atygnak (Afognak), Kodiak, and on the Aleutian Archipelago. At first the Americans

thought they were Indians. Only later did they realize that they were descendants of that famous Ukrainian chivalry—the *kozaky*.[10]

The claims of Honcharenko and Luciw, attractive as they may be to Ukrainians, must be accepted with reserve until they can be thoroughly investigated. Nevertheless, the possibility that there were Ukrainian *kozaky* among the Russians in Alaska is an interesting hypothesis.

Being in New York at the time when Alaska was purchased, Honcharenko decided to travel there, but only reached San Francisco on his journey. In this city the American authorities apparently convinced him that Alaska was unsafe for travel and that he could aid his countrymen more by publishing a newspaper for them in San Francisco. As a result, from 1868 to 1873, the *Alaska Herald* appeared in both Russian and English, supported financially by the government until Honcharenko began to criticize the Alaska Commercial Company, which possessed monopoly rights in Alaska, for exploiting the Alaskans. He continued with an independent publication, *Svoboda*, which was abandoned in 1873, after only a few issues.[11] In his articles Honcharenko also wrote of Shevchenko and matters of interest to Ukrainians. His contacts with Alaskans through his paper showed him that the Ukrainians in Alaska were sufficiently numerous to be interested in such articles. Only the presence of a large number of Ukrainians in Alaska and Siberia, moreover, can explain his efforts to convince the American government to set up a state combining Alaska and eastern Siberia under the name of "Pacific Ukraine", a map of which he had printed on his calling cards.[12]

The presence of Ukrainians on the Aleutian Islands, Alaska, and along the whole western coast of North America is also noted by other researchers and historical writers about Ukrainian emigration, the most important of these being I. Telman,[13] A. M. Shlepakov[14], P. Krawchuk, and Yu. O. Zhluktenko. The first two did not give any specific information and added nothing new to what we have already learned from Honcharenko's writing. Krawchuk makes a contribution by bringing into the picture the Russian sailors Ivan Fedorov and Michael Gvodzdov who "in 1729 were the first to add to the map of the world part of the northwest coast of North America including the west coast of Canada." He adds further: "Without question there were also Ukrainians from Russia in this expedition who undoubtedly were the first Ukrainians to set foot on Canadian soil, this event taking place 200 years ago".[15]

More was written by Yu. O. Zhluktenko who, basing his conclusions on an article written by Matsiyevich entitled "Ukrainians in Canada"[16], asserts that:

> In the ninth decade of the last century in the Canadian province of British Columbia one could still find descendants of Ukrainians who had lived in "Russian America".[17]

If the author could have told us who had met those descendants and where, and could have mentioned at least one name (either the one who had met the descendants or the descendant himself), he would have performed a great service to history. Unfortunately, he was silent on these matters.

Recognizing that Zhluktenko is a researcher in linguistics and not history, we might be led to believe that he could have missed such information in Matsievych's contribution. In investigating this article, however, we find no support for Zhluktenko's findings. Matsievych actually wrote as follows:

> Courageous Russian sailors reached the western coast of North America about the middle of the seventeenth century, long before the English (Cook and Vancouver) and the Spaniards. In the eighteenth century there were already established Russian settlements ("Russian America"). Among these settlers there could have been, undoubtedly, also kozak-Ukrainians. These were established settlers and not new immigrants. In the Canadian province of British Columbia Ukrainians often met "Russians" whose forefathers had settled there "at some unspecified time", hundreds of years before. It was thus that Russians and Ukrainians appeared on the American continent, which also includes Canadian soil, about two hundred years before there arrived in Canada the "first" Ukrainian, the immigrant Ivan Pylypiw, who came from western Ukraine, then under the yoke of the Austrian monarchy.[18]

As we see, Matsievych does not assert that in the 1890s the Ukrainians in British Columbia met descendants of these former settlers, and also does not claim categorically that there were Ukrainians among the Russian settlers. He states only that there "could also have been kozak-Ukrainians". In view of these unsupported and even unclear statements of Matsievych, Zhluktenko's conclusions lose their validity.

It can be accepted without question that Ukrainians played an active role in the whole life of Russia, including the civil service, army and navy, as well as their judicial, economic, religious, and educational institutions. The best example of this is the previously mentioned Petro Poletyka, a member of a noted Ukrainian family who distinguished himself in the diplomatic service to such an extent that he became the Russian plenipotentiary in negotiations with the American government which delineated the boundaries between Russia and the United States, part of which later became the boundary between Canada and Alaska. A second outstanding example is that of Yuriy Lysiansky who came from the Ukrainian kozak regimental town of Nizhyn. He served in the Russian naval service in Kronstadt on the Baltic Sea and distinguished himself in the ser-

vice to such an extent that he was one of a group commissioned by the czar
to travel to England to learn something of British naval technology. While
engaged in this pursuit, he had an opportunity to visit many parts of the
world, returning to Russia with the rank of captain. The czar then appointed him to accompany Captain Krusenstern, an Estonian, in an expedition which was to circumnavigate the globe.

It is also interesting that the czar sent Lysiansky to Germany to purchase two vessels suitable for such an expedition. After they brought them
to Kronstadt, Krusenstern was appointed captain of one of the ships, the
Nadezhda, with a crew of sixty-five men. Lysiansky became captain of the
other ship, the *Neva,* with a crew of fifty-four. They embarked on their long
journey at the beginning of August 1803. On these vessels there were several
scientists who were to carry on various investigations. Sailing from the
Baltic Sea and crossing the Atlantic Ocean, they rounded the southern end
of South America and finally arrived in the Hawaiian Islands. Here they
agreed to sail by separate routes to meet in the Chinese port of Macao. Lysiansky reached New Archangelsk at a time when the natives rose against
Baranov, the governor of "Russian America". It can be imagined what
Baranov's fate might have been had Lysiansky and his crew not arrived in
time. From here Lysiansky sailed to Macao where, having again joined
Krusenstern, they crossed the Indian Ocean, rounded the Cape of Good
Hope, and returned to Kronstadt during the summer of 1806.[19]

During his journey, Lysiansky discovered an island in the Hawaiian
Archipelago which still bears his name. He was the first Russian sailor to
describe the Hawaiian Islands and upon his return to Kronstadt he wrote an
account of the whole journey. Understandably, he wrote the account in
Russian but later translated the book into English, and it was published in
1814.[20] In addition to the island in the Hawaiian Archipelago, the name of
Lysiansky was also given to one of the peaks on Sakhalin Island and to one
of the peninsulas on the sea of Okhotsk.[21]

It may be of interest to add that Lysiansky considered himself a
Ukrainian *kozak* because, in discussing languages, he expressed the opinion
that the *kozak* (Ukrainian) language was purer than Polish, Russian, and
other Slavic languages.[22]

Probably the most authentic record of the first "Russian" settlements
on the west coast in what is now British Columbia, in which there could also
have been Ukrainians, is found in Okulevich's work from which the following is quoted:

> The period of exploration on the north-west coast of America by Russian
> sailors, and its colonization by hunters and traders, ended at the beginning of
> the nineteenth century. At that time the Spaniards from Mexico and the
> English had reached the Pacific coast from the east and were surging north-

ward in waves. The scattered Russian settlements were drowned in the mass of other European settlers. As an example, there is still a tradition, handed down among the pioneers of Vancouver, that this city had its beginning in a small Russian settlement of which no trace now remains. They (the Russians) became assimilated and were lost in the overwhelming numbers of new arrivals.[23]

To these informative conclusions of Okulevich we can also add the already cited works of Huculak about Petro Poletyka, responsible in part for the boundary between Canada and Alaska, in which he asserts that the Russians came by ship from the Black Sea.

From the above it is certainly conceivable that since the Ukrainians played an active part in most Russian affairs, they could also have been included in the various Russian expeditions. Accordingly, they could have been in the Aleutian Islands in Alaska, and even in British Columbia. This most western area of Canada became its sixth province in 1871 and, with the completion of the railway in 1886, its economic development advanced rapidly. This economic development of the province, and especially that of Vancouver, could have attracted both Russians and Ukrainians. When we also take into consideration that there was much feverish activity in the search for gold, it would be surprising if some Ukrainian had not ventured there during these years.

Of course, all this is supposition and it will remain so until some researcher stumbles on some state archives, whether it be Russian (or even American, Spanish, Mexican, or Canadian), describing these expeditions and the settlement of "Russians" on the American continent. This would finally give scholarly support to the theory of Ukrainian settlements on Canadian soil during that period.[24]

Did Ukrainians Emigrate to Canada from the United States Before 1891?

Since Ukrainian immigration to the United States antedated immigration to Canada by about fifteen years, it is also conceivable that a few Ukrainians could have entered eastern or western Canada from the United States before 1891. At mid-century, western Canada (then known as the North-West Territories) was still controlled by the Hudson's Bay Company and was very thinly settled. The most densely populated area was that portion from which the province of Manitoba was formed in 1870, its population then being almost twelve thousand, with 1,565 whites, 588 Indians, and the rest English and French-speaking Metis.[25]

An immense territory with no direct means of communication with eastern Canada, western Canada's links were with St. Paul and Chicago;

this situation was further reinforced by the building of the first railway between St. Paul and Winnipeg in 1878. The first railway connecting Manitoba and eastern Canada was the Canadian Pacific Railway, which reached Winnipeg in 1881. The boundary between Canada and the U.S.A. being largely nominal, Canadians crossed freely for trading purposes and Americans settled without hindrance in Canada.[26] It is therefore entirely possible that Ukrainians entered Canada long before Ivan Pylypiw and Wasyl Eleniak. Alexander Royick, a lecturer at the University of Saskatchewan from 1965 to 1969, reported that a Transcarpathian Ukrainian, George Hazuda, knew of another Transcarpathian Ukrainian from Priashiw (Presov) in Slovakia, who played a part in the Indian uprisings of the 1870s in what is now Alberta, and also worked in the coal mines around Lethbridge. Hazuda added that twelve Transcarpathians had emigrated from Grand Forks in Montana in 1885 to work in the coal mines around Lethbridge, a group that is still remembered by old miners in this area.[27]

If one discounts Grand Forks (North Dakota) as the point of origin, Hazuda's account of these miners at Lethbridge might well be true. It is confirmed by Joseph K. Kirschbaum, a Slovak historian:

> It would seem however that the first large Slovak colony known as such was established in Lethbridge, Alberta, by Slovak miners who came to Canada in 1885 from the coal mines of Shelby, Montana ... At the beginning they were organized in Slovak organizations which had their offices in the United States, but later Lethbridge became a strong centre of Slovak-Canadian organizational activity, and by 1922, the colony had its own church. The Lethbridge colony passed into the history of Slovak Canadians, not only as Slovak, but also as one of the best organized and best known, especially in the Slovak-American Press.[28]

Further, Kirschbaum related that this was the only Slovak church of the Byzantine rite in Canada before the end of the Second World War. It was established in 1921, in the presence of Bishop Budka, with the understanding that the people would be permitted to use their Slovak language in the church. Later, when the parishioners received the document from the bishop confirming the establishment of the parish, which was formally designated as "Ruthenian Greek Catholic", it was returned to the bishop with the demand that another document be prepared in which it would be explicitly stated that this church had been served and would continue to be served by Ukrainian Greek Catholic priests.[29]

In describing this "Slovak" church parish in Lethbridge, Kirschbaum recognized that its parishioners were from eastern Slovakia (actually Transcarpathian Rus, Transcarpathian or Carpathian Ukraine), in which inhabitants practised the Byzantine rite and celebrated mass in the Old Slavonic tongue. However, he and other Slovaks regarded the Lethbridge colonists as Slovaks[30] and did not identify them as "Rusnaks" of Ukrainian origin.

On the other hand, Kirschbaum does mention Rusnaks when he describes other so-called Slovak colonies in Canada. Thus in 1885 Count Esterhazy, a Hungarian, recruited two groups of Pennsylvanians to come to Canada, one consisting of thirty-five families and the other of twelve. Both settled in Manitoba, north-east of Minnedosa, in a district known for a long time as Huns Valley (later renamed Polonia and Mountain Road).[31] According to Kirschbaum, these settlers included many different nationalities from the Austro-Hungarian Empire who had emigrated to the United States and were scattered throughout Pennsylvania mining areas. Among them were Magyars, Slovaks, Rusnaks (Ruthenians), Czechs, and Yugoslavs. The number of Rusnaks is unknown but their separate identity from the Slovaks is unquestionable and both government sources and individual research on Canadian settlement explicitly refer to Ruthenians, or as they are now known, Ukrainians.[32]

There is also little doubt that these Rusnaks or Ruthenians were included in the third Slovak colony founded by Count Esterhazy in 1886, which still bears his name. This settlement, located north-east of Whitewood, now in the province of Saskatchewan, was almost twice the size of that in Huns Valley and, according to Kirschbaum, "these settlers in their ethnic origin were similar to the first two groups" (in Huns Valley).[33] Therefore, it is evident that there were Rusnaks or Ruthenians in this group. Furthermore, other historians of Czech and Slovak settlements in Canada reveal that the names of these colonists may be found in the monument built to commemorate the founder, and that names such as Babiak, Horniak, and Krupa, which appear Ukrainian, also may be found among those names.[34]

Esterhazy organized an additional group of Pennsylvania miners in 1885 with the intention of strengthening the settlement, but a prairie fire destroyed a large part of the buildings so that there was no place to shelter the newcomers. As a result, they were directed to mines in Alberta, but they endured such hardships there that they scattered far and wide. A number of them returned to the United States, some settled on other farms, and some drifted to Winnipeg.[35] Many of those who had settled in Esterhazy earlier also did not remain there long. The winter of 1886-87 was so severe that almost two-thirds of the colonists abandoned their farms and dispersed in like manner.

From the above, one may certainly conclude that there were Ukrainians in Canada before 1891. They came from present day Transcarpathian Ukraine and eastern Slovakia, and were known as Carpatho-Rusyns, Ruthenians, or Rusnaks. Though they were ignorant of their national heritage and never regarded themselves as Ukrainians, they adhered to the

Eastern Rite in the Catholic Church, which distinguished them from both Magyars and Slovaks. They did not draw closer to the Ukrainians, even when the latter entered Canada in substantial numbers and developed their own way of life. They did not rejoice with other Ukrainians at the proclamation of a united and independent Ukraine in 1918 or at their success in becoming an influential ethnic group in Canadian life. Even though Greek Catholic priests ministered to their churches for many years, they continued to ally themselves with Slovakian and other non-Ukrainian organizations.

With reference to the whole list of individuals whom Marunchak discovered in the records of the Parish of the Immaculate Conception in Winnipeg, it must be admitted that they were no more Ukrainian than those of Lethbridge, Huns Valley, or Esterhazy. Marunchak writes of them as follows:

> In the parish records (Parish of the Immaculate Conception) we find a long list of Ukrainian names. As early as 1884 we come across such names as Maria Shweresko, Michael Kolishar, and in 1886, Maria Bubnyk. There is not the slightest doubt that two marriage records refer to *bona fide* Ukrainian inhabitants. On page 17 of the first volume of the registry, office records of 1883-94, under the date November 1, 1887, the following is written in connection with the marriage record of Toma Matliuk, son of Toma Matliuk, and Anna Chapets from Bily Potik (clear brook) near Arva in Austria on the one hand ... in the presence of Matii Sharpii, Maria Bubnyk, and Andrii Kopara. On page 74, under January 9, 1888, there is a record of another marriage, this time of Mykhailo Maketa from Stolitsa in Czekhia and Theresa Tsarstiak, daughter of Anton and Susanna Tsarstiak from Bily Potik in Austria, the entry being made in the presence of Maria Myshak and many friends and acquaintances. Those signing are Joseph Trapay, Maria Chopyk, and Franko Polnitsky.

Marunchak includes a list of names recorded from 1888 to 1891, including Andriy Kopys, Yosyf Piliak, Mykhailo Tsytsora, Eli Krawchenko, Nelli Slota, Anna Maliuta, Yakiv Styrchaliuk, Anna Shpak, Ivan Holub, Anna Chopyk, Anna and Varvara Kozel and Maria and Yosyf Holysh, and declares:

> We are listing these names in detail because, for the time being, they are the best official record to indicate to us how far back in time our immigration stretches in the Winnipeg area.

The author further explains in a footnote that Bily Potik (from where both Toma Matliuk and Theresa Tsarstiak arrived) is a village in Bilobozhnytsky *raion* (county) in the *oblast* (province) of Ternopil.[36]

Although the names of these individuals as transcribed in Ukrainian appear to be Ukrainian in origin—much more so than in their original form—they do not provide a sufficient basis for an assertion that they must be such. The names can be Ukrainian but they may also be Czech, Slovak, or Polish. Furthermore, it is Bily Potik (clear brook) near Arva in Austria that is mentioned and not a river in Galicia, and especially not in Ternopil county. The fact that Maketa arrived from "Stolitsa in Czekhia" leaves no doubt that we are not dealing with people from Ternopil, or even Transcarpathian Ukraine. Arva or Black Arva is found in northwest Slovakia, which does not even border on Ukraine. Accordingly, the most that one can claim about Ukrainians in the Parish of the Immaculate Conception is that there may have also been some Ukrainians among the Slovaks who came from Bily Potik by the Arva and the Czechs who arrived from Stolitsa, but the parish records do not reveal a single name of anyone actually from Transcarpathian Ukraine.

This contention is further supported by the fact that the "fathers" of Ukrainian immigration to Canada, among whom are Oleskiw, Genik, and Reverends Dmytriw and Tymkevych,[37] who gathered information on all Ukrainian immigration to Canada, and particularly Winnipeg, made no reference to any Ukrainians in the Parish of the Immaculate Conception. From 1884 to 1890 Winnipeg was still a small city and they would most certainly have sought out the Matliuks, Chapetses, Myshaks, Sharpiis, and others if the latter had claimed any affinity whatsoever with Ruthenians or Ukrainians.

Could Ukrainians Have Arrived in Canada Before 1891 Together with the Poles?

Polish immigration to Canada became particularly numerous after two unsuccessful rebellions against Russian rule, one in 1830, and the other in 1863. Defeated, the Poles emigrated to Canada and the United States to escape from both Russian and Prussian oppression. After the first rebellion in 1830, the immigrants were chiefly the Kashuby.[38] As they were settled closely around the Baltic Sea, it is unlikely that there were any Ukrainians among them. Following the second uprising, however, Polish immigration came from all areas of Poland,[39] including its former possession, Galicia. Since the Poles often lived as neighbours of the Ukrainians here and were even relatives of Ukrainians on occasion, it is quite probable that some Ukrainians did accompany them to Canada before 1891.

Beginning in 1864, Poles began settling in the Barry's Bay district in Ontario where they founded their own settlement of Vilna which, according to Makowski, contained nearly two hundred families within a short time. Others emigrated to the larger cities in Ontario, such as Hamilton, St.

Catharines, Kitchener, London, Windsor, and Toronto. In 1871 a substantial number of Polish names can already be found in the mortgage records of the city of Toronto.

In the immigration records after the second Polish insurrection it is possible to recognize names which might be Ukrainian. Vasyl Burianyk claims on this basis that the first Ukrainians arrived in Canada fully twenty-six years before Pylypiw and Eleniak. Leaning on the research of a prominent Toronto lawyer, Teodor Humeniuk, he writes as follows:

> The first Ukrainian to enter Canada was Roman Bachynsky, twenty-four years old when he reached port in Quebec on May 30, 1865, on the ship *Belgium.* Next to arrive was Joseph Wozny, twenty-three years old, on the ship *Necker,* also in the port of Quebec, on May 27, 1867. Still later, on October 8, 1882, there arrived in Quebec a Jacob Rii, thirty-seven years old, on the ship *Lake Nipigon.* With him came Karol Lesiuk, twenty-eight years old, and Matvii Kishchatsky, whose age was thirty-eight. Unfortunately, nothing more was heard of them again, and we can only assume that Canada was but a brief stop on their journey to the United States of America. The ages of the first two immigrants give some support to the conjecture that they could have been persuaded to enlist in the ranks of Polish insurgents.[40]

In writing about early Ukrainian immigrants before Pylypiw, Alexander Royick refers to Burianyk's statement.[41] Unfortunately, no matter how interesting the listing of these men in the Department of Immigration archives may be, until these names can be further identified they can only be considered material for further research.

In this connection, V. J. Kaye (Volodymyr Julian Kysilewsky), who has a good deal of experience with research into immigration records, informed the author that he had attempted to verify the information regarding Bachynsky and had discovered two errors in the above information. Not only was the ship on which Bachynsky arrived wrongly listed, as it was the *Belgian* and not the *Belgium,* but his name was recorded as Backensky and not Bachynsky.[42]

The matter of Polish connection in the possible arrival of Ukrainians in Canada was still another and even earlier dimension growing out of the War of 1812, in which the United States attempted to annex Canada. To defend Canada, England dispatched troops, among which were two regiments, the De Watteville and the De Meuron, both of special interest to Ukrainians. Both were named after their commanders, and although known as Swiss regiments, they were really mercenary troops and included soldiers from many European nations. Furthermore, just prior to their departure for Canada, their numbers had been boosted by the inclusion of soldiers taken prisoner in the Napoleonic wars. Among these, as was revealed almost a hundred years later, there were also Poles.[43]

These troops distinguished themselves in battle, and upon demobilization at the end of the war in 1814 those who did not wish to return to Europe were given the choice of highly productive land and a money grant to aid in becoming established. Some of these so-called Swiss soldiers settled in the Perth district of Ontario along the Rideau River.[44] Another smaller group, entirely composed of men from the De Watteville regiment, joined an expedition consisting of eighty men, recruited by Lord Selkirk mainly from the demobilized Scottish Glengarry regiment. The goal of this expedition was to secure the Red River at the point where Winnipeg now stands.[45] After pacifying the Metis, who had been incited by the hostile North-West Company to attack the settlers of the colony and thus discourage further settlement, the soldiers themselves became settlers in the colony, having obviously received generous treatment from Lord Selkirk.[46]

Though the members of the Glengarry regiment had no difficulty in adapting themselves to the new conditions in the company of their countrymen, the De Watteville group did not feel very comfortable. Most of them, since they were neither Scottish nor Presbyterian and were unable or unwilling to intermarry with the Metis or Indians, never became a part of the colony. After nine years of varied hardships, locusts, Indian and Metis attacks, internal jealousies and isolation, and finally a major flood in 1826, almost all of them left for the United States and were forgotten for a long time.[47]

It was not until 1885 that Professor George Bryce provided the names of these settlers in reporting to the Manitoba Historical and Scientific Society, probably being the first to note that there were people with foreign names among the Selkirk settlers.[48] Later, in 1909, there appeared an article in the *Winnipeg Free Press,* entitled "Land Laws in the Selkirk Colony", based on Bryce's report and the foreign names were again listed.[49] Following this, a Polish newspaper in Winnipeg, *Gazeta Katolicka,* printed an anonymous article which revealed that there were Poles among the Selkirk settlers.[50] Though this statement aroused enthusiasm in Polish circles, forty years passed before a young Polish historian, Victor Turek, in a well-documented research study entitled "Poles Among the De Meuron Soldiers", gave conclusive proof that at least ten names among the Selkirk settlers were unquestionably Polish.[51] Turek revealed that the author of the anonymous article in *Gazeta Katolicka* was a well-known Polish doctor, B. Gerzabek. He also listed the following Polish settlers among the De Meurons: Michael Bardowicz, Pierre Gandrosky, Andrew Jankofsky, Michael Kaminsky, Martin Kralich (or Kraluk), Woitchech Lasota, Laurent Quilesky, John Wasilofski, Michael Isaak, and Antoine Sabatzky.

These names are repeated in many forms in different documents because the individuals could not sign their names and different officials spelled them according to what they imagined that they heard. Accordingly, Bardowicz appears also as Bardavitsch, Bardovitche, or Borokovitz. Similarly, other names appeared in different forms and variations.

Coinciding with the appearance of Turek's article, Senator Paul Yuzyk, then a professor at the University of Manitoba and an editor of publications of the Manitoba Historical and Scientific Society, wrote a short review of Turek's work. Yuzyk volunteered the conjecture, and it was only a conjecture, that among the ten Polish names, three of them could have been those of Ukrainians from Galicia: namely, Wasilowsky, Jankofsky, and Kaminsky.[52]

With Marunchak, the conjecture became a theory. Basing his argument on the Selkirk Papers,[53] he concluded as follows:

> Over ten names on the list of De Meurons are purely of Slavic origin. Among these are Semen Dazio, Toma Dyma, Martin Isak, Andrij Wijojko, Petro Komdrowski, Ivan Wasilowsky, Jankofsky, Kaminski ... Some of these names are so mutilated in transcription and the writing is so illegible, that the names can be read in many ways ... Some of the numbered and some of the unnumbered names indicate an indisputable Ukrainian origin.[54]

Without doubt these names in Ukrainian transcription appear quite Ukrainian but the certainty disappears when the original signatures are examined. Instead of Petro there is Pierre, which Poles claim is actually Piotr and therefore Polish. Instead of Andrij Wijojko the original has Andreas Vioiga which Italians, Spaniards, or Portugese can also claim, and this process can be repeated with other names. Accordingly, we are forced to admit that, as pleasing as it would be to find Ukrainian roots in Canada among the Selkirk settlers, this cannot be maintained on the basis of names that are merely similar. As Marunchak himself acknowledges, the matter requires further investigation.

Royick did proceed further, confining himself explicitly to the names of Jankofsky and Wasilowsky, which he considered to be Ukrainian. He based his conclusions on Haiman's research, who reported not only that there were "Ruthenians from the former Eastern Galicia and Little Russians from Korsakow's corps"[55] among the De Watteville settlers, but also added their birthplaces: Andrew Jankofsky was born in Ternopil and John Wasilowsky—in Tuchyn—which is in the *oblast* of Rivne. Royick, therefore, has more reason to claim that these two individuals were Ukrainians as his argument is based not only on names but also on place of origin. He has support for his theory on both philological and geographical grounds.

On the basis of such proof the name of Martin Kraluk, also found on the agreement drawn up between Selkirk and his settlers, could be added. It has a unique attraction for the Ukrainian researcher. Although Turek submits other variations for this name such as Kralich, Kralic, Crallig, and even Garlic, and numbers him among the Poles, his name is not necessarily Polish. It has a much closer resemblance to a Ukrainian name and it could be a derivative of the word *"kralia"* (beauty), from which there may be many derivatives. In Haiman we meet another form of the name, Kralisz, and discover that Kraluk or Kralych comes from "Pestritz". Haiman himself questions this information and speculates that it might be Bystrzyca (Bystrytsya). No other such name can be found in either Poland or Transcarpathian Ukraine. On the other hand it is a very common name of villages in Ukraine. It may be found in the districts of Mukachiv, Lviv, Symy, Rivne, and twice in each of the districts of Stanyslaviv (Ivano-Frankivsk) and Zhytomyr. Furthermore, "Pestritz" need not be Bystrytsya. It is closer to the name of Bestritz, a village which is a few kilometres south of Zhabia in Ivano-Frankivsk *oblast*. Thus, Kraluk could have been a true Carpathian highlander or *"hutzul"* who became an English prisoner of war as an Austrian soldier, and as Haiman reports, had joined the De Watteville regiment at the age of thirty-nine in 1810. He was already forty-seven years of age when he reached the Red River.

Apparently, Swiss regiments did not record the religious affiliations of the soldiers or, if they did, research has been unable to uncover them. When the census figures began to show this aspect in 1832, Wasilowsky and Kraluk had apparently left the colony because there is no mention of them. On the other hand, Jankofsky was regarded as a Pole and a Catholic, essentially a Roman Catholic. As a matter of course, once he found himself in the regiment with Poles he could have been recorded as a Pole automatically. It might even have been dangerous for him to differentiate himself from his fellow soldiers. This is quite understandable, especially to any displaced person who found himself in a German camp at the end of the Second World War. There were many Ukrainians who were quite aware of their ethnic origin but who were forced to identify themselves with the Poles and call themselves Roman Catholics to avoid enforced repatriation to the Russian "motherland".

Royick claims further that there were Ukrainians among the De Watteville soldiers who settled along the Rideau River near Perth in June 1816. Among the one hundred fifty who settled there were over twenty with Slavic names. Of the latter, Royick identifies three as Ukrainians, namely: Ivan Diakowsky, Petro Barko or Barkov, and Andriy Michaliuk. Unfortunately, we find the same difficulty with these variations in signatures as we discovered with signatures in the other records: Diakowsky is listed as Jean Giacoffsky, Giakifsky, and John Diakossky; Barko is written as Pierre Barko and Barkiw; and Michaliuk as Andrew Michaluck and Micheluc. As to birthplace, we find that Diakowsky was born in Brody (*oblast* of Lviv), Barko in Ternopil and no birthplace is listed for Michaluk. Diakowsky settled in the township of Drummond, Lot W 1; Barko in the township of Burgess North, Lot E8; and Michaluk in Burgess North, Lot 3. They are all listed as Poles but their names and birthplaces provide a strong basis for theory that they could have been Ukrainians.[56]

In connection with the War of 1812-14, there is still another name that has received so much attention in Ukrainian publications that it is difficult to omit in this study. A writer signing himself as S.P.H. (later revealed to be Stefan P. Hevak) published a sensational article in *Kanadiisky Farmer* in 1965 about "The First Ukrainian on Canadian Soil". In this article the author claimed that he came across a painting of a battle scene from the War of 1812-14, in the Historical Museum in Dundurn Castle, Hamilton, in which are depicted battles which took place between American and British armies in the areas around Hamilton and Stoney Creek. At the bottom of the painting it was claimed that the artist had listed a number of names, among which the author claimed that he had seen that of "Captain Johanus Strilbytsky'.[57] As this would indicate that Strilbytsky had defended Canada in that war, it was natural for S.P.H. to regard him as the first Ukrainian on Canadian soil (although he conceded in the article that the matter required further research).

Since it appeared certain that the Strilbytsky family had played such a distinctive role,[58] the article aroused the interest of Alexander Royick. His investigations unfortunately came to naught, as the curator of the museum informed him that in his fifteen years as curator at Dundurn, he had never seen such a painting, had never heard of it, and had never seen any record of it in the museum records.[59]

Did Ukrainians Emigrate to Canada with Mennonites or Germans from Galicia or Bessarabia Before 1891?

Mennonites from Ukraine began to emigrate to Canada in 1874,[60] settling first in southern Manitoba. Within a short time 6,000[61] had arrived and built settlements at Gretna, Altona, Winkler, Steinbach, Blumenfeldt, Obertal, and Chortitz.[62] Since the Mennonites knew both the Russian and Ukrainian languages, the Ukrainian settlers who arrived in Canada later found them a convenient group for whom they could work for wages, a circumstance that often led to the theory that some Ukrainians had arrived in Canada with the Mennonites.

In his research on Ukrainian settlement in Canada in 1953, Professor Jaroslav Rudnyckyj visited Wasyl Eleniak in his declining years at Chipman, Alberta. In an interview recorded on tape Eleniak denied that he and

Pylypiw had been the first Ukrainians in Canada. As proof, he reported that when he and Pylypiw had visited Assiniboia (now southern Saskatchewan) they had met a Ukrainian named Kotsur who "had already been there for twenty-three years, as he already had three acres under cultivation." This Kotsur was "from Russia where he had been employed by the Germans, and he arrived (in Canada) with them as a hired man."[63]

On the basis of this interview with Eleniak, supported by the name of the colony, Chortitz, some supported the theory that Ukrainians had arrived in Canada with the Mennonites in 1874. Probably relying on Eleniak's statement, Olya Woycenko wrote in her annals of Ukrainian life in Canada, with respect to the year 1874, as follows: "Kotsur—the earliest known Ukrainian to settle in Canada."[64] Her statement had two implications: first, that there may have been other unknown Ukrainians who had come to Canada; and second, that Kotsur had actually arrived with the Mennonites in 1874.

The above theory was supported by Rudnyckyj, in an article published in the almanac of *Kanadiisky Farmer* in 1963,[65] in which he speculated on the probable time of Kotsur's arrival in Canada. Though he admitted that further research was necessary for conclusive proof, he did not question the theory that Kotsur had actually arrived with the Mennonites in 1874, "together with his family". He even speculated that it might have been Kotsur's idea to give the name of Chortitz to one of the colonies.

Since it was generally accepted that Kotsur was the first Ukrainian immigrant and that he had arrived with the Mennonites, M. Marunchak added the name of another Ukrainian, Nelidow, who might also have arrived with the Mennonites at the same time.

In his research based on the reminiscences of Ivan Romaniuk, Marunchak reported that "there were Ukrainians among the Mennonites who had arrived in 1874, and that the Mennonites had spoken of this freely, making no attempt to conceal the matter... In Obertal, Romaniuk stated, there was a Ukrainian by the name of Nelidow, who had introduced himself to Romaniuk's parents as a Ukrainian who had arrived in Canada with the Mennonites... There was more. On the passage across the ocean they (Ukrainians) offered their services to the Mennonites." Marunchak further states that Nelidow had been on such friendly terms with his father that the two had been in a photograph together. Marunchak included the picture in his research study with this caption: "A symbolic picture of Ukrainian pioneer immigrants. Nelidow, seated, arrived with the Mennonites in 1874 from eastern Ukraine. Standing is Michael Romaniuk from Nebyliw, western Ukraine, who arrived in 1892. The photo was taken in 1895."[66]

Marunchak must have concluded that some of the information given by Romaniuk was not strictly accurate because, in a later account, he has occasion to refer to Nelidow as a "legendary Ukrainian".[67] His doubt was fully justified because Nelidow was well-known both to Kyrylo Genik and Father Dmytriw, the first leaders of Ukrainian immigration to Canada, and a report is found about him in *Svoboda*. He was understood to be an agent of some American railroad company who travelled through Canada, often in the company of a Russian Orthodox priest, Maliarewsky. They attempted to persuade Ukrainians to emigrate to Minnesota and North Dakota. Genik referred to him as "the Russian nobleman" and warned Ukrainian settlers against him, admonishing them to pay no heed to Nelidow's blandishments to induce them to abandon their farms.[68] At no time did these two regard Nelidow as a Ukrainian, and even Ivan's older brother, Wasyl, knew him as Nelyldorf.[69] Furthermore, we cannot even accept the claim that he arrived with the Mennonites in 1874 since V. J. Kysilewsky (Kaye) affirms that he came originally from a German colony near Odessa, arriving in Canada from the United States during the winter of 1896-97, under the name of Nelidorf or Nelindorf.[70] In the light of such evidence, the theory that Nelidow was the first Ukrainian to arrive in Canada, in 1874, must be abandoned.

It is almost certain, too, that Kotsur did not accompany the Mennonites on their arrival in 1874. V. J. Kaye checked all steamship records of Mennonites arriving between 1874 and 1878, a list which totalled 7500 names, and found neither Nelidow, nor Kotsur, nor any other name which could be similar to a Ukrainian surname.[71]

The above research provides a basis for the supposition that Eleniak either had a physical difficulty which prevented him from pronouncing "chy" correctly or that he spoke a dialect in which "tsy" was used instead of "chy". His statement that Kotsur had arrived twenty-three years earlier could accordingly also be interpreted as meaning two or three years earlier. Support for this view comes from another book. Might not this Kotsur be the Kochur of whom Vera Lysenko writes in *Men in Sheepskin Coats*? She states that "the first Ukrainian immigrant was Wasyl Kochur and his wife Anna, both hired hands of the settler, Landetz, with whom they emigrated to Canada in 1888. Kochur did not write to anyone and vanished without leaving any trace in Canada."[72] It is regrettable that the author did not quote the source of her information. If she had, she might have settled the question of Canada's first Ukrainian, for if a Kotsur or Kochur had not arrived with the Mennonites in 1874 one might have come in 1888, which would mean that he had arrived in this country before Pylypiw or Eleniak. That Kotsur or Kochur could have arrived in Canada only two or three years before is further supported by the fact that he had only two or three acres under cultivation when settlers in Assiniboia (Saskatchewan) were able, apparently, to cultivate from three to fifteen acres annually.

Unfortunately, no support has been found for Eleniak's story from other sources. Efforts to find the name of Kotsur or Kochur (and Landetz) among applications for homesteads in the Langenburg area have met with complete failure. This does not prove that Eleniak's story is false, since Kotsur could have been on his homestead for years and then cancelled his application. Very often no record of cancelled applications was kept. Nevertheless, the absence of any record of Kotsur in the area where Eleniak and Pylypiw visited him weakens to a considerable degree the claim that he was the first Ukrainian settler in Canada.

Reports About Other Ukrainians Who Could Have Arrived in Canada Before 1891

From time to time other individuals have been reported as arriving in Canada before 1891. Wasyl Czumer has this to say about one N. Koroluk:

> Early settlers in the Bruderheim district in Alberta related that two Ukrainian brothers from Bessarabia appeared in the summer of 1891, one of them being N. Koroluk who married a German girl and settled with her parents south of Fort Saskatchewan. By religious affiliation he was a Stundist (Baptist) and did not communicate with other Ukrainians. As a result nothing further was heard of him.[73]

Five years later Vera Lysenko repeated the same information[74] but again neglected to quote her source, although it was almost certainly based on Czumer's account.

To throw more light on early settlement, Toma Tomashewsky wrote an article in his newspaper, *Ukrainsky Pioner*,[75] in which he identified the name "N. Koroluk" as Nykola Koroluk, whom he knew personally. He related that Koroluk was a Ukrainian from Bessarabia who arrived in Canada in 1888 and farmed in the Bruderheim district of Alberta. He had moved to Edmonton upon retirement and had died a few years ago at a very advanced age. Tomashewsky therefore concluded that Koroluk had preceded Eleniak to Canada by three years. Unfortunately, although Tomashewsky had known Koroluk personally and was aware that it was important to obtain proof of Koroluk's arrival in Canada before 1891, he neglected to record on which ship he sailed, the port at which he had arrived, the month of arrival, or the name of his wife and parents.

Attempting once more to substantiate the information concerning Koroluk, Kysilewsky reviewed 86,000 names from homestead records, finding among them 2026 names that were Ukrainian. He did not discover among them any Nykola Koroluk from Bruderheim but did find one who settled in Star on May 28, 1898, and had later moved to Cracow. A search in the naturalization records was no more successful. Of course, this does not indicate that Nykola Koroluk was never in the Bruderheim area. If he had worked as a labourer, he could have saved money and purchased a farm. To purchase land he would not have had to have been naturalized and therefore his name would not be found in either the homestead or the naturalization records. While he did not find a N. Koroluk, it is quite significant that he discovered a Stefan Koroluk who had obtained his naturalization papers on May 11, 1895. This would indicate, according to Kaye, "that he must have settled on the homestead in 1892 or earlier".[76]

J. G. MacGregor, the most recent author of an account of Ukrainian settlement in Alberta, casts further light on the matter of Stefan or Nykola Koroluk. He writes, unfortunately, without quoting his source of information, that Stefan Koroluk arrived in Canada in 1888, having married Margaret Hennig of German parentage before emigrating. He had first settled with the Germans in the Medicine Hat area in Alberta and when the Germans resettled in Josephburg he had moved with them. In their company there was also a Ludvig Kulak, whom MacGregor also regards as the son of a Ukrainian who had a German wife. Koroluk preempted a homestead, SE 34-54-21 West of the Fourth Meridian, south-east of Josephburg, and Kulak settled nearby.[77]

The arrival of Stefan Koroluk and Ludvig Kulak with German settlers in 1888, first at Medicine Hat (actually near Dunmore) and later at Josephburg, is confirmed by Hilda Mohr, the author of a 1967 account of the pioneers of Josephburg (which borders on the Bruderheim settlement).[78] A descendant of the first German pioneers in this area, she should know the origin of her people. Although her account makes no mention of Bessarabia, there is a clear statement that her people came from villages not too far apart in Galicia: Josefburg and Brigidau. Regarding Stefan Koroluk and Ludvig Kulak, she relates that they did not accompany the first group of settlers in May 1891 but followed a few months later, likely in the fall of that year, with Joseph Krebs and others. She mentions very little about Koroluk, probably because he had no children to carry on the family tradition. On the other hand, she has a full account of the family of Ludvig Kulak (1868-1940), who married Elizabeth Unterschultz. They had a large family consisting of three sons, five daughters, thirty-four grandchildren, and many more great-grandchildren. In the district there are still many descendants of the original Kulaks but they are obviously not Ukrainians because none have ever identified themselves as such.

Accordingly, on the basis of research by Kaye and the newer sources of MacGregor and Mohr, the legend about "Nykola Koroluk and another man" must give way to the actual fact that Stefan Koroluk and Ludvig Kulak did arrive in Canada in 1888, settling first around Medicine Hat and later in Josephburg. This would mean that they arrived before Pylypiw and

Eleniak. The additional legend about Bessarabia being their homeland must also give way to the positive assertions of MacGregor and Mohr that the German colonists, including Koroluk, came from Galicia in Austria, and that one of their leaders was Johann Krebs, a school companion of Pylypiw in Stanyslaviv (now Ivano-Frankivsk) in Galicia.[79]

Another individual about whom there has been much debate was Ivan Matviiv (Ivan or John Matthews), mentioned for the first time in the English-language *Ukrainian Canadian Review,* under the editorship of John Danylchuk.[80] In this article it was claimed that one Ivan Matviiv (Matthews) was born in Brant River, Ontario in 1888, and that his parents had come from the village of Ulashkivtsi, county of Chortkiv, Galicia. In Canada he had worked in the mines and had become quite wealthy from the prospecting activities he undertook in his free time. Impressed by this information, Toma Tomashewsky revealed in his article, "More light on an obscure matter,"[81] that he had had the pleasure of meeting Matviiv in Toronto in 1952. Royick repeated this information in his article in *Northern Light*[82] but when he sought to verify the information from Matviiv's widow and daughters he discovered that Matviiv, though born in 1888, was born in Galicia and not in Canada. He also learned that Matviiv had not come to Canada until after the beginning of the twentieth century.[83]

There were other rumours, mainly in British Columbia, of a Ukrainian engineer in the government civil service during the last century. Upon investigation, Royick uncovered a Charles George Horetzky who had arrived in Canada in 1858 to become an employee of the Hudson's Bay Company. Later he became a government surveyor and won recognition for his survey of a proposed railway from Edmonton through the Peace River area to Kitimat in British Columbia. He also left behind some published works, all under the name of "Horetzky". Nevertheless, he was not Ukrainian. He was born in Scotland in 1838 and was descended from Polish-Scottish ancestors of the Roman Catholic faith. His father was born in Ruski Horyshiv, near Hrubeshiv, now in eastern Poland, and was descended from Bielorussian and Russian gentry from the village of Horky. Though he was known as Horetzky (not Goretzky), and his name appeared Ukrainian, he regarded himself as a British Canadian.[84]

To complete the list of Ukrainians who may have arrived in Canada before 1891, two more names should be considered. In an article by M.C. in *Novyi Shliakh* (New Pathway) it was stated that Toma Tomashenko, living near Winnipeg at that time, had been born in 1886 near Winnipeg to parents who had arrived from Kishinev in Bessarabia.[85] Although the information was repeated by Leonid Biletsky in a jubilee volume published by the Ukrainian Canadian Committee in 1951,[86] and later by Royick in his article about Bachynsky,[87] it has never been confirmed. No one knows where Tomashenko and his parents lived or where he was born.[88]

Professor Biletsky also referred to an article in the Winnipeg *Free Press* of July 20 (he provided no year) that claimed that "a Mykhailo Hrynyk from Manitoba had arrived in Canada more than sixty years ago", which would have placed his arrival before 1891. Attempts by Royick and Olga Woycenko to discover the source of this information proved fruitless; no trace could even be found of the *Free Press* article on which it was supposedly based.[89] Kysilewsky's archival research uncovered a Michael Hrynyk, born in 1862, who arrived in Canada with a wife and three children on April 26, 1899.[90] Whether this is the Hrynyk to whom Biletsky made reference is unknown.

From all that has been written or related about Ukrainians who arrived or could have arrived in Canada before Pylypiw and Eleniak, it is certain that there were Ukrainians in Canada before 1891. Records of Ukrainians who were not conscious of their national origin can be found in Lethbridge, Huns Valley, Esterhazy, and probably in Winnipeg. It is also certain that Stefan Koroluk arrived with his wife, though we may still question whether he came from eastern Ukraine, Bessarabia, or Galicia.[91] There is also a strong basis for the claim that Ukrainians were here as soldiers of Swiss regiments from which a few (Diakowsky, Barko, and Michaliuk) settled in the Perth area, and a few (Jankofsky, Wasilowsky, and Kraluk) joined the Selkirk settlers in 1816 and established themselves along the Red River.

However, neither the soldiers of the Swiss regiments, nor the Transcarpathian Ukrainians, nor Koroluk or Kochur began any mass movement of Ukrainians to Canada. Credit for that achievement belongs to Pylypiw and Eleniak, especially Pylypiw.

4

Pylypiw and Eleniak Lead the Way for Ukrainian Immigration to Canada

Professor Ivan Bobersky Discovers the "First among the First" Ukrainian Immigrants

Whether we choose to accept that the history of Ukrainian settlement in Canada began with the Transcarpathian Ukrainians in 1885 or that Ivan Pylypiw and Wasyl Eleniak opened the door to a massive influx of Ukrainian immigrants to Canada in 1891, it appears that for many years none of the Ukrainians in Canada knew anything about any Transcarpathian group nor about anyone else who might have been responsible for directing the subsequent flood of Ukrainian immigrants into Canada. Even Dr. Oleskiw, the father of the Ukrainian mass immigration movement to Canada, who toured this country in 1895 and listed almost every Ukrainian in Canada at that time, did not leave any record of the time of arrival of the first immigrants or of the area where they had settled.[1] Nor did Father Nestor Dmytriw, who is considered to be the first chronicler of Ukrainian settlement in Canada.[2]

Finally in 1906, when the number of Ukrainians in Canada had reached about 80,000,* Osyp (Joseph) Megas, then editor of the Winnipeg newspaper, *Kanadiisky Farmer,* published an appeal asking readers to send photographs and information about themselves and the development of their communities, particularly concerning those who might have been first to arrive in Canada. To enhance this appeal, Megas announced that he was planning to write a history of Canadian "Rus". Unfortunately, although there appeared in 1907 a forty-six page history, entitled *Western Canada,*

---

* The author apparently was skeptical of the accuracy of this figure, as it is followed by a question mark in the original Ukrainian text. (Ed.)

there was no mention in it of any "firsts" in spite of the fact that both men, later discovered to be the first arrivals, were still alive. Furthermore, although the beginnings of Ukrainian life in Canada are described in some detail by numerous correspondents to the American newspaper, *Svoboda*,[3] it is curious to note that it never entered anyone's mind to investigate and record the arrival of the first Ukrainians in Canada.

Many years were to pass before anyone identified individuals who gave the impetus to the immigration of Ukrainian settlers into Canada. The discovery was made by Professor Ivan Bobersky, who had arrived on this continent in 1920 as the representative of the Ukrainian Citizens' Committee of Lviv to appeal to Canadians and Americans of Ukrainian origin for financial aid for their motherland. After completing his mission for the Ukrainian Citizens' Committee, Bobersky remained in Canada, occupying himself in Ukrainian social and cultural activities, in the course of which he became interested in the early immigration of Ukrainians to Canada. Having come by chance on reports which indicated that Ivan Pylypiw and Wasyl Eleniak were really the first immigrants, Bobersky proceeded from Winnipeg to Lamont, Alberta, where he interviewed Pylypiw on April 2, 1932, and Eleniak on the following day. The *Providnyk* almanac[4] for 1933, published Bobersky's interview with Eleniak but his interview with Pylypiw was not published until 1937, when it appeared in the almanac of *Kanadiisky Farmer*.[5]

Pylypiw and Eleniak Reach Canada in 1891

On the basis of information obtained first by Bobersky and later by others, Ivan Pylypiw and Wasyl Eleniak, both from the village of Nebyliv, county of Kalusz (Kalush), province of Halychyna (Galicia), arrived in Montreal on the ship *Oregon,* September 7, 1891. It should be noted that the passenger list in the vessel recorded their names as Ivan Pylypiwsky and W. Illilik.[6] Pylypiw's name was correctly stated as he later revealed that he had shortened his name soon after his arrival in Canada. Eleniak's name, of course, is incorrectly written. It was really Ilyniak as only this form of the name can be found in the village of Nebyliv.[7]

Without doubt, the initiative for the long journey came from Pylypiw. He was born in Nebyliv in 1859, a son of Havrylo Pylypiwsky, a comparatively prosperous villager and a good farmer. Havrylo owned about forty morgs (about fifty-five acres) of land, which raised him above the class of the ordinary peasant in those days. Even if he had parcelled out his land among his six sons, each would have received a comfortable estate, a sufficient base from which comparative affluence could have been attained in later life. Ivan completed school in the village, where he also learned some German,[8] and learned the blacksmith's trade before starting to farm on his own at the age of twenty. To supplement a meagre villager's income, he engaged in trade, travelling across the Carpathian Mountains into Hungary to buy and sell hogs and cattle, especially oxen. He also worked as "a contractor in logging operations, felling timber and delivering logs to the bank of some river".[9] In one of these undertakings he entered into a contract with the government to supply 26,000 logs.[10] To accomplish this he engaged forty labourers, including Wasyl Eleniak and other German colonists from Galicia. These activities would indicate that farming, on the scale it was carried on in the village, failed to satisfy him. His restless nature drove him into other enterprises.

Pylypiw learned about the United States and Canada from his teacher at school and later from German labourers, who related that some of their countrymen had emigrated to Canada and had prospered. Having obtained the address of one such colonist in Canada, Pylypiw wrote to him[11] and received in reply the information that there was indeed much land still left in Canada which could be obtained at little cost. This information convinced Pylypiw that he must travel to Canada to ascertain the possibilities of settlement for himself. Not only was this decision a courageous one but it was also momentous.

Pylypiw did not have far to search for companions in his adventurous undertaking; he found them in his own village. One of these was Wasyl Eleniak, a young man of Pylypiw's age (both had been born in 1859), who had been one of the men hired by Pylypiw to help in his logging business. Although he was illiterate, Eleniak was prepared to seek a better destiny elsewhere. As he related later, he had heard of opportunities available in Canada from German acquaintances and had been waiting for an opportunity to travel there.[12] Another who wished to accompany Pylypiw was Tyt Ziniak. The three resolved to leave their wives and families at home and visit Canada alone.

To obtain money for their fares, they sold some of their land and set out on their journey through Stryi, Peremyshl, Krakiw (Cracow), Osviencim, Berlin, and Hamburg. Unfortunately, Ziniak was detained at the border, possibly at Osviencim, and was not permitted to continue his journey as he did not have enough money to satisfy the Austrian government's laws on emigration.[13] Pylypiw and Eleniak were successful in reaching Hamburg, where they embarked on a steamship which first stopped in Liverpool and then, after eleven days travel, arrived in Montreal on September 7, 1891.[14]

On the same day they boarded a train bound for the west and arrived in Winnipeg on September 10. Here the immigration authorities assigned them an agent with a knowledge of both Ukrainian and German, with instructions to guide them to an area where there was land for settlement. Their first visit was to Langenburg,[15] where they were fortunate in meeting some of the Germans who had been logging with Pylypiw along the Limnytsia River. One day of searching was sufficient to find land that was satisfactory. They immediately returned to Winnipeg and each of them paid ten dollars to file on a homestead.[16]

In Winnipeg, a German shoemaker advised Pylypiw to investigate homestead areas in the area which is now Alberta, near Edmonton. The land there, according to him, was not only more fertile but the climate was more moderate. When they applied to the immigration authorities, arrangements were made to pay their fare to Calgary. Although they reached Calgary, they did not travel to Edmonton since there was no railroad to the German settlement. Therefore, they decided to return to Winnipeg. On their return journey they stopped over at Grenfell, about sixty miles southwest of Langenburg, an area also occupied by German settlers.[17] In Grenfell they viewed a large expanse of territory where one could take as much land as desired and begin ploughing immediately, if one only had plough and oxen.

Upon their return to Winnipeg, some Russian Jews advised them to investigate land areas around Gretna, south of Winnipeg, close to the United States border. Proceeding there, they found that the area was already settled by Germans who could also speak Ukrainian. The settlers informed them that they were now in comfortable circumstances, although there had been hardships at first. Though our travellers had already visited many areas, they were once more fascinated by the possibilities of settlement here. Pylypiw wondered whether he could not obtain a whole township to settle 144 families.[18] His plan was never fully realized but it was in Gretna that both Pylypiw and Eleniak finally resolved to bring over their wives and children. Since it was the harvest season and there was a demand for labourers, they were hired by the local farmers to help in threshing operations and were able to earn some money. Pylypiw worked for almost two months and was paid two dollars per day. Leaving Eleniak at work, Pylypiw returned to Winnipeg on December 1 and made plans to go back to Nebyliv and return to Canada with both of their families. On December 15 he set out on his journey, proceeding by way of Montreal, Boston, London, and Hamburg. From there he retraced his steps through Berlin, Osviencim, and Cracow to Krekhovych, where he hired a rig and arrived in Nebyliv on January 12, 1892.

Pylypiw's Imprisonment and the Beginning of Group Immigration

Pylypiw's return from Canada, after being absent for less than five months, stimulated unprecedented interest not only in Nebyliv but also in neighbouring villages. A steady stream of people came to question Pylypiw about Canada. Not only did he relieve their fears about leaving their native land and crossing the ocean but he urged them to go, stressing that "there was plenty of free land there, merely waiting to be ploughed." In preparation for the trip, he counselled them to take with them a plough, milling stones, mortars, scythes, sickles, flails, axes, and anything else useful in farming. As people heard about the free land, agitation increased. In their impatience, some made haste to sell their property and prepared for the journey overseas. Pylypiw established contract with a shipping agency, which offered him five dollars per person for all heads of families and two dollars for each single person if travel arrangements were made through the agency. They also provided him with a fare schedule.[19] Pylypiw accepted advance payments for fares, remitted the money to the shipping agency, and helped people to obtain their passports. In a short time over ten families were ready to start on their journey.

Not all of the Nebyliv villagers were ready to accept his story. There was suspicion in the minds of some of the villagers as to whether Pylypiw had really visited Canada as he claimed, and whether his collection of advances for fares was not outright swindling. Some years previously, thirty Ukrainian families had left Galicia for Argentina. On their arrival there, they were so grossly disillusioned with the living conditions that their protests compelled the Austrian government to advance money from the public treasury for their return fares. Accordingly, there was some justification for the government authorities to attempt to verify the ostensibly fantastic account of Pylypiw that, somewhere in some unknown land called Canada, there was so much land that anyone could emigrate there and obtain some, practically without cost. Therefore, it is not surprising that Pylypiw's home was visited one day by the village elder or mayor, the priest, the village clerk, and the bailiff. Extending a map on the table, they questioned him in regard to his destination, his route in travelling to Canada, and how he had returned. Although they initially appeared to be satisfied with his answers, Pylypiw and his brother-in-law, Tyt Ziniak, who had supported him in encouraging people to emigrate, were arrested soon after on May 12, 1892, and charged with inciting people to emigrate to America and defrauding them of their money for advance payments for their fares. The gendarme delivered them to Kalush where the judge, Karatnytsky, conducted an investigation into their actions which lasted until July 1. On this day they were formally indicted and taken to Stanyslaviv (now Ivano-Frankivsk) where the formal trial took place on July 21, ending in their committal to a month's imprisonment. As they had been arrested and confined long before the case was heard, they actually spent 101 days in prison.[20]

Departure of the First Group for Canada, 1892

Pylypiw's arrest did not dishearten the Nebyliv villagers who had planned to emigrate, and interest in Canada continued to grow. Longing for a better fate for themselves and their children, people explored every channel which might enable them to reach Canada, the new country where there was free land for all. While the two men were still in prison, six men with their families and one alone, all listed below, were already on their way to Canada. They were the following:[21]

1) Antin Paish, his wife and six children
2) Mykhailo (Michael) Romaniuk, his wife and four children
3) Dmytro Wyzhynovych or Wiznovych, his wife and six children
4) Mykhailo (Michael) Eleniak, a cousin of Wasyl's, his wife and three children
5) Mykola Tychkowsky, his wife and five children
6) Yuzko (Joseph) Paish came alone, having left his wife temporarily at home

They embarked on the steamship *Numidian* on June 2, and arrived in Quebec on June 13, nine months after Pylypiw and Eleniak had reached Canada.[22] All with the exception of one, a son of Mykhailo Eleniak, were illiterate. He had attended school and signed his own name as "Ilyniak".[23] Arriving in Winnipeg in the middle of June 1892, the immigrants immediately sought to learn which lands were available for settlement and whether they could obtain jobs to earn money as most of them had found travelling expenses quite burdensome on their limited resources. According to Ivan Romaniuk's memoirs, still not thoroughly substantiated,[24] his father, Mykhailo Romaniuk, Mykhailo Eleniak, and Dmytro Wiznovych filed on homesteads in the Stuartburn area in Manitoba "in the spring of 1892". The other immigrants were eager to proceed to Alberta. Leaving their families in the Immigration Hall in Winnipeg, they travelled west, their fares having been paid to Edmonton, to investigate land east of Fort Saskatchewan toward present-day Bruderheim and the Beaverhill Creek valley. This valley then had the appearance of an impenetrable jungle but the luxuriant growth indicated a fertile soil beneath. After studying various locations, they finally chose homesteads closer to Josephburg at Deep Creek, where Romaniuk filed on SE 12-55-22 W3 on June 27, 1892,

Tychkowsky on SW 22-55-21 W4 on August 5, becoming a neighbour of
Johann Krebs, and Paish on SE 28-55-21 W4 on August 29. (Whether
Mykhailo Eleniak chose a homestead here is unknown).[25]

Satisfied with their success in discovering good land, they returned to
Winnipeg. However, not all of the Nebyliv settlers planned to proceed to
Alberta immediately as only Paish and Tychkowsky left for their homesteads that autumn. At what later became Deep Creek they built a house on
the Paish farm in which both families spent the winter.

The remainder of the group remained in Manitoba. Romaniuk, Wiznovych, and Eleniak found work among the Mennonites in Gretna. Later
they were joined by Wasyl Eleniak and his two brothers, Petro and Ivan,
who accompanied Wasyl on his second trip to Canada in 1893, when he was
returning with his wife and family. It was here that Mykhailo Romaniuk
became acquainted with Nelidov, mentioned earlier, who was already an
agent for some American land agency and was urging Romaniuk and the
others to settle in Minnesota. Romaniuk actually visited the area and was
quite ready to settle near Minneapolis, but changed his mind because of his
reluctance to leave his fellow villagers, who had resolved to settle in Edna
where Mykola Tychkowsky and Antin Paish had already settled.

Pylypiw Arrives with His Family in 1893

Ivan Pylypiw, the initiator and hero of Ukrainian immigration into
Canada, having served his prison sentence, began immediately to prepare
for his return to Canada. Unfortunately, the time lost in prison, and the
money wasted on his defence had been too great a strain on his financial
resources, and he was compelled to seek some way of earning more money
in order to be able to provide for the cost of transportation for himself and
his family. Fortunately, he was again able to return to logging and entered
into a contract to deliver logs to a buyer in Odessa. Together with five
others, he cut and hauled logs to the bank of the Limnytsia River, a
tributary of the Dniester flowing through his village. Along these two rivers
the logs were transported to the Black Sea. To fulfill the contract he worked
until the winter of 1892. Finally, three days after Easter in 1893, he and his
family embarked on their long journey to Canada. Accompanying them
were Yurko Panischak with his family and Stefan Chichak.[26]

In Winnipeg he made haste to rent a house for his family and proceeded to North Dakota, where work was available. Returning in December, he
bought a team of oxen, a cow, a plough, a wagon, and such provisions as
flour, salt, and sugar. He obtained a freight car for forty dollars to
transport his belongings to Edmonton but travelled the rest of the way to
Deep Creek by ox-team. Only Stefan Chichak accompanied him and his

family as Yurko Panischak had elected to remain in Winnipeg. He filed first on a homestead at Deep Creek but cancelled his application six months later in the summer of 1894 and moved east to Edna, later known as Star, where more land was available for his growing family. Here he settled on SW 22-56-19 W4 and became a prosperous farmer, acquiring altogether 800 acres. Here he died at the age of seventy-seven on October 10, 1936.[27]

Meanwhile, as we have already learned, Wasyl Eleniak, after working for two years in Gretna, returned to Nebyliv on May 9, 1893, to bring out his family. According to Eleniak's statement,[28] Romaniuk's memoirs,[29] and Marunchak's research,[30] it would appear that six or seven other families prepared to accompany Eleniak to Canada, including his two brothers, Petro and Ivan; three Melnyk brothers, Fedir, Mykhailo, and Mykola; Mykhailo Pullishy, and Vasyl Feniak. Although all of them set out together, only three of the families, including those of Fedir Melnyk, Mykhailo Pullishy, and Vasyl Feniak were permitted to continue the journey. The remainder, including Wasyl Eleniak, were turned back because of insufficient funds. It was not until a month later that the other families were able to leave for Canada.[31]

After they had arrived in Canada, the three Eleniak brothers went to work among German farmers in Gretna, but Pullishy, Feniak, and the Melnyks left for Edna; the Eleniak brothers did not follow until the end of 1898 or the beginning of 1899.[32]

On January 12, 1956, at the age of ninety-eight, Wasyl Eleniak died and was buried in the same district in which he had settled. At the time of his death, his descendants numbered eight children, over fifty grandchildren and sixty great-grandchildren.[33]

Ivan Pylypiw did not play a conspicuous role in the life of Canadian Ukrainians although he had played such a heroic part in directing their settlement, and it must be admitted that Eleniak's influence was not any more conspicuous than Pylypiw's. Had it not been for Professor Bobersky and Wasyl Czumer, both Pylypiw and Eleniak would have remained comparatively unknown.

In Canada the two friends separated when Pylypiw returned to Galicia to bring out both their families. When Pylypiw returned to Canada in 1893, he came under the influence of a church movement from the United States then regarded as progressive and became alienated from the Greek Catholic Church because it had come under the jurisdiction of the French Roman Catholic hierarchy. He joined the Russian Orthodox Church which was fundamentally Russian in spirit, and propagated Russian imperialism or muscophilism, as it was then called. He remained with that church until his death and did not abandon it even when the Ukrainian Orthodox Church was revived, providing a haven for most Ukrainians who had been alienated from the Greek Catholic Church. On the other hand, Eleniak, who was working for the German Mennonites in Gretna and separated from the large mass of Ukrainians, was never influenced by the new religious movements in the United States and Canada and remained a Greek Catholic. It appears that this division on church grounds was deep enough to prevent them from meeting freely again, although both lived in the same district.

Notwithstanding the above, they both became a part of the history of Ukrainians in Canada after their "discovery" by Bobersky. Above all, the role of Pylypiw deserves not to be forgotten. With his restless nature, his initiative, and his agreeable personality, Pylypiw played an important part in awakening Ukrainians to the advantages of emigrating to Canada. His merit lies in the fact that, in the company of Eleniak, he dared to travel abroad to a land which was unknown to Ukrainians. He ascertained the possibilities of settlement and, having evaluated the situation, returned to his village to bring out his family, and prevailed upon others to emigrate. Of course, his achievement was unwittingly boosted by the action of the Austrian and Polish authorities who brought about his arrest, trial, and subsequent imprisonment. News of his arrest spread to all corners of Galicia and Bukovyna, setting in motion an emigration movement to one of the remaining choice areas of the earth.

After Pylypiw's death, when there began to be a greater appreciation of the contribution of pioneers, Wasyl Eleniak, who had outlived Pylypiw, remained the only survivor of the lonely pair that arrived in Canada in 1891. Accordingly, on January 3, 1947, in commemoration of the eightieth* anniversary of Confederation, Prime Minister Mackenzie King presented personally to Eleniak, as a representative of all Ukrainians in Canada, a special certificate of citizenship at a ceremonial occasion in Ottawa.

---

* The original Ukrainian text incorrectly stated that the year 1947 was the seventieth anniversary of Confederation. (Ed.)

Ivan Pylypiw

Wasyl Eleniak

FIRST TWO UKRAINIAN SETTLERS IN CANADA

Dr. Osyp Oleskiw

Kyrylo Genik

Sir Clifford Sifton

Father Nestor Dmytriw

5

Dr. Joseph Oleskiw, the Prosvita Society, and Ukrainian Immigration to Canada

Why People Emigrated?

The economic condition of the peasant in Galicia was not enviable at the time when the thirty-two year old peasant, Ivan Pylypiw, sought a better destiny for himself and his children by emigrating to Canada. When serfdom was abolished in Austria in 1848, peasants were set free from their feudal obligations and, in theory, they were supposed to receive land but, in actual practice, they were only given the right to purchase land. If they did not have sufficient money, they were forced to go into debt which had to be repaid in installments at a high rate of interest. In addition to debt charges, the peasant now was obliged to pay taxes. Therefore, he could find himself in very distressing circumstances in the event of a crop failure. Crop failures could result from a number of factors. They could be the result of unfavorable weather conditions or the infertility of the soil. Even if weather or soil were favorable, poor crops were harvested if the peasant knew nothing of general soil improvement or fertilization methods. In attempting to discover the causes of economic decay in Galicia, one author suggests an additional factor. He claims that no less harmful than other reasons was their mistaken piety which led peasants to devote half of the year to church holidays. A questionnaire sent out from Lviv in the 1870s revealed that most Galician counties averaged between 100 and 120 such holidays during the year: in twenty-two counties the number varied from 120 to 150, and in sixteen counties the number went as high as 150 to 200.[1] The tragedy of the situation is illustrated by the fact that between 1873 and 1883, 23,237 peasant holdings were lost to their owners through debts and taxes. If we also take into account the custom according to which the father divided his property among his sons, it is evident that holdings decreased in size with each generation, without taking into account all other factors. Even with more wealthy villagers the situation was fast approaching the stage where sons would inherit too little land to raise a family. The peasants really had reason to consider their position in regard to the future. Accordingly, they were only too ready to sell whatever they had to travel to other "worlds" where they could find "free land" and brighter hopes for survival.

However, the lack of material possessions was not the only reason for migration. All Ukrainian writers, including Stefanyk, Cheremshyna, Franko, and others, even memoirists and publicists, have ascribed too great a role to the lack of material possessions, as if people abandoned their native land and emigrated to unknown regions because of poverty alone. Especially is this claim made by communist writers such as Krawchuk and Telman, who stress poverty alone as being the cause of emigration. Actually, this was only one of many reasons for leaving, which may have also included social, national, political, religious, and even psychological factors. Many motives, either separately or in combination, played a part. For instance, any person resents being placed in a menial or subordinate position from which there is no hope of emerging. He desires to be a master in his own household. Accordingly, he will not tolerate a social system with a class division based upon an all-powerful aristocracy on the one hand and a politically and economically helpless population on the other. He will also be incensed at any condition under which he can be treated with scorn or disdain because of his political, religious or national heritage. Other individuals possess not only courage and daring but also an enquiring mind or a love of adventure. They are the frontiersmen who abandon known trails and frontiers to venture into distant lands, impenetrable forests, or unknown oceans to seek new adventures, uncharted trails or shores, and destinies. Their motives are in their characters. Their courage and resolution impels them to search for something better than what they have experienced.

If unfavorable economic conditions were the primary influence for the emigration of the Transcarpathian "Rusyns" and their neighbours, the "Lemkos", and if religious intolerance was responsible for the arrival of the "Stundists" from eastern Ukraine just as it was for the settlement of Mennonites and Doukhobors in Canada, then the movement of settlers from Galicia and Bukovyna in western Ukraine had a social, national, and a psychological basis as well as an economic influence. Among the villagers, as well as the intelligentsia and city dwellers, there were adventurous souls who were anxious to try their fortune in a new land. The restless, good-natured and, by no means the poorest peasant in Nebyliv, Ivan Pylypiw, is a good example of this type of adventurer who initiated the immigration movement.

Furthermore, it should not be forgotten that the agents of shipping companies and plantation owners from far-off countries in their search for cheap labour contributed in no small measure to the strength of the immigration movement. As an example of a country where there was a demand for labour on plantations, we can cite Brazil. In 1888 the king of Brazil abolished slavery and emancipated the Negro slaves in spite of the resentment of landowners and planters. Though the king was forced to abdicate and a republic was proclaimed, the planters were unable to restore slavery and sent agents far and wide to European countries to recruit labourers for their fields and encourage settlement. Some of these agents also appeared in Galicia. Sentiment played no part in their campaign to lure people away from their native land. They were totally indifferent to the fate of the emigrants and unconcerned as to whether they would fare better in the new land than had been their lot at home. Their main interest was to obtain as many passengers as possible for the steamship companies and the maximum number of labourers and colonists for the foreign country because their reward was based on the number they had recruited. Understandably, they exaggerated economic possibilities in Brazil. Not only did they report that there was plenty of opportunity for labour with high wages and free land for settlement, but they had a further advantage in their recruiting campaign in the fact that they could offer free transportation. It is obvious that such an attractive offer, even from distant Brazil, would fascinate the poorest peasant or any individual in search of adventure. They were charmed by visions of a country where "corn grew as tall as spruce trees, summers were cool, and winters were sultry". It was only when they reached Brazil and had endured the free but impenetrable jungle, its unbearable climate, and the exhausting labour, that they became disillusioned and began to bewail their misfortune. Conditions were almost identical for those who chose Argentina.

There were also numerous agents from other lands. While some urged the peasants to emigrate for labour to the plantations of Brazil, others proclaimed the advantages of Matabeleland or Bechuanaland in present-day Zimbabwe (Rhodesia). Ukrainians from the western part of Ukraine, from Lemkivshchyna and Transcarpathia, had journeyed to the United States much earlier and knew about free lands and settlement possibilities both in the United States and Canada, as we saw with the "Slovak" colonies in Lethbridge, Huns Valley, and Esterhazy. People had reason to be agitated and confused.

Emigration Arouses Concern in Austria-Hungary

The emigration movement reached such proportions that it aroused the Austrian government to action. It was fully justified in doing so as it had to protect itself from the actions of unscrupulous agents; indeed, it had already been compelled to provide the return fares of one disillusioned group from Argentina. Support came from a number of quarters. Since emigration depleted the number of cheap labourers who were indispensable in the cultivation of large estates, Polish landowners were concerned, though they did not advance this reason for their concern. Instead, they adopted the role of defenders of the unfortunate peasants, whom dishonest agents sought "to exploit and defraud". As a result, the emigration question was raised both in the provincial Diet in Lviv and in parliament in Vienna. The landowners were even successful in amending the Criminal Code by incorporating a section which forbade unauthorized individuals to encourage people to emigrate, making any infraction under this section subject to heavy penalties.

It must be admitted that Ukrainian leaders were also disturbed. Some opposed emigration on the grounds that it depleted the numerical strength of Ukrainians when their numbers were so necessary to carry on the struggle against constant Polish pressure. Others favored emigration but felt that countries which welcomed new settlers should be thoroughly explored and investigated. They also considered that such emigration should be planned to avoid the bitter disillusionment and suffering which had been the lot of emigrants to Brazil and Argentina.

Oleskiw and the Prosvita Society Direct Emigration to Canada

Dr. Osyp Oleskiw, a qualified agronomist and economist, and a professor of agronomy in the teachers' seminary in Lviv, was a representative of the second group. Considering that living conditions in Brazil and Argentina, on the basis of information which he had collected, were totally unfavorable for Ukrainians, he resolutely opposed emigration to those countries. Arousing his countrymen's interest in Canada, he visited there himself, investigating settlement from the Atlantic to the Pacific oceans, and finally urged them to emigrate to that country.

Canadian Ukrainians owe him a debt of gratitude not only for the number of their compatriots in Canada but also for much of their success, including their material, cultural, and political achievements. Unfortunately, after only a few years devoted to the cause of Ukrainian emigration, he died at the early age of forty-three. After a short period his services were largely forgotten, though we are not certain whether this lapse of memory can be attributed to his untimely death. Although people remembered him in the beginning and named libraries, schools, and post offices after him, they seemed to forget his achievements with the passage of time, and the names of those institutions were later replaced by others. It is true that there remained short, general, and sometimes inaccurate references to Oleskiw, but they did not go far toward enlightening us in regard to the actual role he played in Ukrainian immigration to Canada, and particularly about his attempts to provide the immigrants with moral, cultural, as well as economic aid. The more we became separated from the beginnings of settlement, the more did traces of his labour disappear until, finally, people lost all hope of ever finding any precise records of his service. Fortunately, these records lay in the state archives in Ottawa and were discovered by accident by Dr. V. J. Kaye (Kysilewsky), an employee of the Department of Citizenship and Immigration, after the Second World War. As related by him, there were nineteen files, two of which were labelled "Oleskiw".

Having already become interested in Ukrainian settlement and having already written extensively about Ukrainian pioneers in Canada, Kaye utilized these materials in a masterly fashion by compiling these original documents into a very valuable reference work for both historians and the general public entitled *Early Settlements of Ukrainians in Canada, 1895 -1900.*[2] Just as Bobersky earlier revealed the stories of Pylypiw and Eleniak so did Kaye disclose the role of Oleskiw. This role he relates as follows:

1) How Oleskiw diverted Ukrainian emigration from Brazil and Argentina to Canada.
2) Where and how Ukrainians founded their first settlements.
3) What were the beginnings of Ukrainian pioneer life.

His research will always remain a cornerstone for any investigation by a historian or researcher of Ukrainian immigration to Canada.

From this source we discover that Oleskiw wrote to the Department of the Interior on March 16, 1895, for information about Canada. In his letter he revealed that many thrifty and industrious Ukrainian villagers were seeking to emigrate to some country which still had free lands for settlers. Accompanying this information, he informed the department that the Brazilian government had been carrying on an intensive propaganda campaign in Galicia, offering free land to immigrants and free transportation from Italy to the place of settlement, including material aid until immigrants became established on their farms. Oleskiw further disclosed that a committee for prospective immigrants in Lviv had resolved to investigate possibilities of settlement in Canada and he requested on their behalf that the department send him the following:

1) The latest census figures for the population of Canada.
2) Information about free lands in various provinces.

3) Maps of areas where these lands are available with information on
    railways, forested areas, climate, and the price of work animals.
He enquired whether there was any possibility of a reduction of fares for
groups of immigrants. He concluded his letter by stating that if conditions
in Canada were more favorable than those in Brazil, the committee would
recommend Canada to prospective immigrants, where there was a more
stable government. He also announced his intention to visit Canada to investigate areas suitable for settlement.[3]

Oleskiw's letter was business-like, to the point, and created the impression that the writer had a good grasp of the problems involved. The officials
of the Department of the Interior were quite impressed by it and called attention to its importance in forwarding copies to other departments involved in immigration. They forwarded to Oleskiw the required information and directed a copy of the letter to the High Commissioner of Canada
in London,[4] instructing him to communicate with Oleskiw. At the same
time Oleskiw was advised to get in touch with the High Commissioner.

Following his instructions, Oleskiw wrote to London on May 7, 1895,
informing the High Commissioner that he had corresponded with the
Department of the Interior in Ottawa in regard to emigration from Galicia
and that he had received the literature about Canada. Nevertheless, he insisted that it was still necessary for him to visit Canada personally before he
could report on his findings, and that many people had postponed their
departure for Brazil while awaiting his conclusions in regard to Canada.

In a second letter to the High Commissioner on May 14, 1895, Oleskiw
enclosed his article on Canada in the *Narodnii Chasopys* and informed him
that the widely known Ukrainian association "Prosvita" was in total agreement with his view that Ukrainians should emigrate to Canada rather than
Brazil. He also added that he was preparing a pamphlet on Canada which
"Prosvita" would publish and distribute to its members in July 1895.

The "Prosvita" Association was organized in 1868 with the aim of
enlightening Ukrainians on national, economic, and political matters. The
organization became very powerful numerically within a short time and had
nine branches in Galicia with a membership approaching 12,000 at the time
of Oleskiw's and the organization's common interest in emigration. The
association carried on its activity by publishing booklets once a month and
in organizing libraries and reading rooms in villages where those booklets
could be read and discussed. Oleskiw's first booklet, entitled *About Free
Lands,* was published in July 1895 as planned and went to all the branches
and reading rooms in Galicia.

This pamphlet was prepared by Oleskiw on the basis of information
received from the Canadian government. It had thirty-eight pages and was
divided into three chapters. In the first chapter the author raised the ques-

tion of whether his native land was capable of supporting its population, calling attention to the distressing economic condition of its people, especially of the peasants who constituted the majority of the population, and concluded that emigration was the only solution. He offered two solu-- tions: some inhabitants should emigrate only for limited periods in organ- ized labour groups to earn money which would strengthen the economy in the villages; others should leave for other lands for permanent settlement.[5] In the second chapter he described the appalling conditions which were the lot of Ukrainian immigrants in Brazil where people died like "flies". He regarded Brazil as the grave of the Ukrainian immigrant and emigration to there as virtual suicide. He warned people not to be misled into emigrating to Brazil by the offer of free land. The third chapter was devoted to Canada. He described its almost unlimited extent, climate, inhabitants, government, schools, and above all, its land, outlining the terms on which it could be obtained. He closed his account with the information that he would visit Canada in the near future accompanied by other delegates, who were experienced farmers, to assess possibilities of settlement on the spot. He hoped to give more precise information after his return and recommend- ed that no one should leave for Canada independently and that all should await his report.

It must be admitted that emigration was a daring notion for the average Ukrainian man or woman. Some of them, having married only as far away as the neighbouring village and being forced to live there sang forlornly of the sadness of one's fate in having to die in a "foreign land". The thought of colonizing lands elsewhere was a totally foreign concept which even the Zaporozhians who had been forced to move beyond the Danube could not endure.[6] Instead of welcoming the opportunity of remaining in the new land with the prospect of extending boundaries of areas inhabited by Ukrainians, they constantly dreamed of the time when they could return "to quiet waters and bright stars". The exploits of Spanish Conquistadores, who con- quered distant lands beyond the ocean for themselves and their coun- trymen, had no attraction for them.

The Ukrainian Representatives Leave for Canada

At the end of July, 1895 Oleskiw arrived in London together with a peasant delegate, John Dorundiak, a prosperous villager and an experi- enced farmer from the county of Kolomyia, who was an expert on land and agricultural economics. His responsibility was to make a critical assessment of the possibilities and conditions of settlement for Ukrainians in Canada. On July 29 Oleskiw called on Sir Charles Tupper, with whom he had already corresponded in London, and informed him of the purpose of his journey, producing at the same time his plans for the settlement of villagers from Galicia in Canada. In addition to a letter of recommendation in his possession from Spiro and Company in Hamburg, he now obtained others from John Dyke, in charge of the Canadian Government Agency in Liverpool, and from George Hannah of the Allan Lines, a steamship company in Montreal. Tupper wrote a very favorable account of this meeting with Oleskiw and sent it to the Minister of the Interior in Ottawa by that same boat which took Oleskiw and Dorundiak to Canada.

They left Liverpool on August 1 on the *Sardinian,* arrived in Montreal on August 12, and reached Ottawa on August 13. Unfortunately, neither the Minister of the Interior, Hon. T. M. Daly, nor his deputy, A. M. Burgess, were in Ottawa at that time and Oleskiw was received by the Acting Deputy Minister, J. R. Hall. Hall already knew the purpose of Oleskiw's visit as he had already received and read Tupper's report.

Having toured the city and visited the experimental farm in a two day visit to the capital, the two travellers headed west, reaching Winnipeg on August 17. At the station they were met by Hugo Carstens, a German interpreter in the Dominion Land Bureau in Winnipeg, who had been assigned as a guide for their journey through western Canada. In Winnipeg Oleskiw had a conference with H. H. Smith, Director of Dominion Lands in Winnipeg, from whom he learned that the Minister of the Interior would be pleased to grant him an interview in Edmonton between August 26 and August 28, 1895.

Oleskiw and Dorundiak Tour Western Canada

Carstens' report[7] reveals that he left Winnipeg with the two visitors on August 19, reaching Calgary on Wednesday, August 21. As this area did not meet with Oleskiw's approval because of its arid appearance, they proceeded further, arriving in Edmonton on August 22. From here they followed a schedule of visits to survey land suitable for settlement prepared by R. A. Ruttan, Dominion Land Agent.

Beginning with the district of Stony Plain, west of Edmonton, where they found nearly 150 German families from Galicia, they continued for four days, questioning the German settlers in regard to living conditions and crop yields. The settlers informed him that they were completely satisfied with the land and living conditions in their area. On August 26 Oleskiw and his companions returned to Edmonton to meet the Minister of the Interior that same evening at the Edmonton Hotel.

In his letter to the Acting Minister, J. R. Hall, the Minister revealed that he had a two-hour interview with Professor Oleskiw with the help of Carstens as interpreter. At that time Oleskiw felt that the land bordering immediately on Edmonton was unsatisfactory for settlement but the district of Stony Plain met with the approval of both delegates. They felt that if there were comparable lands elsewhere, they would be satisfactory for the immigrants from his country. Nevertheless, Oleskiw stipulated that the government guarantee an initial grant of ten dollars for each head of a family, ten dollars for his wife, and five dollars for each child above the age of twelve. He also thought the government should make some provision to open an office in Galicia and also to defray the cost of printing advertisements and pamphlets about Canada and of the salary of an official who would receive and investigate applications for immigration to Canada. The minister replied that no money had been assigned in his department for such an unforseen expenditure, and even if he did recommend to the Cabinet the expenditure of as large a sum as $10,000, it would be very difficult to authorize under existing circumstances.

Nevertheless, Daly advised Oleskiw to prepare a comprehensive statement and to include in it the purpose of his visit to Canada, the condition of the proposed immigrants to Canada, the amount of capital each family would likely bring with it, and the amount of aid they would require from the government. Oleskiw was to leave this memorandum in Ottawa before returning to Galicia about the middle of October, at which time it would be submitted to the Cabinet for their consideration.

During this interview the number of prospective immigrants was also discussed. The Minister considered that 100 families, about 500 persons, would be sufficient for a beginning, but Oleskiw insisted that the first group should consist of 400 families or close to 2000 persons. He also contended that the government must have an official whose duty would be to publicize emigration to Canada.

Though Oleskiw's requests were modest and quite reasonable, the government was still unwilling to agree to them, not only because no money had been authorized for such a purpose but also because one earlier attempt to aid settlers had ended in total failure. Kirschbaum reports that the Hungarian Count Esterhazy had negotiated for financial aid for his settlers, of whom there were 95 families, in 1885 and 1886.[8] They had been recruited in Pennsylvania to settle in the district of Esterhazy in Saskatchewan. On this occasion the Canadian government had agreed to a loan of $25,000 to enable each family, before settling, to buy in Winnipeg a team of oxen, two cows, one wagon, one plough, and one shotgun with shells. In addition, each group of two families was permitted a loan of $1,000 to build houses and barns for themselves. Thus endowed, these settlers arrived in Esterhazy in July 1886 prepared for winter but endured only until spring. As we noted earlier, the winter was long and bitter. Having survived until spring, a large number left the colony, leaving behind all the equipment they had brought from Winnipeg. They abandoned their possessions just as easily as they had acquired them. Accordingly, it was not surprising that the government was loath to repeat the experiment with Oleskiw.

Accompanied by Dorundiak and Carstens the next day, Oleskiw continued on his tour, this time to the north-east of Edmonton in the district of Beaver Creek, where there were already sixteen families from "Boikiv-shchyna", a common name for a part of Galicia which bordered on the eastern stretches of the Carpathian Mountains. Then they proceeded south along the west side of Beaver Lake to Demay Lake, Dried Meat District, and on to Wetaskiwin. Though all of this territory attracted Oleskiw and Dorundiak, they were particularly attracted by the Indian reservation which they observed on August 2 just south of Edmonton.

Having surveyed almost all areas around Edmonton, the three travellers left for Calgary on September 3. In Calgary, Carstens gave Dorundiak letters of recommendation to German settlers at Balgonie and Grenfell, now in Saskatchewan, where Dorundiak was anxious to go. Meanwhile Carstens and Oleskiw continued their journey to Vancouver, arriving there on September 5.

In British Columbia, Oleskiw visited New Westminster where he obtained information about available land along the railway. Then he and Carstens continued their journey to Victoria where he interviewed the Minister of Immigration in regard to suitable land on Vancouver Island. On their way back they visited Nanaimo where Oleskiw saw two coal mines in operation before they returned to Vancouver. Two days later we find them around Vernon in the Okanagan Valley. On their journey east they also stopped in Banff for a day, where Oleskiw was probably the first Ukrainian to visit this health resort. From Banff they continued east, stopping in Indian Head for a day to visit the experimental farm before returning to Winnipeg. He remained there for another day before continuing to the German colony in Gretna, where he explored land on both sides of the Red River. As this district also attracted him, he spent several days in studying it, returning to Winnipeg on September 20.

Oleskiw and Dorundiak Return to Galicia

From Winnipeg, Oleskiw travelled to the United States to confer with Ukrainians, before arriving in Ottawa on October 1. There he again met with the Acting Deputy Minister of the Department of the Interior, J. R. Hall, who reiterated his minister's request that Oleskiw prepare a memorandum, outlining his proposals regarding immigrants from Galicia, which the minister could submit to the Cabinet.

Either because he was pressed for time or because he was exhausted by the two-month journey, Oleskiw prepared a brief memorandum which could hardly be called a complete proposal. His main request was that the Canadian government provide a grant of sixty dollars for every head of a family, including also single settlers, if the proposed settler filed on a homestead and arrived with a group whose members would settle near one another and form a type of cooperative. This grant or subsidy was not to be paid to the individual settler but to the directors of the cooperative settlement who would guarantee that no one would abandon the settlement after they had received the grant. The money was to be used in providing the settlement with the basic capital to build a mill, an elevator, a creamery, and a cheese factory. This would ensure that every settlement would become self-sustaining and financially independent from the beginning.

If we compare the terms of this proposal with those he had submitted to the minister in Edmonton about a month earlier, we find quite a wide divergence. Though the minister had already raised objections to an outlay of $10,000 for the whole immigration project, Oleskiw's second proposal had increased the proposed expenditure to $30,000 for one group of five hundred persons, a request which the minister would find still more difficult to accept. The memorandum must have inspired the conviction that Oleskiw was a highly impractical visionary. In return the Acting Deputy Minister merely informed him by letter that he would refer the submission to the minister who, after consultation with the members of the Cabinet, would inform Oleskiw of his decision. Though Oleskiw had been promised another interview with the Minister of the Interior before he returned to Europe, there was no further invitation for that purpose. It is probable that the minister concluded that he could add nothing more to what he had stated previously.

Oleskiw left Ottawa on October 4, embarking on the *Parisian* in Montreal on October 5, somewhat disappointed that he had been unable to reach any definite agreement with the government in Ottawa. On the instructions of the minister, he met John Dyke, the Canadian agent in Liverpool, on October 14, to discuss further the immigration possibilities for his countrymen in Canada. John Dyke even expressed a desire to accompany him to Galicia.

Though Oleskiw did not achieve any concrete results in regard to his proposals, he certainly visited Canada and had made a positive appraisal of its possibilities. He could now recommend Canada as a suitable area for settlement with a clear conscience. With this action he performed a priceless and unforgettable service for his countrymen who settled in Canada. However, this great service is clouded by one shortcoming. Neither he nor the Prosvita Society in Lviv succeeded in enlightening their emigrants as to their national identity, whether this might be under the name of Ruthenian or that of Ukrainian. As a result they came to Canada not as Ukrainians or

Ruthenians but as Galicians, Bukovynians, Austrians, Roumanians, and Russians, while the Canadian immigration authorities and the government designated them almost entirely as Galicians. Accordingly, it was subsequently impossible to calculate exactly how many Ukrainians came to Canada or the time of their arrival. Ukrainian-Canadian leaders were compelled to continue their efforts for twenty years to acquaint their countrymen with their national origin before the Galicians, Bukovynians, Austrians, Hungarians, and Russians began to regard themselves first as Ruthenians and later as Ukrainians.

6

Events Following Oleskiw's Visit to Canada

The Formation of a Committee to Aid Emigrants

When Oleskiw returned to Galicia, he exploited every opportunity to inform people about Canada. Immediately after his return, a conference of leading Ukrainians in Galicia was held in Lviv on November 14, 1895.[1] At this conference, Oleskiw reported on his visit and strongly recommended Canada to those who had awaited his report before emigrating. At the same time a committee to aid emigrants was also formed with Vasyl Nahirny as chairman. Nahirny was a noted economist and, at the same time, the founder, architect, and director of the largest Ukrainian cooperative in Galicia, the Narodna Torhivlia (The People's Market). Some of the other members of the committee were: Viacheslav Budzynovsky, Osyp Markiv, editor of the daily *Halychanyn* (The Galician), and Kost Levytsky, a lawyer and later a member of parliament in Vienna where he was also elected president of the Ukrainian Parliamentary Union; Lonhyn Rozhankivsky, also a lawyer, and Fathers Stepan Kachala, M. Hirniak, and Oleksander Stefanovych.[2]

Although the Canadian government had received favorable reports in answer to their enquiries regarding Oleskiw, and although there was no question in regard to Oleskiw's concern about emigration as he had even involved himself in the formation of the above committee of distinguished Ukrainian leaders, they were still hesitant at first as they continued to question whether Oleskiw and his committee were really competent to set in motion a mass immigration movement to Canada. That these enquiries were initiated partly to discover the attitude of the Austrian government is also understandable. Nevertheless, even after enquiries had fully convinced the Minister of the Interior that Oleskiw could be trusted, the government continued to postpone any decisive action. Subsequent events prove that this hesitation about Oleskiw's proposals was based on other considerations, some political and others a matter of policy. In the first place Oleskiw's demand for a subsidy was unacceptable because its acceptance would set a precedent for other national groups to follow in requesting the privilege. The other difficulty was the internal crisis within the Cabinet over the question of leadership. Under such conditions there was a disposition to limit rather than increase financial obligations. Although the political considerations were hardly understood by Oleskiw, the government was in no position to accept his somewhat uncompromising demands.

Oleskiw's Brochures: "O Emigratsii" (About Emigration) and "Rolnictwo za oceanem..." (Farming Beyond the Ocean...)

Toward the end of 1895 there appeared in print Oleskiw's second Ukrainian-language brochure, *O Emigratsii*. This booklet had seventy-two pages, of which Oleskiw's contribution filled sixty-six pages, divided into twelve chapters. The remaining six pages were added by the publishing group, the Kachkovsky Society.[3] In this brochure the author describes his journey through Canada and contrasts Brazil with other countries to which emigration was possible. He comments on the absence of class distinction in the American world in contrast to that of Austria, and cautions his countrymen about manifesting any signs of servility before foreigners, urging them to maintain their self-respect. He proceeds to describe the broad expanse of western Canada, how the land is divided, where there is fertile soil, and where the climate is suitable for settlement. He calls attention to Manitoba, where soils are heavy but fertile because Manitoba was once the bottom of an ancient lake. He writes about the steppes further west which are also fertile but warns against settlement in southern Alberta because of drought conditions. On the other hand, he stresses the suitability of the soil around Edmonton where a number of Germans and a few Ukrainians had already settled. All of the settlers had informed him that they found both soil and climate very satisfactory.

In closing, he describes his brief visit to the United States and announces his willingness to give prospective emigrants information regarding land in Canada. He adds that not only peasants but also certain members of the intelligentsia are preparing to emigrate and that the latter have expressed a willingness to serve as dependable guides en route as well as to aid emigrants in matters related to their settlement in the new land.

Oleskiw's brochure has a special interest for us because he describes the Ukrainians who were already in Canada. There were approximately ten families in Winnipeg, mostly from Nebyliv, and he lists them as follows: Wasyl Jaciv (Yatsiv), who had arrived in Canada in 1892; Yurko (George) Panischak and Yurko Paish, with no mention of the year of their arrival; Dmytro Widynovych, who arrived in 1893, probably the Wiznovych or Wizhnovych who has been reported as arriving in 1892; Yurko Rozhko, 1894; Hnat Dmytryshyn, Luchka Kulchicki (Kulchitsky), and Ivan Barsky, all arriving in 1895. All of them were happy that they had come to Canada and each one took pride in disclosing the amount of money he had already saved. Jaciv owned a house and had acquired two cows while Panischak also had a house and one cow. Although these families had arrived as early as 1892 and 1893, and Winnipeg was still a small town, they apparently knew nothing about earlier Ukrainian immigrants and Oleskiw did not mention such names as Shweresky, Bubnyk, Slota, Matliuk, Sharpii, Kolishar, Holub, Maliut, Kravchenko or any others with Ukrainian names who belonged to the Parish of the Immaculate Conception.

Oleskiw also did not omit listing those Ukrainians whom he had visited in the Edmonton district. He listed the following: Antin Paish, who lived among Germans near Josephburg; and further east in the Edna district, Fedir, Mykhailo, and Mykola Melnyk from Nebyliv; Petro and Matey Melnyk from Perehinsko; Andrii Paish, Stephan Chichak, Wasyl Feniak, Ivan Pylypiw (to whom Oleskiw fails to ascribe any credit for the arrival of Ukrainians in Canada), Mykhailo Pullishy, Mykola Tychkowsky, all from Nebyliv; "a Mykhailo from Sambir", and Ivan Dubrowsky from Zolochiv.[4]

There is also an account of a small settlement of Ukrainians near Neudorf, Saskatchewan, then known as Pheasant Forks, about twenty miles south-west of Melville. Though Oleskiw was not there himself, the settlement was visited by his travelling companion, Ivan Dorundiak, whose account of his visit Oleskiw merely repeated in his book. This was another group of Ukrainians who had arrived with German immigrants in 1892 and 1893. As related by Dorundiak, this group was composed of Pavlo Shymko, his wife and two brothers whose family name was Huminilovych (but Dorundiak omitted to record their first names); also the larger family of Ilko Pylypiw with two sons, Fedir and Tymko, and a daughter, Anne, whose name also appears to have been unknown to Dorundiak.[5] The family arrived from the village of Ulychne, county of Drohobych.

Though Oleskiw only lists Ukrainians in Winnipeg, Edna, and Pheasant Forks, this does not mean that there were no other Ukrainians in Canada. For instance, *Svoboda* in 1894 published the following overlengthy statement of thanks:

> Ruthenians in Mount Carmel, Pa., extend their heartfelt thanks to their brothers in Canada for their generous donations of forty-four dollars and fifty cents which were collected for their church. They wish to give particular thanks to the collectors, Nykolai Bakosh (Vakosh?), and Yosef Mowfliar.
> — The Church Committee[6]

Following this, the same newspaper included this announcement in a later edition:[7]

> To the newspaper, *Svoboda,* the following have donated sums for the Emigration Home in New York (and here, among other names from the United States, is that of Ann Hrabynska, Canada, $1.00).

These two announcements leave no doubt in our minds that there were other Ukrainians in Canada at the time of Oleskiw's visit but their location, their numbers, the time of their arrival, or their place of origin are still unknown. Nevertheless, there can only be one conclusion in regard to these names: these people must have come from Pennsylvania since they had a feeling of kinship for their church group in Mt. Carmel, but they could have been residents of Lethbridge, Huns Valley, Esterhazy, or even Winnipeg. Apparently, Kaye did not attempt to determine where the collectors Vakosh or Bakosh and Mowfliar lived, but he tried to locate Anna Hrabynska. After some unsuccessful research, he concluded that she must have been a housemaid who had arrived in Canada from Pennsylvania and probably returned there, for no further trace of her can be found in Canada.[8]

Returning to Oleskiw's efforts to divert the attention of his countrymen from Brazil to Canada, we know that he published not only the two booklets, *About Free Lands* and *About Emigration,* in addition to other articles in the Galician press, but he also prepared a brochure in Polish, *Rolnictwo za oceanem a przesiedlna emigracja* (Farming Beyond the Ocean and Transplanted Emigrants). Judging from the review in *Svoboda,*[9] Oleskiw elaborated on the following:

1) Agriculture — production overseas and Europe
2) Particulars of American agricultural production
3) The settlement of North America
4) Agricultural machinery
5) Cattle-feeding overseas
6) Colonization of the Parana in Brazil
7) Emigration to Brazil
8) Emigration to Canada
9) The criminal code and emigration fever

Obviously, the theme of this publication in Polish was similar to that of its Ukrainian counterpart. Its aim was not only to inform Polish peasants about emigration possibilities in the new world but also to warn the Polish aristocrat-landlords that neither the Ukrainian nor the Polish peasant was forced any longer to accept the living conditions which had been dictated to them by their overlords.

The first Group of Oleskiw's Immigrants to Canada

Since Oleskiw had advised prospective settlers to postpone their emigration plans until he had returned from Canada and reported on his findings, the appearance of his publication was awaited with eagerness. When the brochures in the two languages appeared, they were received with enthusiasm and read avidly. People flocked to Oleskiw from all corners of Galicia to seek additional information while some impetuously sold all their belongings in preparation for the journey to Canada. As early as February 1896, Oleskiw informed the Department of the Interior that he was sending thirty immigrant families to Canada. On April 11, ninety-four persons, including twenty-four men, nineteen women, and fifty-one children, embarked on the ship *Christiania* which arrived in Quebec on April 30, 1896.[10] With the exception of three families who chose to remain in Beausejour, Manitoba, all the rest continued west and settled in Edna[11] district though Oleskiw had planned to locate at least half of the group near Dauphin.

This first group produced a favorable impression on Canadian officialdom. Oleskiw had promised that his immigrants would be selected on the basis of their capital possessions to ensure that they would not become a financial burden to the new country. Furthermore, he had written that they would have a guide who would advise the immigrants en route and after their arrival in Canada. He kept his word on both promises. Among the new settlers, there were people with some education including Antin Savka, who had spent four years in a *gymnasium* (secondary school) and it is not surprising that he became a correspondent to *Svoboda* almost immediately. The same is true of Luts Keryk (Kyryk) of this group. The immigrants also brought a good deal of capital with them. Some families brought as much as 200 dollars, others 300, and some 500. Among the wealthiest were Kost Nemirsky who arrived with 700 dollars and Ivan Lakusta with 800. The list of settlers, as provided by Kaye, shows that the total capital possessed by the group amounted to $7250.[12]

The most striking detail about the new arrivals is that their guide was Volodymyr Oleskiw, Osyp's brother, a restless, enterprising, and adventurous personality. During the earlier period of his life he had worked in a chemical plant in Kiev. Following this period, he spent eight years in the United States where he learned the English language. Of course, when he returned, he was instrumental in informing his brother of conditions in that country.[13] Considering his past experience he was a very suitable choice to guide the first contingent of immigrants despatched by his brother. Not only did he help them to reach their destination and settle there but he also continued the negotiations with the Canadian government on behalf of his brother in regard to the requests he had forwarded to the government in the previous year.[14] However, Volodymyr returned to Galicia after settling this group and did not visit Canada again.

Oleskiw's Continuing Concern for the Canadian Immigrants

Oleskiw was conscientious in his attention to immigrant problems and continued to press the Canadian government for changes in dealing with those problems but, as we have already learned, the government continued to be dilatory. Though most of his recommendations included practical and useful economic measures to aid the settlers, he did not forget their spiritual needs. He knew that Edna district already had a considerable number of settlers; other families had settled among German immigrants at Neudorf and Lemberg, and there were already Ukrainians in Winnipeg and district. He also knew other prospective settlers were on their way to Canada. Accordingly, he informed the Minister of the Interior on May 16, 1896, that a Father Ostap Nyzhankivsky had expressed his willingness to emigrate to Canada with his wife and child to look after the religious needs of the immigrants. Oleskiw stated that he could recommend him not only because of his spiritual and social qualities but also because he was a noted musical composer and only thirty-five years of age.[15] Oleskiw asked the government whether any financial aid could be made available to subsidize the support of a priest among the Greek Catholics. In reply, the Minister informed Oleskiw that no subsidy was possible and that no exception could be made for the Greek Catholics. The best that could be done, according to this letter, was the payment of a grant of 100 dollars to cover Father Nyzhankivsky's personal expenses and a commitment that the railway company would give him either free transportation or provide it at a lower rate. Nevertheless, this offer was available only if he accompanied a group of immigrants on their journey to Canada.[16] As there is no further mention of this matter, it is obvious that nothing came of these negotiations, and that Father Nyzhankivsky did not come to Canada.

As the above official letter was written one day before the general election, the government could hardly commit itself to further obligations. It was just as well, since the Conservative government suffered defeat in the election on June 23, 1896, and the Liberals took over with Sir Wilfred Laurier as the new Prime Minister. Fortunately, the new government was not hostile to schemes for increasing settlement in western Canada. Two months after the election, the Prime Minister appointed Sir Clifford Sifton, a lawyer from Brandon, to the position of Minister of Immigration. There was also a new post created, that of Commissioner of Immigration, to which W. F. McCreary was appointed. He played a very important role in the settlement of Ukrainians in western Canada. In addition W. T. R. Preston was given the post of Inspector of Canadian Immigration Agencies in Europe with an office in London, England. All of these men were wholly dedicated to the promotion of immigration. Furthermore, since there were no longer internal troubles within the Cabinet, these officials could commit themselves wholeheartedly to the problem. Nevertheless, before they could launch any program, they had to become acquainted with the plans and activities of the previous administration, a pursuit which lasted a few months.

Ignorant of these internal Canadian problems, Oleskiw became increasingly disillusioned with his activities in the promotion of immigration and informed the Canadian government of his disappointment. Fortunately, he did not abandon all hope and continued his correspondence in which he included practical suggestions to improve upon the immigration policy. Recognizing that his attempt to obtain direct help for a priest had failed, Oleskiw wrote to the Commissioner of Dominion Lands in Winnipeg, recommending the appointment of an immigration officer in that city who, in addition to German and English, would also know the Slavic languages and about whom prospective immigrants could be informed before they left home. He also insisted that this individual should be someone they could trust and respect.[17] Such an agent could lighten the load of immigration officials and benefit both the immigrants and Canada. Oleskiw had in mind for the job Kyrylo (Cyril) Genik, a teacher from Bereziv, thirty-nine years of age, who had been at the conference in Lviv when Oleskiw had reported on his journey to Canada and who had led a group of immigrants to settle in Stuartburn, Manitoba, in July 1896.[18] Nevertheless, he did not refer to Genik by name as he was certain that the immigration officials would recognize his ability on his arrival in Canada. This is exactly what happened. When Oleskiw wrote later to remind the Minister of Immigration of the necessity for such an appointment, he was informed that Genik had already been hired as an interpreter and was assisting immigration officials in the settlement of immigrants.

Before Oleskiw had received an answer from the Commissioner in Winnipeg, he had written another long letter to the Minister of the Interior[19] proposing that the government reserve certain blocks of land for settlers whom he was sending to Canada. He felt that people who had already disposed of their property in their homeland should know exactly where they were going and what land would be available to a settler in selecting a homestead. He could not see any virtue in the policy whereby immigrants were compelled to remain in the Immigration Hall in Winnipeg until the leaders of the group returned after finding an area for settlement. While awaiting the return of the survey parties, the immigrants sank into despondency and despair. In this state they were subject to the influence of local malcontents who spoke disparagingly of Canada. Some had already been influenced to return home with the conviction that there was no free land available in Canada as had been advertised. Others had settled in unfavorable areas such as Brokenhead (near Winnipeg) and also returned home when they saw no future in the land which was offered to them. Still others, tired of waiting, bought "dwarf farms" of ten to fifteen acres in size along the Red River and paid large sums for them. Oleskiw was especially critical of the Roman Catholic priests who had sold small fractions of land in St. Norbert (near Winnipeg) to nearly twenty families. He believed these small allotments were too insubstantial for the immigrant to achieve self-sufficiency, let alone economic independence. Not only did he denounce these transactions as "economic nonsense" but he also warned the immigration authorities that buying this land from Roman Catholics would place these immigrants, who were Greek Catholics, in a position of material and moral dependence on the Roman Catholic Church. But the Greek Catholic Church was totally different from the Roman Catholic. Oleskiw pointed out that even the language of the liturgy in the Greek Catholic Church was different from that of the Roman Catholic, as Greek Catholics used Slavonic while the Roman Catholics used Latin. News from Canada that Greek Catholics were dependent on the Roman Catholic Church would deter emigration of many Greek Catholics. He ended one section of his letter with these words: "In this country (in Galicia) these two Churches are in a state of struggle."[20]

Disorder as the Result of Haphazard Policy

To appraise the value of Oleskiw's advice and foresight with regard to the difficulties in allocating settlers, one need only examine the case of two groups of immigrants which arrived in Winnipeg on May 1, 1897: 633 from the S.S. *Arcadia* and another 435 from the S.S. *Scotia* six hours later. Since the passengers from the first ship had been organized and arranged for by Oleskiw, they were directed to the district of Dauphin, where most of them settled. Passengers from the second ship, chiefly from Bukovyna, had been brought together by steamship agents and no arrangements had been made to settle them. As noted by the letter of the Commissioner of Immigration, W. F. McCreary, to the Minister of the Interior,[21] these people had been informed by agents that the Crown Princess of Austria[22] lived in Montreal and that she would ensure that every immigrant obtained land with a house, two cows, and subsistence for a year. If these were not immediately available, they were told to send a telegram to the Austrian princess and she would provide for the fulfillment of these promises. McCreary sent a group of 46 individuals to explore land around Stuartburn and managed to settle about twenty families there but the rest, nearly 200 persons, refused to settle on land without the promised house and cows. They remained in the Immigration Hall in Winnipeg for an additional two weeks without the permission of the authorities, demanding that they be transported back to Bukovyna.

Unfortunately for them, the immigration authorities received a telegram from Ottawa warning them to prepare for a further contingent of 1200 immigrants from two ships. As room had to be made for new arrivals, the matter of allocating the protesting group became very critical. The authorities directed that they must either leave for the Yorkton district (around Wroxton and Calder), where there was good land both for grain farming and cattle raising, or leave the Immigration Hall and seek their fortune without the help of the immigration officials. This meant looking for work to support their families. When the group refused to budge, force was used to evict them. Some of the immigrants lay on the floor in protest and had to be carried out, together with their belongings. Obviously this caused a disturbance with "a great deal of yelling, crying, and shrieking". One of the women could not stomach such "brutality" so she took off her boot and hurled it at McCreary. Fortunately, she missed him but this action provided a pretext for summoning the police. With the arrival of a police sergeant and five constables, the protesters were finally evicted and informed that they could board the train which would leave for Yorkton the next day. McCreary related in a second letter[23] that it was one matter to evict these people and another to persuade them to enter the railway cars. When the officials loaded the baggage trucks, the malcontents upset the trucks, took their baggage, and carried it north along Main Street, squatting along the street and taking possession of two vacant houses not far from the Immigration Hall. With the coming of night, it was necessary to find food and shelter, but the local troublemakers who had incited the immigrants were unwilling to accept them in their homes and support them for an indefinite period. To add to the immigrants' misery, there was a heavy downpour of rain and it turned cold. Consequently, one after another, the protesters boarded the train, and almost all were in their places in the designated passenger cars by morning. The train left for Saltcoats, a station near Yorkton.

Understandably, the newspaper reporters did not neglect to sensationalize this incident. The *Winnipeg Tribune*[24] gave full coverage to the story of the shouting Bukovynian woman who had thrown her boot at the former mayor of Winnipeg, and of the officials who had conducted the immigrants off the premises with the help of the police in order to make room for the new arrivals.

7

Ukrainians Gain
Recognition as Settlers

First Unfavorable Impressions Give Way to
Gradual Acceptance

Oleskiw's reference to the outward appearance of North Americans—their clothing and their neat appearance—in his brochure, *About Emigration,* was deliberate. Accordingly, those immigrants whom he was instrumental in sending to Canada sought to pattern their appearance to some extent after what they anticipated would be the appearance of Canadians they would meet. On the other hand, immigrants who had been recruited by steamship company agents embarked heedlessly into a novel world in their national costumes—in sheepskin coats with fur on the inside, in long white shirts tied around the waist over their trousers, with a broad pleated or solid leather belt, and in heavy boots rising to the knees. To the English- or French-speaking inhabitants of that period, these were strange outlandish costumes in which there must be concealed an uncommon or outlandish people similar to the aborigines of this country, either Eskimo or Indian. Accordingly, the outward appearance of these first Ukrainians, both from Galicia and from Bukovyna, did not evoke a favorable attitude in the Canadian population and it is not surprising that they were labelled "men in sheepskin coats". It should also not surprise us that many Canadians who had arrived in Canada a generation or two earlier feared that these immigrants would never become useful citizens of this country.

Regardless of the fears as to the quality of the newcomers, the Galicians and the Bukovynians continued to arrive in hundreds and thousands. After the passengers of the S.S. *Scotia* disembarked, three additional transports of immigrants from the same provinces reached port within a month's time: 622 on the S.S. *Prussia*, 558 on the S.S. *Arabia,* and 717 on the S.S. *Armenia.* After them came still others as the immigration authorities reported the number of arrivals in 1897 from Galicia and Bukovyna as being close to 6000.[1]

The colonization officials hastened to allocate land to these settlers as early as possible to give each one an opportunity to prepare a small plot for the next year. Not only did they help the newcomers to settle but they returned later to determine their progress. To some they extended material aid and made reports of the circumstances to their superiors. It is of interest to note that these reports were generally sympathetic and favorable. R. A. Ruttan, Dominion Lands and Immigration Agent in Edmonton, wrote the Commissioner of Dominion Lands in Winnipeg as follows:

> They are good settlers and I should like to see more of them. Their frugality, modest ambition and industry fit them to meet in the best way the difficulties this remote locality (Edna) presents.[2]

Lord Strathcona (Sir Donald A. Smith) in his letter to Hon. Clifford Sifton, Minister of the Interior, makes the following observations:

> We must set ourselves in one way or another to get as many immigrants as possible from the Continent of Europe and none I believe have turned out better in our North-West than the Galician settlers.[3]

Though it is true that Lord Strathcona wavered in his support of these settlers, immigration figures rose steadily during the period that he held office. C. W. Sutter, Dominion Lands and Immigration Agent in Edmonton (likely Ruttan's successor), has the following in his letter to the Commissioner of Dominion Lands in Winnipeg:

> On my way back to Edmonton I met Mr. Porte, President of the Fort Saskatchewan Agricultural Society. He had been to every house (of Ukrainian settlers) to ascertain how much crop per acre each farmer would have and he informed me that he had never seen a more contented and happy lot of farmers than the Galicians. They are all doing well, had considerable crop and land cultivated for next spring.[4]

What may be of more interest is that the Austrian Consul in Montreal, Eduard Schultze, was also following closely the fortunes of Austrian immigrants in this country. In the summer of 1897, during a two or three month period, he visited almost every Ukrainian settlement and gave the Canadian government a report on his visits. He was so pleased with the condition of the immigrants in the Yorkton and Saltcoats districts that he hastened to express his satisfaction by dispatching the following telegram to McCreary, the Commissioner of Immigration:

Have inspected colonies at Saltcoats and Yorkton accompanied by officer Speers from Whitewood. Am delighted for what I have seen. Beautiful country, specially adapted for settlement; far exceeds my expectations, good houses, splendid farms; am very thankful for your wise policy in placing these people. Mr. Speers had taken great pains to show every advantage of the people, the work done reflects great credit, is really wonderful. I extend to you the congratulations of my government for what I have seen.[5]

Of additional interest is the report of Ignatius Roth, a representative of a steamship company in Montreal, who acted as interpreter for Consul Schultze. In his letter dated September 5, 1897, he relates the following to his superiors about the visit to 180 families in the Stuartburn district:

I find that the people are doing fairly well, all have good houses and gardens, also cattle with the exception of a few Bukovyna families, who reached the Colony this year without any means whatsoever. Almost all the men are out harvesting and earning $20 to $25 per month and board, some getting $1.50 per day. I visited all those that can write and do the writing for others, and explained to them the necessity of their writing home to their friends and relatives that this country is good and there is plenty of room here for more. In answer I was told that it is their wish to have their friends come out here and leave Galicia, "that bad country", as soon as possible. It is really wonderful what progress these people are making and what fine houses they have built with only an axe.[6]

The Deputy Minister of Immigration, James A. Smart, also expressed his approval in a letter to Lord Strathcona:

...the Galicians have, so far at all events, shewn themselves to be possessed of qualities which will ultimately make successful settlers ... I am inclined to think Prof. Oleskiw ought to be shewn that his work has been appreciated, because so far as I am aware he has sent only those of the better class to this country.[7]

The Canadian Government Finally Recognizes Oleskiw's Services

The immigration figures and the favorable reports about immigrants whom Oleskiw had sent to Canada convinced the Canadian government of the seriousness of his intentions in promising further immigrants and in advising how to deal with them when they arrived in Canada. Accordingly, Sir Clifford Sifton, the Minister of Immigration, gave instructions that Oleskiw be requested to come to Canada to assume control of "Galician immigration".[8] Complying with instructions received from Ottawa, Lord Strathcona wired the offer to Oleskiw. However, whether from disappointment with the earlier indifference with which the government had treated his proposals or because it was impossible to abandon his classroom in the middle of a school year, Oleskiw declined the offer. He proposed instead a meeting with Lord Strathcona in London to discuss immigration problems. On receiving Oleskiw's reply, the minister agreed to the meeting and gave Lord Strathcona full authority to negotiate an agreement.

Taking advantage of the Christmas and New Year's break, Oleskiw reached London on January 4, 1898. In London, a number of conferences were held with Lord Strathcona, and an agreement was reached which enabled Oleskiw to continue to promote immigration. The Canadian government was to provide a subsidy of between 500 and 600 pounds sterling to defray the costs of printing suitable brochures and advertisements, their circulation, and wages to personnel. In addition the government agreed to pay Oleskiw a bonus of $2.50 for every immigrant above the age of eighteen. It was stipulated that the agreement would remain confidential, an arrangement which was probably intended to protect Oleskiw from harassment by Austrian government officials.[9] The agreement was ratified soon after, and an advance was forwarded to Oleskiw to cover expenses.

On the basis of a statement by the accountant of the Department of the Interior, as reported by V. J. Kaye, the sum received by Oleskiw from the Canadian government during the three year period (1898-1900) to cover travelling and printing costs, including wages for himself and his assistants, was $5,745.59.[10] Though this might appear a large sum in total, it was quite modest if we take into account the period of time, the amount of work involved in obtaining varied information and advice, the cost of travel, and payments to assistants.

It is probable that Oleskiw's contribution was assessed most accurately by S. W. Coryn, the European representative of the C.P.R., whose letter to his superior contained the following appraisal as early as 1896:

> Oleskiw ... has done an immense amount of travelling, has answered innumerable letters, and spent considerable money in the interest of immigration, and the sub-agent's commission which he may have received from Spiro & Co. would not in any way compensate him, or reward him for practically giving up his profession.[11]

Oleskiw's Role Diminishes as Immigration Increases

With the beginning of 1898, immigration from the two provinces revived again. On April 10, the ship *Bulgaria* brought 931 immigrants to our shores but other ships continued to arrive. By the end of 1898, statistics revealed that 6000 immigrants had reached Canada from western Ukraine in that year alone. So rapidly did the number of new arrivals increase that the 1901 census, taken about the middle of the year, indicated that there were already 28,407 immigrants in Canada from Austria-Hungary; ninety percent of these were probably Ukrainian, the remaining ten percent probably being Poles and Germans. Obviously, they all corresponded with relatives and friends, the majority eulogizing Canada and some even grossly exaggerating the blessings of life in Canada. These letters served as propaganda in favor of immigration to Canada as we have already learned from the correspondence of the interpreter accompanying the Austro-Hungarian consul.

In addition, the agents of the steamship companies, profiting from the information broadcast by Oleskiw and his organization, intensified their efforts. The consequence of all this effort was that immigration numbers increased and continued unabated until the First Great War. The following table, taken from government statistical records for the years beginning July 1, 1900 until June 30, 1907, shows clearly how immigration grew and the groups among which Ukrainians were to be found. From this table, it is impossible to calculate the number of Ukrainians who came to Canada during the years listed in this table. However, there is not the slightest doubt that Bukovynian Ukrainians are listed in the column headed "Roumanians". Under the heading "Austrians", Germans constituted the largest proportion in the first four years but, after 1905, Ukrainians would be in the majority because many began to identify themselves as Austrians rather than Galicians at that time. Unquestionably, there were also Ukrainians under the heading "Russians" in a large majority of cases. Ukrainians would also constitute close to ninety percent of the total number in the column under "Galicians", leaving ten percent to be divided among Germans and Poles. The same percentage would apply in the category of Bukovynians, with the remainder divided among Germans and Roumanians. Not until 1904-5 do Ukrainians begin to identify themselves by their territory or state of origin and give their ethnic origin as *Rusyny*, or "Ruthenians" in English. There

IMMIGRATION
(July 1, 1900 - June 30, 1907)

Year	Roumanians	Austrians	Russians	Galicians	Bukovynians	(Rusyny) Ruthenians
1900-1	152	228	1044	4702	128	—
1901-2	272	320	2467	6550	550	—
1902-3	437	781	5505	8382	1759	—
1903-4	619	516	1955	7729	1578	—
1904-5	270	837	1887	6926	1123	3
1905-6	396	1324	3152	5656	1355	266
1906-7	798	1426	4414	13376	1856	729
TOTAL	2944	5432	20424	53321	8349	998

were still no "Ukrainians". The late appearance of the latter name gave the Canadian population the impression that they were an additional ethnic group among the nationalities which originated in Austria.

Under whatever national or ethnic origin they came, they arrived in Canada by the thousands, and the greater the number of arrivals, the greater was the number who came to Canada independently of Oleskiw. It was not only the numbers that weakened the influence of Oleskiw. Having left Lviv in 1900 to become the director of a teachers' seminary in Sokal, he was too far removed from Lviv to continue his efforts for the cause of emigration. Sokal was only a small centre in comparison to Lviv, which was then the administrative and economic capital of Galicia.

In Sokal other misfortunes awaited him. Not only did his wife die soon after their arrival, but he also became ill before long and died on October 18, 1903, at the age of forty-three and in the prime of his physical and intellectual powers. His death meant a great loss, not only to the Ukrainian settlers in Canada but also to people in his native land. Ukrainians in Galicia manifested how highly they valued his services by providing for the internment of his body in the Lychakiv cemetery in Lviv rather than leaving him to be buried in Sokal. In the Lychakiv cemetery are buried the remains of many eminent sons and daughters of western Ukraine and it was fitting that he be numbered among them. On the other hand, they could have shown more insight into the nature of his services had they made some provision for research to explore Oleskiw's role in the emigration movement of Ukrainians to Canada on the basis of his own records and those of the state archives in Lviv and Vienna, where documents must have been available.

The Canadian Ukrainian community began to show some appreciation of his colossal service with the appearance of V. J. Kaye's *Early Ukrainian Settlements in Canada, 1895 - 1900,* which will now ensure that he will not be forgotten. Just as they have acknowledged Pylypiw and Eleniak's role in opening Canada's door to Ukrainian immigration, they now recognize Oleskiw's contribution in directing mass immigration to Canada. Not only did he direct settlers there, but he also sought to lessen their hardships once they had arrived. He continued to correspond with the Canadian government, offering advice on how immigrants from his homeland should be received and how they could be settled most quickly. Since he foresaw that the new arrivals would feel lost and neglected, he sought to provide them with available leadership sending with the settlers men like Genik, Bodrug, Negrych, and others who played a very important part during the insecure and experimental pioneer period.

Of particular interest, however, was the fact that Oleskiw also attempted to make some provision for the religious life of the Ukrainian settlers.

Having sent forth his first group of settlers, he immediately urged the Canadian government to make provision for a priest. When nothing came of these negotiations, Father Nestor Dmytriw arrived from the United States, almost certainly with the connivance of Oleskiw, who so arranged matters that Father Dmytriw was able to serve his people in the capacity of a priest at no cost to the pioneering settlers since he earned a salary as an official of the Department of Immigration in Winnipeg. With this convenient arrangement, Oleskiw, as a lay person, did more to fulfill the religious needs of these first Ukrainian settlers than their church authorities in Galicia. In evaluating Oleskiw's achievements, it would not surprise anyone if the Canadian Ukrainian community suddenly awoke to the necessity of giving some form to their belated appreciation of his services to his people by becoming concerned about the erection of a suitable monument in his memory not only in Canada but also on his grave in the Lychakiv cemetery in Lviv.

8

Administrative Divisions of the
N.W.T. and the Formation of
the Western Provinces

Administration of the North-West Territories

In order to understand better how Ukrainian immigrants were settled, we
must remember that all territory in western Canada, excluding the province
of Manitoba after 1870 and British Columbia after 1871, from the United
States border to the Arctic Ocean, was given the name of the North-West
Territories. In order to make provision for more efficient administration in
such a wide area, to allocate districts for settlement more precisely, and to
initiate a postal system in widely scattered settlements, the Canadian government created in 1882 four provisional districts in the southern part of the
territory.

West of Manitoba along the United States border was Assiniboia, approximately rectangular in shape, which extended west to just beyond
Medicine Hat in present day Alberta, and to a few miles south of Saskatoon
on its northern border. Bordering on the north was another rectangular-
shaped district which was given the name of Saskatchewan. Its western
border was a continuation of that of Assiniboia and its northern boundary
was the fifty-fifth parallel. To the west of Assiniboia and Saskatchewan, extending to the Rocky Mountains in the west and to the fifty-fifth parallel in
the north was the district of Alberta. All the territory between the fifty-fifth
and sixtieth parallels lay in the fourth district, which was named Athabasca.

In these districts, settlements began as early as 1882, chiefly with arrivals from Ontario. These consisted of larger or smaller groups of
courageous individuals who sought a happier destiny in the wide expanses
of this territory independently or through colonizing efforts under the

guidance of various English church organizations.

The Formation of the Provinces of Alberta and Saskatchewan

The North-West Territories became more densely settled with settlers from various European countries, including many Ukrainians, toward the end of the nineteenth and the beginning of the twentieth centuries. As a result, the Dominion Government created in 1905 two new provinces, Alberta and Saskatchewan, from the four former districts. Assiniboia, Saskatchewan, and the eastern part of Athabasca became the province of Saskatchewan, which now extended to the sixtieth parallel. The eastern boundary of Alberta became the one hundred and tenth meridian, which meant that portions of the former districts of Assiniboia and Saskatchewan became part of the province of Alberta, the boundary line having been moved twenty-five miles east of Medicine Hat. The western part of Athabasca also became part of Alberta, bringing its northern boundary to the sixtieth parallel.

This formation of the two provinces left Manitoba with a small area in the shape of a postage stamp on the map of Canada. It was not until 1912 that its northern boundary also became the sixtieth parallel. In the east, additional territory was added by establishing a boundary which ran from the north-east corner of its former territory in a north-easterly direction to Hudson's Bay.

The Survey of Lands in the North-West Territories

Land in the North-West Territories, later the western provinces of Canada, was divided into squares six miles to a side from south to north and from east to west. Such a square was called a township and each township had its respective cardinal number—1, 2, 3, and so on, the number changing every six miles. Numbering began at the American border and continued north.

In referring to these townships as they ran from east to west, the name range was given. Probably to avoid large numbers in numbering ranges from the Ontario border to that of British Columbia, and also because of geographic reasons (which will be explained later), the survey began with an arbitrary line on the 97.5° meridian west longitude, which became the principal or first meridian. It runs from south to north about twelve miles west of Winnipeg. For the second meridian 102° west longitude was chosen (already in eastern Saskatchewan). The remaining meridians—the third, fourth, fifth, and sixth—each came four degrees west of the previous one.

Thus townships are numbered in order from the American border to the north, but ranges are counted from one of the arbitrary meridians to the

east and are shown as the range west of a certain meridian. Only in
Manitoba, in that territory east of the principal meridian up to the Ontario
border, are the ranges indicated by a number east of the meridian.

Every township is divided into squares, a mile to each side, and is
thirty-six square miles in area. Each of the squares in a township is called a
section and the sections are also numbered in order from one to thirty-six.
They are numbered beginning with the south-east corner of the township
and moving west. Therefore, the first row of sections has the following
numbers: 6, 5, 4, 3, 2, 1. In the next row, the numbers go in order from west
to east: 7, 8, 9, 10, 11, 12. In the third row the numbers again run from east
to west, and again in the opposite direction in the fourth row. This continues until the number 36 is reached in the north-east end of the township.

Every section is divided into four quarters but these are not numbered.
They are identified according to their position—south-east, south-west,
north-east, and north-west. Considering that each section has 640 acres,
there are 160 acres in each quarter, approximately 113 morgs in Galicia.[1]
Land in Manitoba was surveyed on the same plan as in the North-West Territories. When Oleskiw wrote about *"Vilni Zemli"* (Free Lands), which the
Canadian Government also advertised widely in Europe, it was in reference
to these quarter sections. After paying ten dollars for a filing fee, a prospective settler was free to choose any quarter which was open for settlement.
However, to become a full owner of such a quarter section on his homestead, he had a number of duties to perform: he had to break twenty-five
acres; he had to build some sort of living accommodation; he had to provide
proof that he had resided on the homestead for three years; and he had to
become a Canadian citizen.

In discussing these "Free Lands" one should remember that only even-
numbered sections were designated for homesteading: 2, 4, 6, 8 and so on.
From these sections, 8 and 26 were alloted to the Hudson's Bay Company.
Nearly all odd-numbered sections were the property of either the Canadian
Pacific Railway or the government, except that sections 11 and 29 were set
aside as school lands. In every township opened for settlement, only sixteen
sections or sixty-four quarters were alloted for settlers.

These early government regulations were never understood or appreciated by the pioneer settlers. They were especially disliked by Ukrainians who would rather have had every section free so that their relatives and
friends could become close neighbours. However, after a few years it
became evident that this policy was sensible and showed foresight, since a
quarter-section of land became too small an economic unit. After they had
established themselves, many began to extend their farming operations by
buying lands from the Hudson's Bay Company, from the Canadian Pacific
Railway Company, and from the government.

9

The First Ukrainian Colony — Pheasant Forks

Location and Origin

Hitherto, so much has been written about the settlement of Ukrainians at Edna in Alberta that it could lead to the mistaken notion that Edna was the first colony. Such a conclusion, however, would be false. Chronologically, first place belongs to Pheasant Forks, north-west of Grenfell, at one time in the district of Assiniboia but now in south-eastern Saskatchewan. In its beginning the settlement was also known as Grenfell because settlers, arriving from the east, had to travel to Grenfell, a village on the main line of the C.P.R., and then by wagon to reach their destination.

At the north end of this colony, along a stream known as Pheasant Creek,[1] there was a building in which there was both a store and the post office. The stream originated close to this building from the union of two separate branches or forks flowing from the north. It was on this account that both the settlement and the post office were given the name of Pheasant Forks.[2]

The colony was established in 1882 by a Toronto company sponsored by the Methodist Church which purchased approximately ninety sections of land in townships 19, 20, and 21, and ranges 8, 9, and 10, with the understanding that a railway would be built through the colony within eighteen months.[3]

The area, especially that part within the Pheasant Creek valley, was indeed charming. One of the first settlers describes it as follows:

> I call this God's own land. What more could one wish: rich soil, first class water, splendid climate and cool nights, and God's presence and blessing[4]...

Although the colony of Pheasant Forks, and especially the valley along its stream, was beautiful, the colonization company was not successful in obtaining enough settlers to dispose of all of its land. On the other hand, the government, when disposing of any land to colonization companies, organizations, or individuals, always retained a clause in the agreement stipulating that if land was not settled by a specified time, unsettled areas could be advertised for settlement by other individuals. In this way all unoccupied lands of this area were made available to other prospective settlers.

In addition to lands that had not been settled, many occupied homesteads had been abandoned because of a period of drought which visited western Canada in 1882 and continued for a number of years. Many of the settlements totally disappeared. Some of the settlers returned to Ontario, while others moved into districts where green grass and leaves were still to be seen during the summer. In abandoning the settlements which they had once named God's paradise, they now maintained:

> ... this country ain't no place for a white man ... when y' ain't freezin' ye're burnin' up, and that's what happens in hell. God al'mighty ain't nowheres near here! He didn't come this fur West—stopped down to Rat Portage![5]

Accordingly, just east of this Methodist colony there were wide expanses of uninhabited territory, to which German settlers from Galicia came in 1887 to occupy townships 19, 20, 21, in ranges 7, 8, and 9, naming their settlements Jozefsberg and Neudorf (New Village).[6] In time, climatic conditions underwent a change and this German colony grew in size and extent as new transports of Germans from Galicia arrived to join earlier arrivals. With these later arrivals came two Ukrainian families who became the nucleus of a Ukrainian colony in the area known already as Grenfell or Pheasant Forks.

First Evidence of a Ukrainian Settlement at Pheasant Forks

The first written evidence of the existence of this colony is to be found in Oleskiw's brochure, *O emigratsii* (About emigration)[7] which as we have already learned, appeared in 1895. It is also mentioned in Father Dmytriw's account, *Kanadiiska Rus* (Canadian Rus), published in 1897,[8] and in an anonymous contribution to *Svoboda* (unquestionably by Kyrylo Genik), which describes the first visit of Father Dmytriw to Crooked Lakes in the south-eastern part of Canora district in Saskatchewan. He related further that there was a still older colony in that province, known as Pleasant Forks (probably a printing error), but that it had only a few families.[9] Of the above three sources, however, most information on this colony is to be found in Oleskiw's brochure. Though Oleskiw did not visit the colony personally, it was visited by his travelling companion Dorundiak. In his brochure Oleskiw merely quotes parts of extensive notes which Dorundiak had kept of his visit to the colony and the Ukrainian families who lived there. With some surprise, he noted that wheat yielded well though the soil appeared sandy. He mentioned by name the two settlements of Germans from Galicia, Jozefsberg and Neudorf, and provided an extensive list of their names and origin as follows: Lemberger from near Sambir; Yakob Otto from Stryi; and also Yakob Ulmer, Mattias Hak, Ludwig Wendel, Litsenberger, David Heimer and many others from Hassendorf, Neudorf near Drohobych, Semigeniw, and from Dulib near Stryi. He ends this list by adding, "Beyond the Germans lies the Rus (Ukrainian) colony".

In the latter colony Dorundiak lists Ilia Pylypiw and his two sons: crippled Tymko, who had been a wheelwright in his native land, and Fedir. Both sons had their own homesteads but Fedir was away working for an English settler at five dollars a month. He also reports that Pylypiw had a daughter who was away from home, working for four dollars a month. Dorundiak relates that the whole family arrived in Canada in the company of German settlers in 1893. He also lists another family, that of Pavlo Shymko, a town dweller from Kalush, with whom had also arrived his wife and two brothers, Andrun and Mikhas (Michael).[10] He reported that this family had arrived with German settlers in 1891 but the date is probably an error. Dorundiak devotes particular attention to Mikhas, whom he regards as a "literate town-dweller, naturally inquisitive and adaptable", who was then working for an "Englishman" and earning thirty dollars per month. Continuing his story, he relates that Mikhas had married the daughter of a wealthy German settler by the name of Liniczek, who had arrived in Canada from the town of Zhovkva in Galicia, and that he would soon quit working for others as he had bought a large area under cultivation on his own land and was comparatively prosperous.[11]

Dorundiak really revealed a good deal of information about this Ukrainian colony and probably provided more in his notes which Oleskiw failed to include in his brochure. What Oleskiw did include does not give us a clear picture of the colony. He should have recorded the villages of origin for both the Pylypiw and the Shymko families, as well as the exact date and port of arrival. Furthermore, it would have been of value to know whether Ilia Pylypiw's sons were married and had families, as well as the first name of Ilia Shymko's daughter, about whom we learned that she was earning four dollars a month. It would also have been worthwhile to know something of Paul Shymko's family, especially about his wife's brothers. Were they children or adults? These questions remained a puzzle and without answers to them, it was impossible to determine the composition and extent of this Ukrainian settlement.

Kaye Solves the Riddle

The riddle was once more solved by Kaye seventy years later in an article published in *Ukrainian News*.[12] On the basis of immigration and naturalization records, he confirmed that Ilia Pylypiw's family arrived in Quebec on June 18, 1893, on the ship *Pickhuben,* but the family was recorded as Filipow. It was listed as follows: Ilia, sixty years of age; Fedir, thirty-three; Fedir's wife, twenty-six. Fedir's children were Mary (8), Nastia (3), and Vasylko (diminutive of Vasyl), who was not yet a year old. Ilia Pylypiw's daughter, whom Dorundiak mentions without naming her, was Anne, eighteen years of age at the time of arrival. "Crippled Tymko", Ilia's second son, was thirty-one years of age and married, his wife being Varvara (Barbara), thirty-two years of age. Their infant daughter, Kateryna, was only nine months old. Kaye further reports as follows:

> In the citizenship registration records I discovered the name of Tymko Pylypiw who had settled on a farm in Pheasant Forks district in Assiniboia. He obtained his citizenship on June 19, 1896. In the documents which I examined, I did not discover any reference to any place of origin for the Pylypiw family. It can be assumed that they came from the county or district of Kalush from which also came the German families in the district and from whom the Nebyliv villagers had also learned about Canada.[13]

Kaye believed that Dorundiak had made an error in regard to the name of Shymko as no such name could be found in the records.[14] However, he discovered that a Pavlo Seynkiw (Senkiv?) had arrived in Canada with his wife Rozalia and two children, a four-year old son, Oleksa, and a three-year old daughter, Anastasia. There were also Rozalia's two brothers, Andrun and Mikhas, whose family name appeared in the ship's records as Umoroslavich. Their ages were listed as follows: Pavlo, forty-one; Rozalia, thirty-three; Andrun, thirty-seven; Mikhas, twenty-six. They arrived in Halifax on the S.S. *Mongolian* on April 16, 1892, and not in 1891 as related by Dorundiak. In the naturalization records Kaye discovered that Pavlo Shymko's wife, in applying for her Canadian citizenship, gave her name as Rozalia Seynkiw, a farmer from Tiree, Assiniboia, and listed her birthplace as Kalush. In the same naturalization records for 1896, he discovered two other "Austrians": Andrun Huminolovych from the district of Hyde in the Qu'Appelle Valley, south-east of Neudorf, and also Mykhailo Huminolovych from the district of Tiree, where Pavlo's wife was farming.[15] From all the above information we can conclude that there were seventeen people, ten adults and seven children, in Pheasant Forks after the arrival of Pylypiw which was a very promising beginning for a colony.

There were two reasons why this colony was never recognized as the first Ukrainian settlement in Canada. In the first place, neither Senkiv, Pylypiw, and especially Mikhas Huminolovych, whom Dorundiak treats with special respect, publicized themselves or their colony enough to attract any additional Ukrainian settlers to their area. Dorundiak reproached them during his visit for not informing others about themselves but "having hidden themselves like rats in their holes". However, their answers indicated that this was not the case. Although they had written home to report their success, "their relatives do not want to believe them and ridicule them because they had been landowners in Kalush and had left for Canada where they worked for others more than on their own land".[16] Furthermore, German settlers had populated the area so thickly that there was no longer any land left nearby which was suitable for settlement. If productive land was available, it was either unknown to them or was too far removed from the nearest railroad station at Grenfell.

Pheasant Forks Colony Plays a Role in Further Settlement

Although suitable land was no longer available among the German settlers in Pheasant Forks, Ukrainian immigrants continued to arrive in the colony. Some came by railroad to Grenfell, others by horse and wagon from Brandon, and the rest through Yorkton, to which a railroad had been built in 1890. In the beginning most of the new arrivals were from the village of Ulychne, county of Drohobych, which indicates that Dorundiak's reproach about hiding like rats in their holes had brought results. As early as 1895, there arrived in Pheasant Forks, the Kulchytsky family, gentry from Ulychne. In this family there were four brothers: Mykhailo, Tanasko, Ivan, and Hnat. After lodging with Fedir Pylypiw for some time, they were directed northward to settle in the present district of Fenwood.[17] Others followed the Kulchytskys and Pheasant Forks thus began to extend northward. The majority of the new arrivals continued to be from Ulychne.

As can be expected, the Huminoloviches also corresponded with their fellow villagers to encourage them to emigrate. In 1896 Leon Boikovych and his family arrived in this way. For almost a year he lodged with the Panischak and Khlopan families in Winnipeg while he investigated the possibilities of settlement in the Dauphin district. Since he found it impossible to look for land in that area because of heavy flooding, he settled among the German settlers in the Neudorf-Pheasant Forks area on SE 32-19-8 W2.[18]

Though Fenwood-Goodeve was first settled by Ulychne villagers, fellow-countrymen of Pylypiw, whose numbers grew to about three hundred families, this does not mean that other immigrants from Bukovyna and Galicia did not settle there. When immigration to Canada became a mass movement after 1896, and thousands of Ukrainian immigrants reached Winnipeg, immigration officials had to allocate new arrivals wherever possible to leave room in Winnipeg for new arrivals of Ukrainians. In addition to Ukrainians, there were also large numbers of German, Icelandic, Swedish, and Norwegian newcomers. As a result of this flood of new arrivals, no settlement in those days could be limited to a selected group of villagers. Accordingly, immigrants from many counties in Bukovyna and Galicia came to Goodeve-Fenwood. A number of families from the village of Peremyliv, county of Husiatyn in eastern Galicia, arrived in Pheasant Forks through Grenfell in 1902. These included Fedir Dumka, Yosef Chykrun, Stepan Pyliuk, and Yasko Muzyka. Having arrived in Grenfell, these families were transported by Pylypiw to Pheasant Forks where they were quartered for a time at his home before they left to file on homesteads near Goodeve.[19] A few families from the village of Uvysla in the same county arrived in the same year. The best known of these are Prokip Burak and Panko Davydiuk. Davydiuk's family, including his son Mykhailo, arrived a year later in the company of Yakim Burak from the neighbouring village of Celijiw (Tseliiv), county of Husiatyn.[20]

Lemberg Becomes the New Centre for the Pheasant Forks Colony

In 1903 the Canadian Pacific Railway extended a line through the German colony of Jozefsberg and Neudorf. Unfortunately, it was not directed through Pheasant Forks, as many settlers had fondly hoped, but approximately five miles south where the station of Lemberg was established. Another station east of Lemberg was given the name of Neudorf.[21] Pheasant Forks thus lost all hopes of becoming a railway town and the street plan which the optimistic settlers had prepared was forgotten.[22] Though Ukrainians continued to patronize Pheasant Forks for a time since it was much closer, Lemberg became their railway centre. As Lemberg's importance as an economic centre for the area continued to increase, Pheasant Forks fell into a decline and eventually ceased to exist even as a post office. It became only a historical memory.

As Lemberg was much nearer both to Fenwood and Goodeve than was Grenfell, immigrants who wished to settle in those areas now travelled to Lemberg by train. In this way arrived Ivan Chernecki (Chernetsky), a member of the gentry of the village of Ulychne, with his three sons, Volodymyr, Sabin, and Ludvig, to settle a few miles south of Goodeve in 1903.[23] The two Korchynsky brothers, Evstakhii (Eustace) and Julian, also members of the gentry in the village of Ulychne, arrived in the same year and settled in 1904 in the area where Hubbard was later established, thus laying the foundation of another Ukrainian settlement. They had obtained information about the area from other Ulychne settlers who were already established in neighbouring Fenwood. They spent the summer working for the Canadian Pacific Railway. During the winter Evstakhii remained in Neudorf but Julian returned to his native village, married, and returned to Canada in 1904, not only with his wife but also with his other brothers. They travelled to Yorkton to file on homesteads at Hubbard which later became a railway station. In Neudorf they bought two teams of horses for $350 at a time when most settlers had to be satisfied with oxen. In addition to these two settlers, the following are listed as pioneers of this district: F. Parakhoniak, Hr. Kulykevich, St. Jurysty (Yurysty), Tymko and Ivan Lozynsky, W. Boyko, F. Mandziak, Ivan Simenowski, P. Shoma, Ivan Korinets, Stepan Pavliv, and Ivan Klepak.[24]

According to Yurko (George) Pylypiw, his father was instrumental in directing prospective settlers from Galicia, both Ukrainians and Poles, to Fenwood, Goodeve, and Hubbard. Before coming to Canada, Fedir had been an assistant to German surveyors in the city of Lviv, the capital of the province of Galicia. As he knew German and associated with Germans, *he first learned about Canada from them* and persuaded his father Ilia and the rest of the family to emigrate to Canada. Although he had to work for English-speaking settlers initially at five dollars a month, as noted by Dorundiak, his surveying experience aided him in grasping the essentials of Canadian land surveys very quickly. Obviously this knowledge proved to be of great help to other immigrants but it resulted in a good deal of inconvenience to himself. To obtain a homestead, an immigrant first had to choose his land and then to travel to Yorkton to fill out his application. Fedir played a large role in this process as immigrants asked for help not only in searching for suitable homesteads but also in filling out application forms in Yorkton.[25] At the same time many of the immigrants were encamped in his home while they located homesteads. And the number of these prospective settlers was not small according to a well-known authority on settlement in the North-West Territories. After the railroad through Lemberg was built, Ukrainian settlers poured in so rapidly that they constituted a majority of the population in four townships.[26] Some of the families which came to Fenwood in those years are those of Hnat and Nykola Kozakevych, Buhay, Ogrizlo, Rygus, Korpach, Hawryliw, Pawlyshyn, Kushnir, Kostoriwsky, Kindrakevych, Stelmakhovych, and Halyk. In 1905 a new group of settlers from the county of Javoriw (Yavoriv) in Galicia settled in the district of present day Jasmin.

With the influx of Ukrainian immigrants the new colony grew rapidly and community life quickened to such an extent that the Pylypiws and Andrun Huminolovych also abandoned Pheasant Forks in 1906 to move into Goodeve. In the same year (1906) a large group from the village of Jamnyca

(Yamnytsia) in the county of Stanislaviv (now Ivano-Frankivsk) settled around Bedfordville, north of present day Ituna. Though this district was officially known as Bedfordville, Ukrainian settlers called it Stanislawtsi from the beginning. Among its settlers were Maxim Kozun and his sons, Kost Spilchak and his sons, Ivan Obuch (Obukh), Stepan Smycniuk (Smytsniuk), Oleksa Derkach, and Pylyp Zubiak.

The Ukrainian Colony of Pheasant Forks Is Transplanted and Thrives Along the Railway

The early years of settlement in present day Fenwood-Goodeve-Hubbard were very arduous because of the distance from the nearest railroad. But these hardships were the common lot of both Ukrainian and non-Ukrainian settlers in pioneer times and circumstances changed with the passage of time. During 1907-8 the Grand Trunk Pacific Railway completed its main line through Melville, Watrous, Saskatoon, and Edmonton to Vancouver. With its completion additional settlers, both Ukrainian and non-Ukrainian, poured into the colony to extend the settled area to the north until it joined the Ukrainian settlement around Insinger and Sheho, which had originated in 1897.

Thus the original colony of Pheasant Forks began to extend to the north and north-west and, with the coming of the Grand Trunk Pacific Railway, became the location of the stations and villages of Birmingham, Fenwood, Goodeve, Hubbard, Ituna, Jasmin, and Kelliher. In addition to these village stations there were also the post offices and districts of Plain View, Homefield, Beckenham, and Bedfordville. Pheasant Forks—the original name of the English, German, and Ukrainian settlement—was forgotten. Only Pheasant Creek remains.

10

The Colonies of Edna and Rabbit Hills

Origins of the Edna Colony

We have already noted that Mykola Tychkowsky and Antin Paish were the first Ukrainian settlers and that they filed on homesteads among German settlers from Galicia near Josephburg in 1892. In the next year, they were followed by Ivan Pylypiw and Stefan Chichak, who also filed on homesteads near them. However, in 1894 there arrived a larger group, consisting of Mykhailo Pullishy, Vasyl Feniak, and Fedir Melnyk, to be followed later by Mykola, Mykhailo, and Petro Melnyk, all of whom settled along Beaverhill Creek about twelve miles east of the original settlement. To the early Ukrainian settlers the stream was known as Beaver Creek and its valley was Beaver Valley. Before the end of the year the group was joined by Ivan Pylypiw, Stefan Chichak, and Mykola Tychkowsky. All of them moved to be nearer their countrymen but Mykola Tychkowsky had a special reason in that Petro Melnyk was his son-in-law. Additional families arrived during 1894 and the beginning of 1895 because Oleskiw, on his visit in 1895, listed twelve families in the settlement, a larger number than Dorundiak had found in Pheasant Forks.[1]

When Ukrainians first settled at Beaver Creek, there were already other groups near Edmonton. Close to Edmonton, to the north and north-west, settled the French from Quebec who named their colony St. Albert. To the west and north-east came Germans from Galicia in 1891 and Volhyn in 1894, the first group settling at Josephburg and the latter one at Bruderheim. Most of the first group had moved here from their original colony around Medicine Hat. Prior to the arrival of both Germans and Ukrainians, there had also been some English-speaking settlers, mostly retired members of the Royal Canadian Mounted Police and discharged soldiers from the Riel rebellion. Journeying through Alberta, they discovered large expanses of fertile land and chose to remain there. However, most of these were individual settlers. It was not until 1891, in the same year that Pylypiw and Eleniak first came to Alberta, that a delegation arrived from Parry Sound in Ontario to inspect land around Edmonton. As a result of their favorable report, eighty families arrived in the spring of 1892 to settle south and south-east of the German colonies.

Over and above the relatively sparse French, German, and English-speaking settlements close to Edmonton, there lay large tracts of productive land on which thousands could still settle. In this productive area also lay the Beaverhill Creek district where the first Nebyliv villagers arrived between 1894 and 1895.

Fortunately, there were already partially travelled roads in the area, in particular a trail along which Hudson's Bay Company servants had formerly travelled between Winnipeg and Edmonton. This trail ran in an easterly direction south of the North Saskatchewan River, crossed Beaverhill Creek near the present day village of Star and, after skirting the northern shore of Whitford Lake, continued south-east through present day Lloydminster across Saskatchewan to Winnipeg. A few miles north-east of Wostok another trail branched off from the main trail to Winnipeg, toward the North Saskatchewan River to the settlement once known as Victoria but which is now called Pakan. On the north bank of the river a Methodist mission was established which was known as the Victoria Mission, and the trail to the settlement became known as the South Victoria Trail. Where the trail crossed Beaverhill Creek, travellers had built a number of crude shelters which served as a protection against the elements, and the location became a favorite stopping place. After the area became populated by the Nebyliv settlers, a Norwegian named Knowlton built a store in 1894 which soon included a post office named after his daughter Edna.

Edna store and post office became the nucleus of the most extensive Ukrainian colony in Canada. It became a centre not only for those who had settled there but also for those who, in the next ten years, were to populate the surrounding area and extend the colony in all directions.

?apid Expansion of the Edna Colony

In the spring of 1896 there arrived a large transport of settlers which ad been organized by Dr. Osyp Oleskiw and sent to Canada under the irection of his brother Volodymyr, as mentioned earlier in this history. It is ubtful whether there is anywhere a complete and accurate list of the immigrants in this group but, according to Kaye's research, it included eighteen families and nine single men. In addition to the listed names of Antin Savka, Luts Keryk, Ivan Halkiv, Ivan Lakusta (son of Andrew), Teodor Rudyk, and Ivan Danchuk, there were certainly others whose names appear in correspondence to *Svoboda* and in many later memoirs. Among the members of this group we encounter the name of Kost Nemirsky, a Ukrainian from the county of Borshchiv who could speak German. He had his own store in his native village and became a leading farmer in the Wostok area. Not long after their arrival, his brother Teodor (Theodore) was engaged to assist in the allocation of settlers. Toward the end of 1897 immigration officials noted that he had already assisted in settling 281 families in the Edna district. In 1899 Teodor was able to establish a post office near Edna to which he gave the name Wostok (east in Old Slavonic) and, in all probability, became the first postmaster of Ukrainian background in Canada. It should also be noted that Teodor Nemirsky left an extensive account of the lives of his countrymen in his district, and his memoirs became a primary source of information for J. G. McGregor's *Vilni Zemli*.[2] Teodor Fuhr, born in the village of Vysotske, county of Yaroslav, achieved a place in Ukrainian-Canadian history by not settling with the others in Edna. Instead of filing on a homestead there immediately on arrival, he purchased a partly cultivated quarter section from a German settler south of Edmonton in an area which was then known as Rabbit Hills, but soon became known as the Leduc-Calmar-Thorsby area. A large majority of immigrants from the county of Yaroslav followed him to settle in the same area.

Following in the footsteps of Oleskiw's group other immigrants arrived at the end of 1896 and the beginning of 1897. When Edna was visited by the first Ukrainian Catholic priest in Canada in 1897, Father Dmytriw, there were already seventy-five families in the area. In describing the district he wrote as follows:

> This Ukrainian colony is the farthest north of any Ukrainian colony in the world. Our people of whom there were seventy-five families at the time of my visit, are distributed through the following townships: 55-18, 56-18, 56-19, 56-20, 57-19, 57-20. From east to west the settlement stretches for twelve miles which is the distance from Kost Nemirsky's to Ivan Dombrowsky's. Dombrowsky arrived in Canada from the village of Krasne in the county of Zolochiv.
>
> I will classify these settlers into four groups basing this classification on the time of arrival. The first farmers were from the village of Nebyliv, county of Stryi? One of these, Mykola Tychkowsky, has already been farming for five years while the other nine began farming three years ago, but nearly all of them are from the same village.
>
> 2) The middle group consists of Ivan Dombrowsky from the village of

Krasne; Ilko Senetovych and his son-in-law Tymiak, both from Hlyniany; also Fedko and Petro Kinash from Poliukhiv.

3) A transport of about twenty families, mostly from the county of Borshchiv, arrived under the leadership of Volodymyr Oleskiw.

4) The most recent arrivals are those who arrived during the preceding winter or in the last month.[4]

Dmytriw related further that he continued his journey to the Rabbit Hills colony where he "expected to find eleven families from the county of Yaroslav, largely from the villages of Vysotske, Vetlyn, and Lahzy," who settled among Russian Germans "buying already developed farms equipped with buildings and other necessary farm equipment." However, he did not list their names and limited himself only to describing Teodor Fuhr's possessions and his prospects for the future.

In concluding his account, Father Dmytriw stated that when he reached Winnipeg he learned of the arrival of four hundred new families from Galicia and Bukovyna with a total population of 1081 persons. Sixty of these families continued their journey to the Edna district. As many more immigrants continued to choose Edna as their destination during the summer and autumn of 1897, this colony rapidly outstripped Pheasant Forks in population.

Difficulties of the Immigrants Who did not Have Oleskiw's Guidance

The families which arrived in Edna following Father Dmytriw's visit had not been organized by Oleskiw despite his warning that prospective settlers should not set out Canada without financial means. These immigrants had been assembled by steamship agents whose main purpose was to obtain as many passengers as possible to fill their vessels. As we have already noted, some of these agents had even assured prospective settlers that the Austrian emperor, and particularly the empress, would aid them in obtaining all supplies and equipment to begin farming in Canada. Most of these settlers belonged to the more impoverished strata of village society and did not have the financial means to protect themselves in a new land. Others who did have money at the beginning reached their destinations penniless because they had been swindled of the small sums they possessed or had spent their money while they were being held in quarantine either in Halifax or Winnipeg.

They billeted themselves wherever they could, built houses or, rather, dugouts and huts, and thus prepared to spend the winter. Some purchased a horse and a cow, others only a cow, but the majority were unable to purchase anything. Fathers were forced to leave their families to obtain work, as no money was available. Food was in short supply or totally lacking since those who came late in the year were unable to cultivate any land and had no money to buy food. Five of the immigrants had even lost their baggage en route with all their clothes and were totally unprepared for the severe Canadian winter.

As early as August 1897 the Royal Canadian Mounted Police (RCMP)*, who were responsible for law and order in the North-West Territories, called attention to the poverty of the settlers. After investigating their living conditions, a report was forwarded to the Regina headquarters advising that thirty-five families would require aid in order to survive the winter. According to this report, only one family had two ponies (not horses), two families possessed two cows each, six families had one horse each, seven families possessed one cow per family, while others even lacked a shelter to pass the winter. Only four families were without children. Five families had one child each, four had two, while others had three, four, or five children. One family which possessed two cows and "nothing else" had six children.[5]

The condition of these settlers was certainly very critical and it appeared as if they would have to face the extreme Canadian winter unprepared. The five families whose baggage had been lost did not even have suitable winter clothing.

The commanding officer in Regina forwarded this report to headquarters in Ottawa whence it was transmitted to the Minister of the Interior with the query whether the Minister deemed it advisable to grant any aid, under police supervision, for the winter.

The police report in regard to the condition of the Ukrainian immigrants was not received very favorably by the immigration authorities. Tactfully but firmly, they expressed dissatisfaction with police interference in immigration matters. Moreover, they promptly launched their own investigation to prove that the condition of the settlers was not as drastic as reported by the police. Investigations continued with the police attempting to obtain more accurate evidence of the conditions they had reported previously and the immigration authorities seeking to prove that the police report was unduly alarming or totally incorrect. It was argued that living standards of settlers from Galicia and Bukovyna could not be measured in Canadian terms, and that newcomers were perfectly capable of overcoming early hardships and would demonstrate their suitability as settlers in due time.

These inquiries and counter-inquiries extended over many months, but

---

* Known as the North-West Mounted Police at the time of their formation in 1873 until 1904, when the prefix "Royal" was added to their name. In 1919 they assumed the name by which they are currently known—the Royal Canadian Mounted Police. (Ed.)

the immigrants finally profited since they obtained sufficient aid to survive the winter. Another benefit arising out of these investigations was the fact that the names of settlers were recorded, a boon for future historians, since we can tell *who was already in the district in 1897.*[6]

The Poverty of the Settlers and Their Distance from the Railway do not Inhibit the Growth of the Colony

Though the controversy and the resulting investigation into conditions in the settlement continued, this in no way hindered new immigrant groups from arriving in the colony. In the fall of 1898 the Director of Immigration, C. W. Speers, reported that there were already 360 families in Edna colony, 281 of which had been settled by Nemirsky alone. In August 1903, five years later, Kyrylo Genik, now an immigration official, also toured the Edna and Rabbit Hills districts for three weeks and reported to his directors that there were 2500 families in the colonies with a population of 16,000 spread over fifty townships. He advised that there were no more homesteads available for settlement among the Ukrainians in the fifty townships. All who desired land would have to travel much further east where there was still much unoccupied arable land. However, if they did not wish to travel too far from the periphery of the settlement to obtain homesteads, they should be prepared to buy land from the Canadian Pacific Railway which was selling land at $3.60 per acre or $560 per quarter (160 acres). He revealed that five post offices were already established: Star (formerly Edna), Wostok, Whitford, Vegreville, and Beaver Lake. Settlers in the Rabbit Hills district obtained their mail either from Edmonton or Leduc. In concluding his report, he wrote, "I also visited Edmonton and found here about 100 families, who have bought property and settled in the town, and have made good progress."[7]

We are filled with wonder at the calibre and courage of these settlers. It certainly required confidence in their future success to settle fifty townships (1800 square miles), fifty to seventy miles from the closest railway station at Strathcona. The hardships faced by these pioneers were enormous. Even after they had cultivated a few acres with great hardship and harvested some wheat, there was still the additional task of hauling the grain over great distances by wagon before they could sell it.

Fortunately, they survived until conditions improved. In 1906 the Canadian Northern Railway was completed from Winnipeg to Edmonton. On this railway the following stations accommodated Ukrainians living in the district: Vermilion, Mannville, Innisfree, Ranfurly, Lavoy, Vegreville, Royal Park, Mundare, Hilliard, Chipman, Bruderheim, and Lamont. The next two railways were built north of the North Saskatchewan River. The first was the McArthur Railway, later changed to the Northern Alberta Railway, which was started in 1913. Along this railway the following stations were established: Fedora, Opal, Egremont, Thorhild, Newbrook, Boyle, and Lac La Biche. The areas surrounding these stations were also thickly settled by immigrants from Bukovyna and Galicia. The Canadian Northern Railway followed in 1918 and 1919 with another railway which skirted the northern bank of the North Saskatchewan River. Along this railway the more important stations were Bon Accord, Redwater, Radway, Warspite, Smoky Lake, Bellis, Vilna, Spedden, and St. Paul.

In 1928, comparatively late in railroad building history in the West, the Canadian Pacific Railway finally built a branch through the heart of the earliest Ukrainian settlement to establish stations at Star, Wostok, Andrew, Whitford, Willingdon, Hairy Hill, Kaleland, Two Hills, Musidora, Slawa, Myrnam, Derwent, and Rusylvia, the last station being about thirty miles from the Saskatchewan border.

Long before railways were built, there were already post offices, schools, and churches serving as centres for the settlers' activities. Such centres were Wostok, Skaro, Zawale, Sniatyn, Hunka, Kahwin, Sunland, Shandro, Shalka, Beaver Lake, Ispas, Shypyntsi, New Kiev, Duvernay, Slawa, Luzan, Ukraina, Peno, Delph, Boian, and others. In a few cases Ukrainian names were given to railway stations, such as Wostok and Slawa, but usually such names were found only in farming community centres off the main railroad lines.

The scope of this work does not permit a detailed treatment of the progress and development of any Ukrainian colony in Canada. Its aim is to reveal only how quickly the free lands of western Canada were being settled by European immigrants and, in this chapter, how quickly and in what numbers Ukrainians colonized the Edna area. During the next fifteen years, Ukrainian settlers extended the settled area to the east of the Edna colony until it approached the Saskatchewan border. In breadth it stretched from around Vegreville and Vermilion in the south to districts near Lac La Biche in the north. This includes an area which extends approximately one hundred miles from west to east and eighty miles from south to north. As such, it is the largest bloc settlement area of Ukrainians in Canada.

The extent of this colony and its progress in a comparatively short period under distressing pioneer conditions can best be illustrated and understood from the number of schools which were established. In building these schools the settlers attempted, wherever possible, to give them names from their homeland. However, the actual spelling adopted in the official form of the name was sometimes difficult to trace to its original form as the spelling was influenced by the way it was written by Austrian officialdom, its Old Slavonic variation, or the inability of Canadians or even the immigrants themselves to write the names as pronounced.

As the colony grew, extending continually to the east, north, and south, and with the establishment of postal, school, church, and especially railroad centres, the first name of Edna gradually fell into disuse and was forgotten just as Pheasant Forks, the earliest centre in Saskatchewan, had been forgotten.

Although the Edna district became the largest area populated by Ukrainians in Canada, it would be an error to conclude that all of this territory was inhabited by Ukrainians. In this area, as well as in other Ukrainian colonies about which more will be written later, there were people of many ethnic origins. The names of many of the towns, post offices and schools indicate that there were other nationalities which gave their names to many of these institutions. To one centre, Poles gave the name of Krakow while Duvernay and Lamont definitely came from the French. Governmental agencies were especially cautious about creating exclusively Ukrainian settlements. As a result, the territory is considered to be Ukrainian only because Ukrainians constitute this majority of the population. In some districts the majority could reach ninety percent but in others it might be less than fifty percent. But these districts with a smaller proportion of the population sometimes bordered on another with a larger proportion, and thus constituted a unit. In such cases, districts with a smaller percentage of Ukrainian settlers are often regarded as Ukrainian districts.

Some Reminiscences from the Edna Colony

In these times we have no difficulty in visualizing the magnitude of this Ukrainian settlement, as it is quite simple to locate the settlements on a map, especially if they are connected by railroads. For a more complete knowledge, we can tour the whole area by automobile on good gravel and even asphalt roads. But the earliest settlers possessed none of these conveniences. Until 1906, Edmonton, or rather Strathcona, was the closest railway station for the whole Edna district to the east, north, or south. Prospective settlers, travelling on a hardly recognizable trail, could reach Edna or Pakan only with great difficulty. Having left this trail in search of a homestead, they had to force their way through thicket, forest, and swamp. After they had chosen their land, they had to clear a road, root out the trees, dry the muskegs, and break land before they could harvest a crop in order to make a living. The railways began to come only when they already had cattle and grain for sale. The hardships of these first settlers on Canadian soil, covered by forest and muskeg, can hardly be described. The poorer settlers passed through the longest period of poverty and privation.

Undoubtedly, the wives suffered the greatest hardships. Their husbands had to seek work in unknown regions where some even lost their lives and did not return to their families. In the meantime, the wives remained with their small children in rude shelters without adequate protection against wolves or bears, and often with primitive hoes and shovels to grow vegetables and even grain. Epics can be written about families whose lives were filled with acts of heroism and achievement, and the stories would enthrall the reader.

To illustrate the hardships of the pioneers, some memoirs of pioneer settlers in northern Alberta are included in this section. They reveal how many of the immigrants managed to reach people who were known to them in their homeland, their struggle to build better lives for themselves and their families, and the conditions under which they passed their first years in Canada.

Reminiscences of Kost Zahariichuk of Smoky Lake, Alberta

I arrived in Canada in 1899 from the village of Toporivtsi, Bukovyna. Having arrived with my family, I had to billet them with some Metis in Pakan. We were poor as I had only ten dollars in cash when we arrived in Pakan, eighty miles north-east of Edmonton. It was already autumn when I decided to walk to Fort Saskatchewan where I might find work with some farmer. I was hired by a German farmer and earned ten sacks of potatoes for a week's work. I considered this a great blessing because it guaranteed that we would not starve that winter. When I wrote my wife that I had earned ten sacks of potatoes she could hardly believe it and travelled the fifty miles to find out whether we had really that many potatoes. Fortunately, we did not need to deliver the potatoes ourselves because the farmer agreed to convey them to our home as payment for my plastering of his barn with clay to shelter his cattle over winter.

However, my wife took almost a sack-full of potatoes and walked home to Pakan with the potatoes on her back. I continued to work during threshing and the farmer did not take me home until after snowfall. When the potatoes arrived, my wife knelt down and prayed for almost an hour to thank God for not permitting us to starve in Canada. Next spring settlers came to our home from as far as twenty miles away to beg us to share some of the potatoes with them for planting because news of our good fortune had travelled fast. We portioned out some to everybody. And what do you know! They cut out only the eyes of the potato for planting. The rest was boiled until it disintegrated into a gruel and used to feed their infants because no milk was available. In these times no one will believe stories of early hardships.

Early in the spring of 1899, I selected land ten miles north of Pakan where the village of Smoky Lake now stands. Though the land was still unsurveyed, I wanted to build some sort of shelter in which to leave my family before I set out to seek work. It took a week for us to carry all our possessions on our backs to the homestead. As there was no road, it could not be reached by wagon. That is where I filed on my homestead. After we had settled that spring, I merely built a hut so that my wife and children could shelter themselves from rain and find protection from wild animals at night. In this hut they could sleep in peace, for there were all kinds of animals, chiefly moose, coyotes, and bears to disturb them.

After all our "treasures" were conveyed to the homestead, I immediately started for Edmonton on foot, leaving my wife and children in the wild forest land. For subsistence, I left them a bag of XXXX flour, hence four-ex flour to immigrants, the remaining potatoes, and a slab of bacon, but not a cent of money. The remaining five dollars which we possessed I took with me for my journey.

However, I asked Mitchell, the manager of the Hudson's Bay store in Pakan, where merchandise was kept for the Metis and Indians of the district, to accommodate my wife in case she needed sugar or cornmeal and that I would pay him after I obtained a job. How I explained this to him, I cannot remember. All that I can remember is that he replied, "All right, Kost."[8]

Kost Zahariichuk relates further that he was unable to obtain work in Edmonton. After buying two loaves of bread and bacon, he again set out on foot for Calgary because he hoped he could find work in a larger city. After four days he reached Red Deer, a distance of about a hundred miles. He slept in barns and under hay or straw stacks. In Red Deer Russian-German settlers advised him to seek work in Gleichen, about fifty miles east of Calgary. For a summer's work in Gleichen, he earned forty dollars in cash, a mare in foal, and a cow. He continued:

I cannot describe how precious that stock was to me. To a rich man millions in money and even his children might not have been as dear as my summer's earnings were to me. It took me four days to reach Wetaskiwin on foot while leading both animals on a rope. From Wetaskiwin I rode horseback. My wife was thoroughly alarmed when I brought my stock home. I had to reassure her that I had earned it and it did not belong to anybody else. If my wife was thoroughly astonished at the stock I had brought home, I was indeed taken by surprise by the new house which she and our young son had built during the summer. She had plastered it with clay both inside and outside while she thatched the roof with sheaves of long grass which they had mown with a sickle and carried from a slough half a mile away. Woven from Canadian willow there was a cradle in which lay an infant who had not been there when I set out for work in the spring.[9]

Obviously, other Ukrainian settlers followed Zahariichuk, along with a sprinkling of other nationalities. These settlers were the nucleus of what later became the progressive town of Smoky Lake, in which Nicolas Gavinchuk was to play an important part.

Also interesting and worthwhile are the reminiscences of Maria Yureychuk of Hamlin because it helps us to learn something of the beginnings of Wasel, about twelve miles east of Pakan. The Yureychuks arrived in September 1899 together with one family from Galicia and seven families from Bukovyna. At a cost of fifteen dollars per family, the Bukovynian immigrants were able to leave for present day Andrew within three days but Yureychuk and the family from Galicia remained in the immigration hall in Strathcona because they did not have the money for transportation. After a week of disappointing search for suitable homesteads close to Edmonton, the two fathers returned to their families. Yureychuk's friend found an acquaintance who was ready to accommodate his whole family, but this left Yureychuk without money or friend. During the next few days, he wandered around Edmonton in search of someone who might take him to Pasichney's at Victoria, near Pakan, but had no success. Finally, he resolved to build a raft with which he could reach Pasichney's by floating down the river. Maria Yureychuk continues the story:

> My husband was strong and healthy. We lived in the Carpathian Mountains where my husband floated logs on the Cheremosh River to Moldavia.... He soon constructed a raft on the river in Strathcona and we immediately hastened to carry our baggage on to the raft out of the "barn" hostel where I had spent the last two weeks. It was noon before we steered from the shore and began to drift down the current. Toward evening of the next day, we reached the ferry at Fort Saskatchewan. The water was very shallow in the river and the raft moved very slowly. Germans who spoke Ukrainian advised us that it would take a week to reach Victoria. As we had food for only two days, my husband had to hurry to buy potatoes, lard, and bread in Fort Saskatchewan. On the raft we had a flat piece of metal, on which we made a fire to bake our potatoes which we ate with melted lard. My husband also built a shelter on the raft to protect ourselves from storms.[10]

They continued to drift down the river for three days until the weather changed. Twelve inches of snow fell overnight and it was impossible to see where the raft was going. It drifted into shallow water and grounded so solidly that they were unable to dislodge it and move it into open water again. They had almost given up in despair when they became aware that Indians lived on the bank of the river. Seeing the strange object in the river shallows, some of the Indians rowed out in a boat to investigate more closely. When they saw people in trouble, they took them to their homes, gave them tea, and an opportunity to warm themselves. Though conversation was out of the question, the Indians construed somehow from Yureychuk's attempts at conversation that he was a "Galician" and directed him on the road to the nearest other "Galician" about ten miles away. Yureychuk set out on foot to reach Stefan Ratsoy in Pakan, who had arrived in Canada two years earlier and already had horses. He returned with Ratsoy driving horses and a wagon to where the Indians lived, then known as Pine Creek. The next day Ratsoy again transported them to Pasichney's in Wasel, where the Yureychuks finally settled.[11]

Maria Yureychuk's memoirs do not illustrate the experience of a typical settler. We can regard her husband's experience as an example of the exceptionally difficult circumstances faced by immigrants who came to Canada without money, and the initiatives which they needed to take to overcome the various predicaments they encountered. On the other hand, the reminiscences of Zahariichuk can be regarded as more representative of the experiences of the majority of Ukrainians who settled in Alberta as nearly every settler, once having filed on a homestead, built a simple shelter for his wife and children and then travelled as far as several hundreds of miles to obtain work in order to be able to purchase horses, cows, and rudimentary equipment for his farm.

Ukrainian settlers from Bukovina *en route* to Edna-Star, Alberta, 1897

(Public Archives of Canada)

STUDENTS OF P. MOHYLA INSTITUTE 1916-17

11

Stuartburn—Ukrainian Colonies in Southern Manitoba

The First Ukrainian Colony in Manitoba

Stuartburn is the oldest colony in Manitoba but, chronologically, it is the third in Canada as it follows Pheasant Forks in Saskatchewan and Edna in Alberta. It originated with Oleskiw's third group which he sent under the direction of Kyrylo Genik. The immigrants disembarked in Quebec from the *Sicilian* on July 22, 1896. Three days later they were in Winnipeg, where they met nine other Ukrainian families who had arrived earlier but had not yet acquired homesteads. Both groups decided to remain in Manitoba and elected six delegates to accompany the immigration officer, Wendelbo, with Genik as his assistant, to survey lands south of Winnipeg east of the Red River. Setting out on July 30, the delegation visited German settlements along the way to determine how suitable the soil was for cultivation. After a few days they located a suitable area in Range 6 close to the American border between the present day villages of Gardenton and Stuartburn. After they had reported to the group, twenty-six families and a number of single men set out by train on August 11 for Dominion City from which they were transported by wagon to Stuartburn. The men left their families here while they accompanied the surveyors with whose help they chose their homesteads. Consequently, the whole group settled in Township 2, Range 6 East of the First Meridian.[1]

While most members of this earlier immigrant group were from the province of Galicia, we also find among them a Vasyl Zahara and his wife Vasylyna from Bridok, county of Zastavna, Bukovyna, the first Bukovynian settler to be recorded in Canada.[2] News of his arrival precipitated a

mass movement of Bukovynians to Canada, many of whom settled near
Stuartburn. Their settlement extended the boundaries of the colony to the
south and south-east to lay the foundations of the present day villages of
Gardenton, Tolstoi, Arbakka, Kaliento, and Sundown. Thus, Vasyl Zahara
initiated the first Bukovynian colony in Canada.

Among the settlers were two old country school teachers, Kyrylo Genik
and Ivan Negrych, whose influence probably prompted the settlers to select
the name of Rus for their projected settlement. However, the name was
never used officially and was soon forgotten. Once they had become settled,
the already existing post office of Stuartburn became their first post office
and became widely accepted. Though the district retained that name, less
educated immigrants soon reconstructed its pronunciation into their own
expression, as "Shtonboor".

Although the first settlers arrived late in the year as it was the month of
August, others were to follow them. At the beginning of December of that
year, Carstens, who was sent out to investigate conditions, reported that
there were already thirty-seven families and seven single individuals in the
colony. He also listed their names.[3]

Anxiety and hardship united the settlers at the beginning, inspiring
friendly relations and encouraging mutual aid. These characteristics were
noted by M. Stashyn in his memoirs:

> In those days settlers held one another in high esteem. They welcomed
> visitors and entertained them with whatever was available. They aided one
> another as much as was in their power. And this spirit helped us immigrants to
> survive pioneer hardships and to ease our heartbreak at being parted from
> friends at home.... Desolate was our life.[4]

The newcomers' primary task was the building of some sort of shelter
to house their families over winter. In this effort they helped one another
and every building was the result of cooperative effort. Getting settled and
constructing shelters used up the rest of the summer and fall. So quickly did
time roll by that there was no opportunity to prepare the ground for the
most essential vegetables or to seek work in neighbouring settlements to
earn enough money to procure provisions for the coming winter. Those who
had money bought a cow, or even a horse, as well as necessary provisions
and supplies. But not all were that fortunate. Among the group were ten
families who were penniless and unable to make any provision for winter.
Their condition was comparable to that of the Edna families, and aid was
essential if they were to survive until spring. Having discovered what was
happening, the government arranged for the bringing in of some supplies.
According to the account presented by Carstens, who administered the
relief funds, the total amount spent was $341.55.[5]

It must be understood that this expenditure of money was not welfare in the modern sense, according to which a municipality or even the central government might grant aid in the form of a regular cash allowance, generally limiting the aid to persons of Canadian birth or residents of long standing. Usually these grants are given without any obligation of repayment. The aid granted to these immigrants was in the form of a loan which had to be repaid. Furthermore, it was not a cash payment. Officials distributed to the needy the cheapest flour or other food products and clothing necessities. When the time arrived for the recipient to obtain a title to his land, he was required to repay any indebtedness for aid which had been incurred before the title was issued. As we learn in a later report, this aid caused no inconvenience for the government because Ukrainian immigrants were prompt and even scrupulous in meeting deadlines. As a result of these relations with the newcomers, officials were generally favorable to Ukrainians in their reports and optimistic about their future.[6]

Prejudice Against the New Settlers

Rumours about poverty-stricken immigrants whom the government had to support reached the press. On December 23, 1896, the *Daily Nor'Wester* of Winnipeg published the following editorial with the title, "Undesirable Immigrants".

> Parties of Galician immigrants continue to arrive in Winnipeg. If our foreign immigration agents cannot send us a better class of immigrants than these it is almost time to consider whether we might not dispense with immigration agents altogether. The southern Slavs are probably the least promising of all the material that could be selected for nation building.... There is a class of immigration which retards rather than promotes progress. The uncleanly and illiterate are an evil rather than a good.... Many of them have also arrived in such a destitute condition that the Government has had to support them. It is bad enough if these people come to us of their own accord; but it is monstrous that we should be paying agents to induce them to come.[7]

This editorial sharpened the prejudice of many Canadians against the new settlers. To them, Ukrainians appeared to be alien beings. Not only was their language strange but, as a result of the long journey, they were tired and neglectful of their appearance. The first impression Canadians gained of Ukrainians could hardly have been favorable. As the immigrants knew no English, they could hardly converse with others. Some were even illiterate. Therefore, it is not surprising that some of these Canadians, probably with the best of intentions, formed a "Committee of the Foreign Immigration Association" which claimed to consist of Germans, Poles, Russians, and Ruthenians (Ukrainians). This group forwarded a petition to the government in which they condemned the immigration authorities and their petition contained the threat that "if the government would not do something in this matter, we will get hundreds of this kind of immigrants in the Spring and the City will have to endure them." The committee accused Oleskiw of sending "the poorest class of immigrants into this country," and that he had also sent his assistant Genik, who claimed that the Government had appointed him as a government interpreter.[8]

Neither the *Daily Nor'Wester* nor the committee manifested any understanding of the true situation. Their adverse judgement of the immigrants, based on the newcomers' outward appearance, was false and unjust. Although these newcomers had undergone physical and emotional hardships in coming to Canada, their experience had not broken them. Later years were to demonstrate that these immigrants were of a quality which Canada needed very urgently at this time. Only a type of settler who was physically and morally hardened, as well as persevering, could have felled the forests, drained the swamps, and cleared off the stones to make the soil productive. At the same time they were to provide the labour for the network of railway lines which were so necessary for Canada's economic development.

With their attacks, the *Daily Nor'Wester* and the committee unintentionally supported Oleskiw's efforts to help the immigrants. Foreseeing the difficulties which would be encountered in locating settlers, Oleskiw had advised the government that the settler should know as soon as possible where he would be located in the new land after he had sold his land at home. The effect of these attacks was to prod the immigration authorities to direct immigrants in accordance with some plan. But the government was not entirely at fault because immigrants generally preferred to make their own choice in regard to the district where they would settle. They did not always accept advice and often settled in areas against which they had been specifically warned by immigration officials.

Until recently it was mistakenly considered that no one was concerned with Ukrainian immigration to Canada. The research of Kaye, who unearthed much valuable information about early settlement, reveals that it was quite otherwise. Not only were the early arrivals under the direct guidance of Oleskiw and the Canadian immigration authorities but they were also watched closely by the Austrian government. Almost immediately after the group of immigrants had located themselves at Stuartburn, Austrian authorities instructed their consul in Montreal to obtain information on the group of Oleskiw's immigrants who had left in July and to report specifically on Maykowski and Genik, "both rather prominent men in their circle". Consul Eduard Schultze requested the information and received the reply that the group was located at Stuartburn and also that

Genik and Maykowski had filed on homesteads there. As additional information, Maykowski's address was listed as Stuartburn but Genik's was Winnipeg, "to enable him to send his children to the City schools..."⁹

Father Nestor Dmytriw's Visit

Notwithstanding the temporary privations of the newcomers and the unfavorable attitude of the Winnipeg group, the Stuartburn colony thrived and its Ukrainian population continued to increase steadily. On April 16, 1897, it was visited by Father Dmytriw, who noted the following in his diary:

> There are forty-five families of our people in this district—altogether 175 souls. The first twenty-four families settled on August 19, 1896, but others drifted into this colony in the fall and even in the winter—a few families at a time.

After information on where the families originated, he described the land as follows:

> The soil is generally good. In some places there are stones but they are alluvial in origin and found only on top of the ground. Hay meadows are excellent, arable land is plentiful, and there is sufficient woodland. In the woodland I found plums, cherries and even grapes. Many kinds of vegetables grow here. Wheat, oats, barley, and other grains are also raised. The district is very suitable for pasturing cattle. It is only nine miles from North Dakota where our people go during the harvest season in summer and fall, which enables them to earn from forty to sixty dollars per month. Surrounding this district there are also wealthy farmers who need labourers and pay well.¹⁰

As the number of new settlers increased, the assigned township was quickly populated and newcomers had to move further east in Range 7 East of the First Meridian and later in Range 8 to settle where Vita and Caliento are now located. Some new arrivals also headed west to file on land in Range 5 East of the First Meridian.

The government opened for settlement only the even-numbered sections of each township. Odd-numbered sections were closed to settlement as experience in the past convinced the government that the Canadian farmer would eventually need more than one quarter-section of land and would want to extend his holdings. Odd-numbered sections were thus left vacant to have land for future sale close by. As this regulation also applied to Stuartburn area, the immigrants pleaded that this land be also opened for settlement so they might be as close as possible to other settlers:

> Everyone sought to live as close as possible to some fellow villager or countryman because it was a strange country with strange people. Ignorance of the English language generated fear in our settlers and caused them to

crowd close together in their choice of location. To satisfy these feelings and to accede to the persistent requests of these poor immigrants, not only the odd-numbered but also the C.P.R. sections were opened for settlement. In their desire for close neighbours, some of the settlers even surrendered half of their land, claiming that the whole quarter was too large for them.[11]

Immigrants began to raise the question of homestead entry on odd-numbered sections as early as the first year of settlement. The government resisted the pressure for some time but the continuing requests, petitions, and demands, including recommendations by Oleskiw, finally achieved success.

However, the government had an additional reason for yielding. Before the arrival of the Ukrainian immigrants, many of the odd-numbered sections had already been purchased by earlier settlers who had never kept up with their payments. The land was only nominally purchased; the buyers had made only small deposits and had undertaken to pay the rest in annual installments. From a legal standpoint they could still be considered owners of the land but, because they had not fulfilled the terms of the agreement in regard to annual payments, the government had the right to declare the sales invalid. Among the purchasers there were some who had bought two or even four sections of land, not only for themselves but also for their families and friends. However, they did not keep up with their annual payments, did not settle on the land, or cultivate it—the land was left undeveloped. Since these purchases had become a nuisance, the government cancelled the agreements and opened these lands for homesteading. These earlier purchases had been blocks of land which included all sections both odd- and even-numbered. The government now opened for homestead entry not only lands on which sales had been cancelled but also the remaining quarters of odd-numbered sections, on which settlement had not been permitted earlier. Thus, Stuartburn settlement achieved a more concentrated population as well as an extension of its boundaries. On the basis of a report by Genik, an official of the land department was able to announce in December 1901 that there were already 337 families in this colony.[12]

Although more productive land in this district was occupied in the first two years, immigrants continued to file on less productive land. Some settled here to be close to their relatives; others came to join friends and fellow villagers. Still others settled because they feared to be isolated from other Ukrainians in an alien land without a knowledge of its language. The district thus became populated with Ukrainian settlers within a short period of time.

There were also immigrants from Pennsylvania—Ukrainians who flocked to Canada on the advice of Father Dmytriw. Some of these arrived in Stuartburn, others in Dauphin, and still others in Canora as well as in other Canadian settlements. The majority of these immigrants were Lemkos from north-west Galicia, an area now occupied by Poland. They had arrived in Pennsylvania some years earlier to labour in mines and factories. While in the United States, they had learned enough English to be of great service to more recent immigrants after their arrival in Canada. In many instances they also became leaders of their communities. Among these was Theodosy Wachna (Wakhna) who settled in Stuartburn. Genik reports the following about these settlers in *Svoboda* in 1898:

> During the past year over ten families arrived from Pennsylvania in addition to a number of single men. We have great hopes for these, for they are people who, one can say, have become Americanized and can therefore be of much help to recent arrivals. Some of them are to be found in every settlement.[13]

Two Shocking Murders

A tragic event which brought terror to the whole Stuartburn community was the murder of Wasyl Boyechko and his four children on October 18, 1898. He was murdered by two of his fellow villagers—Semen Chubey and Wasyl Hushchak—who stole fifty dollars from him. All three individuals had arrived from Puste Ivania, county of Borshchiv, in the company of several other families during the summer of 1898 to settle at Stuartburn. This fearful event was fully reported and the perpetrators of the crime denounced by Genik in *Svoboda* on January 19, 1899. Two years later another crime was committed. Joseph Solomon, a farmer, killed his wife, after having found her crippled as the result of falling from a ladder. The settlers were not only frightened because the murders were in their neighbourhood; they also feared that these tragic events would aggravate the hostile feelings which had been aroused against them by earlier newspaper reports.

Beginnings of Social and Church Life

As was the case in other Ukrainian colonies, immigrants in the Stuartburn area missed their own church and its spiritual guidance for their families from the beginning. The services of a priest were urgently required for baptisms, marriages, and funerals. Having arrived from the United States in 1897 to visit Ukrainian settlements in Canada, Father Dmytriw also visited the Stuartburn district where he celebrated mass on Palm Sunday, April 16. This was his second church service in Canada as the first had been at Terebowlia, near Dauphin, on April 12. In Stuartburn mass was celebrated in the store of a Frenchman, with a large crowd in attendance. Dmytriw did not forget the colony, for he visited it again in August of the same year. As a result of his influence during these visits, the settlers began to build a Greek (Ukrainian) Catholic church on NW15-2-6 E, two miles east of Stuartburn, with both Catholics and Orthodox adherents cooperating, on the farm of Mykhailo Dumansky. But it was not completed until 1900. During the same period the Orthodox group built the first Ukrainian church in Canada at Gardenton, the first Bukovynian colony in Manitoba.[14]

The parents were also compelled to turn their attention to education as more and more children began to reach school age. Those living close to the hamlet of Stuartburn could send their children to the existing school but Stuartburn was too distant for most of the settlers. When they failed to obtain any aid for building schools from Franklin Municipality, they applied to the provincial government, where they also met with failure. Since their request for aid had been rejected by both levels of government, they decided to form a separate municipality. The Stuartburn Municipality thus became an entity in 1902 with Theodosy Wachna, the Pennsylvania settler, as its first secretary. Wachna continued to hold influential positions in the community because of his knowledge of the English language.

During the same year the settlers began to construct a number of new schools, most of which were built with logs from which bark had been stripped. Nine schools were completed in the next three years: Pearl Bank, Koroliwka, Shewchenko, Arbakka, Bukovyna, Lukiwtsi, Franko, Becket, and Kupchenko. At the time these schools were built, they were bilingual but there were no bilingual teachers until 1904, when T. Kochan (Kokhan) and D. Pyrch arrived in the district. There were many more teachers in succeeding years.

When immigration from Europe was closed owing to the outbreak of war in 1914, Stuartburn colony was already thickly settled. By that time the settlement extended along the United States border from Emerson to Sprague, close to the Ontario border. Along its northern boundary it stretched from Dufrost in the west to a point six miles south of Steinbach, excluding only small areas settled by Germans and French at Grunthal and St. Malo. From the point south of Steinbach the boundary ran south-east to Sandilands and along the forest reserve to Sundown and Sprague. The following villages may now be found in this territory: Ridgeville, Tolstoi[15], Gardenton, Vita[16], Caliento, Arbakka, Sundown, Sandilands, Zhoda, Sarto, Rosa, Dominion City, and Dufrost. By 1941, the Ukrainian population of this district was close to 6500.[17]

Having overcome initial pioneer hardships, this colony developed rapidly and has produced many leading personalities who played an important part in the cultural and educational life of Ukrainians in Canada.

The first Ukrainian Church in Canada — St. Michael's Ukrainian
Orthodox Church, Gardenton, Manitoba, 1899.

Peter Shkwarchuk and family,
Gardenton, Manitoba
1913

Sandyk Mekelij
Gardenton, Manitoba

12

Dauphin District—Ukrainian Colonies North and North-East of the Riding Mountains

Terebovlia—the First Ukrainian Settlement in the Dauphin District

Ukrainian settlement in the Dauphin district also had its origin in 1896, but it began with fewer settlers and a month later than the Stuartburn colony. Only seven families were in the first group to settle in the Dauphin area as compared to the twenty-seven families who came to Stuartburn. The newcomers chose land along the Drifting River, nearly seven miles west of the future station of Valley River, and gave their chosen area the name of Terebovlia. The architect and founder of this new colony was Wasyl Ksionzyk (Vasyl Ksionzhyk), a literate, able, and patriotic Ukrainian from the village of Zavalia in the county of Terebovlia, Galicia. He was proud of Terebovlia, the county seat in his native land, and made certain that the same name, so well known to people in their area, was given to their post office in the beginning and later to their school in Canada. An account of the early hardships of these families and the long and arduous journey to their chosen land was published in *Svoboda* in 1897.[1]

Father Dmytriw Visits the New Immigrants

For a more profound insight into pioneer hardships in Canadian Terebovlia, we shall quote from Father Dmytriw's account. He visited the colony about six months after it was established and described the journey in his booklet.[2] He arrived in Dauphin by train on April 9, 1897, and reached Valley River station by wagon on Saturday afternoon. He writes as follows:

Further travel by wagon became hopeless; the creek in which there is hardly a trickle of water during the summer was now impassable. There was no other remedy except to travel to the colony six miles distant on foot as the apostles had travelled. Having crossed to the other side of the creek, I chanced on an "English" farmer and hired his horses. For the next three hours through forest and glade, the horses dragged the wagon which rebounded repeatedly from the sides of tree stumps or alternately bounced half a yard on impact with logs. In this way I reached the home of another "English" farmer who lived alone in a very mean dwelling. Beyond his dwelling there was already no trail and to penetrate thick brushwood on a wagon was a hopeless task. Again there was no other remedy except to set forth on foot. The cold rays of the declining sun illumined the large snowdrifts and torrents of water tearing their way through the thick web of willow and primeval turf. For more than an hour I wandered through the forest, wading through water and snowdrifts in an area where only an Indian hunter's footstep had trod previously. As light began to fade, I was overcome with fear, a fear of the dark night in this primeval steppe and forest. I felt the terror of an insect forced to face invincible and unruffled nature. Panic-stricken at the thought of having to spend the night on the frozen snow in the midst of an impenetrable forest thicket, I summoned the last vestiges of energy to flounder further through the snow. Finally, I discovered or rather blundered upon a trail and jubilantly followed it without caring where it led. Half an hour later, I reached a farm-house occupied by two Scottish settlers who lived with their horses and cattle like two hermits. One of the men cheerfully harnessed a team of horses, and we again set out, the horses trudging slowly in the direction of the colony.

A bright moon shone in the sky.... Finally we approached a small habitation. The horses stopped, and I was delighted that we had reached the end of the journey. Partially stripped poplar logs, dove-tailed at the corners, formed the walls of a hut. The roof consisted of poplar boards covered with turf and soil. The distance between the ground and the eaves of the hut was no more than half a meter. A small metal pipe protruded from the roof. Serving as a chimney, smoke belched forth from it continually since there was no problem with fuel. The English iron stove was red hot inside and gave plenty of heat. Strips of dough were boiling on the stove without milk or fat of any kind as the family still had no cow. At the stove stood the mother dressed as in her homeland and the children, obviously very hungry, sat around the stove. The bed, table, the bench on which the father was seated, and the home constituted the entire wealth of our peasant, who had emigrated during winter from his home to seek his fortune. No, this was not his entire property for, underneath the bed, both chickens and pigeons could be heard, and a very attractive dog strode back and forth excitedly through the room. Near the house stood a barn in which there was a team of oxen, the common property of three settlers. In the yard stood a giant wagon which had cost seventy dollars and was also owned in common by the three settlers. I did not remain long with this family as they informed me that the farmer whom I had to contact lived a farm (quarter-section) and a half further.

Finally, I reached the dwelling of the man I was seeking....[3] It was on the other side of the creek. It was somewhat larger than the first habitation and a wagon close by served as a temporary store-house. Under the wagon there were kitchen utensils and one pot was covered with *Svoboda*. The barn was also more spacious as it accommodated two cows, two calves, and a team of oxen. In the yard there were two ploughs, a necessary prelude to husbandry. In the house, the same order prevailed as elsewhere. I made myself comfortable, dried my feet and shoes, carried on a desultory conversation, and fell into a profound slumber. On Sunday morning I was awakened by a rooster crowing persistently under my bed. The people began to assemble in front of the house and soon most of the colony, consisting of fifteen families and seventy-eight persons, congregated in the yard. The Terebovlia immigrants had arrived in autumn and early winter before Christmas from the counties of Borshchiv, Chortkiv, Buchach, and Terebovlia. The fifteen families possessed five oxen, two cows, and two calves but two of the oxen and two cows were the property of one person. Only one wagon and three of the oxen were owned by the rest of the settlers.[4]

Such were the hardships endured by Father Dmytriw in accepting the invitation of Wasyl Ksionzyk, the first Ukrainian pioneer in the Dauphin area. He was already a subscriber to *Svoboda*, a publication in which Father Dmytriw was a collaborator. It is remarkable how Ksionzyk succeeded in reaching this area without previous information, leadership, or any knowledge of the English language. After settling here, he gave it the name of Terebovlia. Furthermore, as we have discovered, Father Dmytriw reached the settlement by travelling to Dauphin on a train. When Ksionzyk and his band of fellow settlers came in the fall of 1896, the last station on the railway was Neepawa, nearly eighty-five miles south-east of Dauphin.

A Leader in the Settlement

When Wasyl Ksionzyk, the leader of this new colony, arrived from Terebovlia in Galicia, he reached Quebec on the ship *Christiania* on August 16, 1896. Before he emigrated, he contacted Dr. Oleskiw who gave him information on the district north and north-east of Dauphin and, on the basis of this information, he chose the district for settlement. Leaving their families in Winnipeg, he and two other members of the group set out to explore the area. A few weeks were spent in selecting suitable land before returning to Winnipeg. After their return, he and six other immigrants with their families set out for the area they had chosen. In Neepawa, the last station on the railroad on the way to Dauphin, Ksionzyk bought a wagon, a team of oxen, and other farm equipment. The rest of the group bought two wagons and two teams of oxen jointly. The whole group then followed Indian trails to the district—not six miles, the distance Father Dmytriw had to travel, but over a hundred miles from the last station.

The first settlers who accompanied Ksionzyk to the Dauphin district were the following: Ivan Sytnyk, NE18-26-20; Ivan Gereliuk, NW20-26-20; Josef Pawlicki (Yosef Pawlitsky), SW20-26-20; Petro Perchaluk (Perkhaliuk) and his son Petro, SW30-26-20; Josef Baszczak (Yosef Bashchak), NE20-26-20. Ksionzyk settled on NE19-26-20. There is no record of the exact location of another settler who was variously known as Nizhalkowski, Nizhalowski, and Nipliansky.[5] They named the settlement Terebowlia but their post office was Rigby, a name given to it when it was established, several years prior to the settlement.

These settlers were joined that same winter by a number of families consisting of Ilia Nimets, Hawrylo Staranczuk (Staranchuk), Petro Huska, Mykhailo Gadzhosa, Ivan Lozinsky, Mykola Jacentuk (Yatsentiuk), and Pant. Czerwinski (Chervinsky). P. Potocki (Pototsky), H. Szewczuk (Shewchuk) and others followed next spring.[6] This explains why Father Dmytriw reports that he found fifteen families in the district encompassing a total population of seventy-eight.[7]

The Continuing Influx of Ukrainian Immigrants

Ukrainian immigration assumed massive dimensions in 1897 as we have already noted. In February of that year 140 immigrants arrived on the steamship *Labrador* and 42 came on the *Scotsman*. The *Arcadia* brought 648 newcomers to Quebec on May 2 and six hours later on the same day 435 more disembarked from the *Scotia*. Within a few hours 1100 immigrants, prospective settlers, crowded into Winnipeg from these two ships. Some of them continued to Edmonton, 475 left to settle in the Dauphin area, and the rest remained in Winnipeg. Some of them were later to play a part in the disturbance which was reported earlier in this volume.

Among those who reached the Dauphin settlement soon after May 6 were two teachers from the village of Bereziv, Ivan Bodrug and Ivan Negrycz (Negrych). On the road to Dauphin or soon after they reached there, they were joined by Yurko (George) Syrotiuk who had already become an interpreter[8]. Leaving their families in the Immigration Hall in Winnipeg on May 7, the men of this group proceeded in the company of a government agent, Paul Wood, to select their homesteads. According to the ably-written memoirs of Dmytro Romanchych,[9] they travelled by train to Sifton, which was then the terminal of the projected railway. From Sifton they travelled on foot another ten miles to the north-west, spending the night in the forest. The country caught their fancy and they decided to settle there. So certain were they that other Ukrainians would choose to settle in the same area that they accepted the suggestion made by both Bodrug and Syrotiuk to give the name of Ukraina to the settlement. Their guide made a note of the suggestion and promised to direct their request to the proper authorities. Subsequently, Vasyl Standryk and Dmytro Rivniak, members of this group of settlers, drew up a petition to support this request. Their efforts bore fruit. When construction was continued from Sifton in a northwesterly direction in the following year, the railway station nearest to them was given the name of Ukraina.

Romanchych relates that they travelled still further to the north-west to approximately where Ethelbert stands today. Finding good black soil in this district the following families chose to remain there: Danylo Syrotiuk with his two sons and his son-in-law, W. Wetzel; Hawrylo Symchych, Gapko, Ivan Malkovych, and Nykola Sulatycki (Suliatytsky). Semen Negrycz (Negrych) and Wasyl Melowsky chose land seven miles south of Ethelbert. Others went still further south to settle at Drifting River, near Venlaw. This colony consisted of Ivan Negrych, a relative of the teacher Ivan Negrych, his brother Wasyl Negrych, Jacob Genik with his two sons, Nykola Pidlasecki (Pidliasetsky), the large family of Hryhorchuks, and others. Thirteen newcomers from the village of Bereziv in the Carpathian Mountains returned to the group without having chosen homesteads. They expressed a wish to inspect land south-east of Dauphin, along the Riding Mountains, in spite of the fact that Wood warned them that these lands were set aside for a forest reserve. Wood's warning did not daunt the Bereziv villagers. They preferred to live near the Riding Mountains because the area would remind them of their beloved Carpathian highlands. After discovering good black soil in an area burned out as far as the Vermilion River, they settled there.[10] In the same month they were joined by over a dozen other families from other villages and counties, principally from the village of Hleshava in the county of Terebovlia.[11]

However, since the settlers were mainly from Bereziv and other villages in the Carpathians, the district was generally known as Kossiw, the name of the county and the county centre in their native land. This name was also given to their post office and the first public school in their new home. Romanchych states further that the name of the post office was later changed to Keld on the advice of a missionary, Father Sabourin.

Although the Kossiw group managed to settle on good black soil near the mountains, they still had difficulties. Some of them located on odd-numbered sections which had not been opened for homesteading. On these sections they had cultivated land and built homes. Fortunately, their determination, appeals, petitions, and finally Genik's support again overcame the opposition of the government and they were permitted to retain their land.

Following the arrival of the *Arcadia* and the *Scotia* in May 1897, there followed the *Prussia* with 672 immigrants from Galicia, the *Arabia* with

558, and the *Armenia* with 672. Thirty-nine families from the *Prussia* who had planned to settle in Terebowlia were immediately directed to the area by the immigration authorities. There is little doubt that many others were directed to these settlements as it was easier to allocate settlers where a beginning had already been made.

With the influx of more immigrants, Kossiw, the southern Dauphin settlement, expanded both east and west. In the east it extended along the Riding Mountains for about thirty-five miles, reaching St. Rose and beyond. To the west, settlement followed along the Riding Mountains through the district of Petlura to the end of the forest reserve. Even earlier than this, the Dauphin settlement had expanded to the north of Valley River and Terebowlia, broadening both east and west. In the north it advanced beyond Sifton, Ukraina, and Ethelbert. In the west it reached the Duck Mountain Forest Reserve, giving rise to the districts of Halych, Venlaw, Zoria, Drifting River, and Mink Creek. In the east it spread to Fork River and Yorkton, reaching Lake Winnipegosis just south of the village of that name.

A Disastrous Fire

The settlers west of Valley River, Sifton, and Ukraina suffered a great catastrophe which hindered the development of the district for some time as it affected almost every settler. In October 1899, after grain had been harvested, hay stacked, and preparations were being made for winter, an unexpected fire broke out in the west. Beginning in Range 20, it raced through forest and prairie to extend its front from Township 26 to 29 and burned itself out finally in Range 22. The homesteaders protected what articles they could by burying them underground or in sloughs and small lakes while they fled west with their cattle.

Philemon Leskiw, who arrived in Dauphin on May 27, 1897, and settled later at Sifton, describes this terrifying experience:

> Thus fared our settlers during the first three years. Having surmounted many difficulties, they embarked on their fourth year. Conditions were beginning to improve. When the haying season arrived, they cut their hay, and heaped it in haycocks; some had even hauled it home and stacked it. As autumn grew near, everything was dry and there was no lack of brushwood in the forest. A fire started somewhere and began to envelop us from two sides, from the west and the south; the whole area west of Sifton was on fire. The flames did not spread along the ground as in a prairie fire; they shot up to heights of twenty or thirty feet. Smoke covered the sun like a cloud during the day. The fire was only partially checked in the sloughs so that everything burned, including the haycocks. People hid in pits and even in wells. As there was very little cultivated land in those days, there was nothing to prevent the fires

from reaching the farmsteads, and the destruction was terrifying. The wind, which continued to blow from the west, was not a strong wind but it was sufficient for the thick dry underbrush. Consequently, the fire which had its origin in the far west of Zoria postal district was not checked until it reached the railroad. In some sections it even crossed the railroad..... Moose and elk, which were trapped by the flames, trumpeted in frenzied agony.... When we travelled on the Indian trail from Sifton to Dauphin a week later, dead rabbit carcasses piled along both sides of the trail five miles south of Sifton had the appearance of crowding flocks of sheep.[12]

This fire was a great disaster to the early settlers as it destroyed their provisions for winter and, in many cases, also their buildings. The government had to advance some aid to the victims to enable them to survive the winter but the destruction hampered progress in the colony for a number of years. However, this misfortune also proved to be of some benefit as the destruction of forests and underbrush aided the settlers in cultivating more land.

In spite of this disaster, new settlers continued to arrive, extending the settled area northward to areas around Garland, Pine River, Duck River, and Slater. From here additional newcomers pushed west to approach Minnetonas and Swan River, then south-west through Benito to the Saskatchewan border, where they almost joined the Ukrainian settlement at Arran. Simultaneously, the southern colony spread wedge-shaped from Grandview to Shortdale and Roblin. North of Roblin it again skirted the south-western slope of the Duck Mountain Forest Reserve to reach the Saskatchewan border once more, as the northern settlement had done. It included more heavily populated centres such as Shortdale, Roblin, and Deepdale, and more sparsely settled areas like Glen Eden, Postup, Merridale, and Zelena.

The Memorial Cross of Freedom

We can no longer find the name of Terebowlia on the map of Manitoba because the settlement did not have the good fortune to become the centre of some economic or administrative unit. Its misfortune was its proximity to both the established post-office of Rigby and the district of Halych in the neighbouring municipality. Only two mementoes remain to remind us of the once thriving settlement: Terebowlia School #1040 and the first cross of freedom in Canada which was blessed by Father Dmytriw on his first visit to the colony.[13] The first cross was constructed from a poplar tree and erected on a hill on the farm of Ivan Gereliuk. Unfortunately, the bottom rotted repeatedly with the passage of time, requiring that it be cut down and reburied on each occasion. To take its place, a large marble cross was erected in the same spot, but the farm no longer belonged to Ivan Gereliuk;

it was now the property of his son-in-law, Stepan Stechishin. The ceremony of unveiling and consecration of this memorial cross took place on July 31, 1966, to celebrate the seventy-fifth anniversary of Ukrainian immigration to Canada. It took place with the participation of church dignitaries, a specially-trained choral group from Dauphin, and a large crowd of visitors from many parts of Canada and the United States who were attending the Ukrainian Festival in Dauphin. The consecration of the cross and the production of the Ukrainian Festival were noteworthy events and a fitting celebration to commemorate both the struggle and the accomplishments of these first Ukrainian settlers.

Although the nearest dwellers of this area know little of the first colony of Terebowlia, this does not detract from its significance as the "mother" settlement of Canadian Ukraina: Kossiw, Halych, and subsequently the whole Dauphin area. Both Oleskiw, who advised Ksionzyk to settle here, and Ksionzyk himself, who settled here and aided the immigration authorities in the allocation of other settlers in the Dauphin district, would be proud to know what a large colony they had brought into existence in this part of Manitoba. Furthermore, the early immigrants of Canadian Terebowlia themselves contributed to give the community historical significance. From among the first settlers there emerged a number of personalities who played a dominant role in the lives of their countrymen and who will be recorded in the history of Ukrainians in Canada.

13

Pleasant Home—the Interlake Region in Manitoba

Ukrainian Colonies in the Interlake Region in Manitoba

Four Ukrainian colonies in Canada came into existence in 1897 almost simultaneously. They were Pleasant Home in Manitoba and three areas in Saskatchewan: Saltcoats, just east of Yorkton, Beaver Hills, west of Yorkton, and Crooked Lakes, north-east of the same centre.

Pleasant Home had its beginning in June 1897 when the director of immigration sent out eleven families to file on homesteads in Township 17, Range 2, East of the First Meridian. The district was approximately forty miles north of Winnipeg and only a few miles west of present-day Winnipeg Beach. At that time the nearest station was Stonewall, nearly twenty miles south of the projected colony, but there was a store and post office in the district. As far as we know, no one recorded the names of the eleven families or where they settled, but Dmytro Drohomoreski (Drohomoretsky) gives the names of some of these first settlers in his memoirs.[1] He lists Petro and Ivan Drohomoreski, Dmytro Genik, Yurko Kuzych, Mykola Romanchych, Stefan Dragan, and Ilia Chreptyk (Khreptyk). Furthermore, Kaye[2] reports that the following settlers from this area were naturalized on September 9, 1900: Stefan Dragan and Ilia Chreptyk, two already listed by Drohomoreski; also Wasyl Porayko, Antin Chreptyk (Khreptyk), Prokip Slusarczuk (Slusarchuk), Fedir Holynsky, and Yurko Lukaszczuk (Lukashchuk). It is evident the last five names must have been members of the first group which settled in 1897. The first settlers were joined by others, either the same fall or later in winter since Kyrylo Genik, in reporting his visit to the colony at the end of March 1898, stated that there were eighteen families in the area.

Pleasant Home region differed from others in that it was more heavily wooded and contained more stretches of muskeg. The forest inspector reported that the district was unsuitable for settlement and advised the government to move the settlers elsewhere but the colonization officials would not change their original decision to colonize this area, and the settlement remained. In this decision they were probably swayed by the wishes of the immigrants themselves who believed that heavy enforestation was evidence of abundant soil fertility.

These settlers also had other worries. As they could not prepare the land for any grain crop or even a garden, those of their number who did not have means to survive the winter had to depend on government aid, usually in the form of a loan. However, the government was prepared for this eventuality; some of the settlers were supplied with necessary provisions while others were given temporary work. In this way they survived the first winter. But this did not end all of their difficulties. In this district as in others many had filed on quarters in odd-numbered sections. Although immigration officials assured them that these sections had been assigned for homesteading, the government made no official pronouncement about this matter for some time. As the newcomers were uncertain about permission to remain on this land, they did not cultivate their land or improve their homesteads in other ways until governmental approval finally came through.

The Rapid Establishment of Other Settlements in the Interlake Area

In the spring of 1898 many more Ukrainian families arrived in this district. Dmytro Drohomoreski lists forty names[3] of these new settlers and describes their lives as follows:

> Exhausted by the long journey, they landed in the wilderness, a district over which spread a dense forest through which the only approaches were the surveyor's marks and clearings. The soil was exceedingly stony with extensive stretches of muskeg. Dark clouds of relentless mosquitoes swarmed day and night so that everyone had to wear a mosquito net or carry a smudge along.... When they had filed on their homesteads, they immediately went into action. They assisted one another to raise the walls and put up the roofs of their homes, using dry poplar logs which had been scorched by fire. They filled the spaces between the logs with moss and plastered the walls with clay. The women cut the long swamp grass with their sickles, tied it into sheaves, and thatched the roofs... Summer came. Everyone who could afford it bought a cow so that their children could have milk. This meant additional work because hay had to be prepared to winter the cow. It was cut in the sloughs

with scythes or sickles and had to be stacked. When autumn came there was still no rest for the newcomers who came together to build roads. They also felled and stripped trees for buildings and split spruces to make three foot shingles to cover the roofs or split the spruce trees to make lumber. During the winter they felled the giant poplars to sell as cordwood[4] and walked on foot to Winnipeg in the spring to seek work... The women remained at home with the children. They dug up the ground with grub-hoes and prepared their garden plots to plant potatoes and other vegetables. The forests swarmed with wild animals—rabbits, deer, elk and moose. Those with firearms never lacked meat for their families. The forest also teemed with fruit—plums, raspberries, and saskatoons. The lakes contained all kinds of fish.

With the arrival of increasing numbers of immigrants, Pleasant Home spread to the east into Ranges 3 and 4 in Township 18, which had been reserved for Icelandic settlers who always strove to settle near the lakes. However, since no one had attempted to settle here for a number of years, the government opened this reservation for homesteading to accommodate new arrivals. As a result, we learn from Father Tymkevych's account in *Svoboda*[5] at the end of 1898 that there were already 150 families in the settlement. From Ivan Drohomoreski's account in the same newspaper in 1903[6] we discover that the number had increased to between 700 and 800 families.

The settlement expanded to the north along Lake Winnipeg and soon by-passed both Gimli and Riverton. It also surged north of Teulon to Komarno, Malonton, Fraserwood, Meleb, and Rembrandt to reach and pass beyond Arborg. At the same time it extended westward toward Inwood, Chatfield, Poplarfield, Fisher Branch, Hodgson, and beyond Dallas. In the northern section the following new districts came into existence: Berlo, Jaroslaw (Yaroslaw), Sky Lake, Zbaraz (Zbarazh), Sylvan, Okno, and Shorncliffe. At present this inter-lake Ukrainian colony spreads over forty townships, an area of 1440 square miles. Yuzyk claims that this region had a Ukrainian population of about eight thousand by 1941.[7]

Their Hardships in this Forest and Muskeg Area

Life was not easy in the region between lakes Winnipeg and Manitoba. The low altitude of between 800 and 900 feet created special difficulties. In the whole area, there are few streams to drain water to lakes or the ocean. The only streams are Netley Creek, which flows south-east near Pleasant Home to enter Lake Netley, and Icelandic River, which skirts Arborg to flow into Lake Winnipeg. This condition created a region of forest and muskeg; forests which were not easy to clear and muskegs which were difficult to drain. One of the pioneers of Chatfield area characterized the district as follows in a letter to his relatives:

Dear Brothers and Sisters!

Together with other of our people from Galicia, Bukovyna, and Transcarpathia, I have arrived in Canada. I landed on farms in northern Manitoba where the sun's rays do not penetrate the thick forest and muskegs stretch so far that one can visit neighbours only with great hardship. If I die in this dense forest, even the black raven will not bring news of my death.[8]

Immigrants left Winnipeg to travel by train as far as Teulon, forty miles north of Winnipeg. From Teulon they travelled by ox-team to Chatfield, another forty miles north-east of Teulon, then to Poplar Field, Broad Valley, Fisher Branch, and Hodgson, all of which are approximately eight miles distant from one another.

Experiences of the Pioneers

One pioneer tells this story about such a journey of a group of immigrants travelling in the direction of Chatfield:

Accompanied by their wives and children, they travelled by train to Teulon with all their farming equipment and other supplies. They passed the night in the station. The next morning two Hebrews with their wagons... from the settlement of Colonia[9] agreed to transport our people to their colony thirty miles north of Teulon. As all equipment, supplies, and children could not be accommodated on two wagons, the immigrants hired an additional driver with a wagon.

Immediately after sunrise they set out with the three teams of oxen pulling three wagons on which were piled crates, parcels, and children. They travelled along what was known as the "government road" though officially it bore the name of a colonization road. In reality, it was only a road clearing where a future road might be built.... This road clearing followed higher land but in places it had to cross swamps and mud-holes.... These were crossed by corduroy roads built of logs cut by Ukrainian settlers who had arrived a year or two earlier. The logs which traversed the mud holes were thickly covered with underbrush to give the oxen a surer footing... The owners of the oxen were in a hurry to reach Colonia before nightfall and the oxen plodded steadily at their slow and measured pace. Accompanying the slowly moving transport was the steady hum of clouds of mosquitoes. The mothers wrapped their children in what they could so that the insects ... would not torment them. The men who walked alongside the oxen drove the mosquitoes off the oxen in turn, otherwise the animals would not have been able to pull the freighted wagons.

Very often during such journeys there were unexpected and somewhat terrifying experiences. When the transport reached Colonia, the following took place:

The people of Colonia sheltered them overnight in their barns and outbuildings. The men spread hay on the ground, mothers pressed against their children, and soon everyone was fast asleep worn out by the hardship of the journey. The next morning ... a child uttered a fearful scream. Awakening immediately, the child's mother added to the terror when she saw a snake on her child. All were immediately awakened and anxiously enquired what had happened. The terror-stricken mother, holding the child in her arms, could only dumbly point to the pile of hay on the floor. When one of the men pushed aside the hay, four snakes slithered away... Fortunately there was no danger since the snakes were not of the venomous type which leave their venom in the wound after a bite.[10]

Mykola Shushkevych, who arrived in Canada in 1903 at the age of fourteen with his parents, Andrew and Kateryna Shushkevych, has the following to say about the lives of the settlers during the first year of homesteading in Chatfield:

When we arrived in Chatfield district in 1903, the green forest welcomed us. We were bound for the home of Ivan Vovchuk, my father's friend, who had arrived in Canada a year or two earlier... He already had a small log home with a hay-covered roof. The house resembled a haycock. One fourth of the interior was taken up by the *"pich"* or oven. Six children of our family, including myself, and two of Vovchuk's children, together with our parents, made a total of twelve persons living together. Consequently, the crowding in that one room home was so close that one can only compare it to the overcrowding of some prison cell.

My parents filed on a homestead adjoining that of Vovchuk. People who followed us, travelled further north across our homestead to settle at Hammerlick, Poplar Field, Broad Valley, Fisher Branch and Hodgson. They arrived from every country of Galicia ... Father set about felling trees to clear a space for our house ... When he left to seek work, mother continued to work in the forest, stripping bark from the felled trees which were to be used as logs for the building; she also cleared the willow thickets and underbrush.

Father returned in December and set about building our house. He erected both the walls and constructed the roof with logs, covering the grass with soil. The roof had to be capped with dry grass so that our house, like Vovchuk's, looked like a haycock... Soon after this, father and other neighbours travelled to Teulon where he bought an iron heater... four window panes, two bags of coarse flour with bran, salt, coal oil (kerosene), and wire for snaring rabbits... The heater was stoked both day and night. ... We finally moved into the house.

We had a house but we lacked food. Mother baked flat bannocks on top of the stove while father and I set snares for rabbits. Rabbit soup was not very appetizing but it was filling and we ate rabbit flesh with the bannocks. We survived the first winter in this way.

Other people on homesteads were in worse straits as they had to live in dug-outs for a whole year or even two. The roofs of these shelters were only partly above ground and looked like dog houses.... In the beginning the forest was so dense that travel was very difficult. There were also swamps and muskegs. Mosquitoes swarmed everywhere. In winter snow could lie to a depth of six feet. Frosts were severe; the temperature often sank to fifty degrees below zero. The extreme frost caused trees to crack with the violence of explosive weapons.

He relates further how he went to Arborg at the age of sixteen to clear land for an Icelandic farmer. It was arduous work and the wages were only fifty cents a day. While returning home, he froze his feet. There were no hospitals and the mortality rate among pioneers was very high. He continues:

> I knew many who died in those years. Oleksa Yanisiw buried both his wife Mary and their child on his farm. Dmytro Kowal also dug a grave for his son on his own homestead. Many of our people rest in the forest. Other graves have become overgrown with grass and even poplars have found root in the graves.
>
> In spring father again left home to find work somewhere while mother and I, with shovel and grub-hoe, cultivated half an acre of land for a garden and plastered a *"pich"* in the house. When father returned from work in the fall, he returned to Teulon with a neighbour to purchase provisions. He bought six bags of four-ex flour (coarse flour with bran), 100 pounds of cracked buckwheat, fifty pounds of salt, and two gallons of kerosene. Since we had our own potatoes and other vegetables, life became more enjoyable. Even rabbit soup was more appetizing when it contained vegetables and cracked buckwheat. Father bought a cow and we had our own milk. When our male calf grew older, father bought another, and within two years we had our own ox-team to pull a wagon. In the fourth year we already had our own work cattle.[11]

Their Spiritual Strength

Such hardships during the pioneer period in Canada were probably not experienced by everyone and certainly not everywhere. As the interlake region was covered by forest and muskeg, some of the settlers were allotted land which was definitely unsuitable for cultivation since the quality of the land was not the concern of the surveyors. They surveyed the land in straight lines and, hungry for land, the immigrants took whatever was available. The above accounts portray very faithfully the lives of the first settlers who arrived in Canada without money. On reading them we are amazed at the courage and persistence of these pioneers who, in a sense, assumed the role of the early Spanish Conquistadores. The only difference between the two was that the Spanish Conquistadores purposely burned their vessels on reaching the new world, so that they could not return to their homeland, and built their lives in the new land by plunder and pillage.

On the other hand, the Ukrainians travelled so far by land and ocean that they used up all their financial resources and were penniless. Since they lacked the means to return to their homeland, they built their lives in the new land by patience, co-operation, persistence, and arduous labour. They felled and uprooted trees, dried the muskegs, and converted the wilderness into fertile land which became the basis of our modern farming communities.

Among the Pleasant Home settlers there were leading personalities under whose leadership emerged the beginnings of social life, first with the establishment of schools and then through the organization of churches. The Pleasant Home settlement constituted a cradle of cultural and educational developments from which organized community life was transplanted to neighbouring settlements.

14

Ukrainian Colonies in the Yorkton District

Three Colonies in the Yorkton District

Three separate settlements in Saskatchewan trace their origin from the beginning of mass immigration in 1897—Beaver Hills, Crooked Lakes, and Saltcoats.

Fifty-one families arrived at the end of May 1897 in the Beaver Hills district, approximately thirty-five miles north-west of Yorkton. Yorkton was then the last station on the railroad which ran from Winnipeg through Portage la Prairie, Neepawa, Shoal Lake, Binscarth, and had already been projected to reach present-day Theodore. A few days later, eleven railway cars, loaded with more immigrants from Galicia and Bukovyna, arrived in Yorkton district. Another three railway cars containing eight families from Galicia and twenty-three from Bukovyna stopped at Saltcoats. These families were scheduled for settlement north-east of Saltcoats near present day Calder and Wroxton. The other eight railway cars with 110 families, nearly all from Galicia, continued to Yorkton, from which they were taken about twenty-five miles to the north-east to a district known as Crooked Lakes. The only traces of former lakes here were ravines, gullies, and rocks. The community is now known as Mazepa and it has become a part of Canora district.

Beaver Hills Colony—Insinger, Theodore, and Sheho

The Beaver Hills colony extended over an immense area. When the railway was continued north-west of Yorkton, Theodore, Insinger, and

Settlers from Halychyna —
Burianyk family members.

Mykhailo (left) and
Myroslaw (right) Stechishin,
1906

Family house of Mykola Kucheriavy from the Sheho, Saskatchewan area — 1910

Sheho stations were established along its route. The region north-west of present-day Insinger was occupied first in 1897 by settlers from the county of Borshchiv in Galicia who settled in townships 28, 29, and 30, ranges 8 and 9 West of the Second Meridian.[1] On the same steamship, families from the county of Kitsman, province of Bukovyna (villages of Valova, Pohory-livka, Luky, Boianchuk, and Horoshivtsi) arrived and settled south-east of present-day Insinger.[2] During the years 1898-1902, new groups of immigrants arrived from Galicia and Bukovyna and settled in the Beaver Hills colony. The majority of Galicians were from the county of Borshchiv and settled east of Insinger, where the post office of Theodore was already established. The families from the counties of Kitsman and Chernivtsi, in Bukovyna, occupied lands to the north-west of Insinger, in townships 29 and 30, ranges 9 and 10, where the present village of Sheho was later established.

Having overcome pioneer hardships, the settlers exerted themselves to extend their farming operations, working collectively where possible both in their farming and community activities. The religious influence of centuries awakened in them a yearning for their own church. To allay this nostalgic hunger, immigrants from Galicia erected a tall wooden cross in 1898 on NE24-29-9, West of the Second Meridian. Two years later, they built a small church on the same spot where both Greek Catholic and Greek Orthodox met jointly for religious services. In those days there were no priests in Canada of either faith but relations between members of both faiths remained friendly. Newcomers from Bukovyna built their own church near Budzinsky's on NE9-29-8 at about the same time.

Saltcoats District—Calder, Wroxton, and Stornoway

A large proportion of the immigrants who arrived in Saltcoats were members of the group which caused an uproar in Winnipeg. The colonization agent who was responsible for the allocation of these settlers was Thomas MacNutt. He was elected to the North-West Legislative Assembly in 1902 and was twice elected, in 1905 and 1908, to the Saskatchewan legislature. In 1911 he became a member of the House of Commons in Ottawa and was again re-elected in 1917.[3] MacNutt left a very revealing account of the allocation of this group:

> In the spring of 1897 I received a wire from the Land Department of the Manitoba and North Western Railway re finding suitable land for a large settlement of Central Europeans. I replied that the former big bush country, averaging about twenty-five miles north-east from here, still contained bluffs of useful timber, hay, good soil, with a good many sloughs but much open land, which had been burnt off. A few weeks later several carloads of Galicians and Bukowinans arrived and a request from the Federal Immigration

Commissioner for me to locate them. My first impressions were that they were an impossible class of settlers and I almost refused. However I thought better of it. I noticed, as soon as the train stopped that the women made a rush for the Lake, with bundles of dirty clothes, and started washing vigorously. A dandified Jew interpreter had been sent along; and I found that he did not realize that these people were under the protection of the Union Jack, and was using a whip very freely. Even the big strong men cringed before him and took the lash meekly, although he was a miserable little runt that a good big lad could handle. I cautioned him not to use that whip any more but he said that that was the only way to manage them. I found him striking the women. I kicked him off the platform and wired to Winnipeg to get him recalled, or I was through with the whole business. He left on the next train, and we saw no more of him. I then found a Galician German named Ratgibber from Bereseena, east of Saltcoats, who talked pretty good English, and after making the people comfortable, at the small immigration shed and in some box cars, I took some delegates from their number out to view the land. They were satisfied and we then moved them all out of the shed and cars and put them in tents which were supplied by the government. The railway company sent me an old transit as the survey marks had nearly all disappeared and the various sections and quarters could not be distinguished. With the help of this transit I was able to locate them. There were thirty-two heads of families or single men of homestead age (18), and the party great and small numbered about one hundred and twenty-five all told. I found I had to get the Bukowinans and Galicians in two separate camps as they were not friendly with each other. The Galicians numbered eight families. One lot were Orthodox Greek Catholics and the other Greek Catholics. I am not sure that I have the distinction right, but any way there was some religious difference between them which appeared to cause friction. Probably, there was some obscure racial trouble as well, tracing back to the past history of these people.

The new settlers started in to cut logs and roof poles, I hired some teams, and had these hauled to the place where they intended to build their dwellings. The teams also ploughed tough sods for the roofing. The settlers all had tools for carpenter work, and knew how to use them, so they made window frames and doors. Wells were dug, and other necessary work done. The people had no stoves but they made stoves, chimneys and all out of sub-soil clay. The ovens of these stoves baked first class bread, but their flour was inferior, being of the lowest quality and costing a dollar fifty a bag.

A few had some money, but the majority had none, and some of these were in debt to the wealthier ones for passage money, but all were very industrious and grateful for any assistance rendered them. They had come out in response to the Sifton propaganda and were proud to think they were in possession of a "farma" of their own. They would not settle on the open sections, preferring those which contained some wood and hay, although they had to contend with a good deal of scrub. I cannot say that their cleanliness was equal to their godliness, for they were very religious. They had a "lay reader" and held services on every Sunday and on religious festival days, the latter of which, in honor of various saints, were somewhat numerous. On these occasions they appeared, men and women, in dazzling thick white linen costumes, embroidered and woven, and made by themselves, and without a speck of dirt; on work days they were not so particular by any means. I may say that all the expenses of settling them and feeding them were charged up against their homesteads and I believe I am correct when I say that every cent was subsequently repaid to the Government.

They had some peculiar and some disagreeable customs to a Canadian. One of the latter was hand kissing. I broke them of this habit and also of some of the others, which I will not pause to particularise. I spent six weeks amongst them, and I then came to the conclusion that these people if decently handled and led would make good citizens.[4]

Although a large section of these settlers were among the immigrants who had fallen for the claims of steamship agents that the Empress of Austria would be their protectress and had accordingly arrived in Canada without financial resources, it would appear that there was no special provision for government aid. This may have been so because the group was small and consequently easy to manage. It may also have resulted from the fact that their immediate neighbours, settlers who had arrived much earlier, were not critically disposed toward them, for we do not find any specific reference to their poverty. If a few families were in need of aid, they likely obtained it without much comment and, as MacNutt claims, they repaid their debts to the last cent. This group was also not faced with exceptional difficulties in regard to distance from any railroad, as was the case with other colonies of Ukrainians in Canada. While some had to travel as far as forty miles to a railroad, others had only fifteen miles. This was not unusual for those times since other settlers in the North-West Territories, including English settlers, were often much farther away from any railroad. Furthermore, the problem of distance was solved in a relatively short time by the extension of the railroad from Russell in Manitoba through the heart of the settlement of Canora. The following stations were established along this railway: MacNutt, Calder, Wroxton, and Stornoway.

The Ukrainians in this district were surrounded by other nationalities, particularly by Germans, which prevented much expansion. However, population within the limited space became so densely concentrated with new arrivals of Ukrainians that there were only three families who spoke English in the area.[5]

Furthermore, in spite of the apparent confinement, the colony stretched to the Assiniboine River in the east, the village of MacNutt in the south, and Stornoway in the north-east, bringing it close to the Ukrainian settlement of Crooked Lakes. In the summer of 1902 the General Colonization Agent informed Ottawa that the number of Galician settlers, obviously including those from Bukovyna, had risen to 200 families, and that some of them had fifty acres of wheat in crop. Among other matters he reported:

> The Galician settlers, whenever I have been in a position to come in contact with the Colonies, either in Saskatchewan or other districts in Manitoba or the Territories, are very prosperous, and among our best settlers.[6]

Crooked Lakes—Mazepa, Canora and district

In July 1897 one hundred families, mostly from Galicia, moved northeast of Yorkton into the Crooked Lakes district, now Mazepa, where they had almost limitless space for expansion. Their settlement spread south to the German colony of Rhein, a ten mile belt which separated Mazepa Ukrainians from those at Calder. This belt of German settlers narrowed with the years to such an extent that the two Ukrainian settlements almost combined. At the end of 1898 the population of this area was estimated at 180 families. From the two original Townships 28 and 29 in Range [2], East of the Second Meridian, the homesteaders expanded north to include Township 30, and to the west to include Townships 29 and 30 in Range 4.

The first newcomers gave the name of New Jaroslaw (Yaroslav) to this new district, probably because Section 30, Township 29, Range 3 was occupied by three immigrants from the county of Yaroslav in Galicia. Oleksa Warcholak (Varkholiak), Ivan Chacholak (Ivan Khakholiak), and Roman Slezhyn[7] immigrated to Canada from Carmel, Pennsylvania, at the beginning of August 1897, approximately a month later than the first 110 families.[8] Most of the immigrants were from Borshchiv and Sniatyn counties in Galicia and the counties of Kitsman and Zastavna in Bukovyna. Among them there were educated individuals who were conscious of their heritage.[9] It was their influence which led to the adoption of the name of the Ukrainian hetman, Mazepa, for their district. Their local school was also given the name of Mazepa which probably contributed to the survival of the name until the present day.

The settlement eventually expanded both to the south and the west. When the railroad reached this area from Dauphin, Canora became a station in Township 30 Range 2. It grew into an important centre when another railroad was built to connect it with Yorkton. Crooked Lakes has been forgotten and almost no one remembers it. But it is still remembered by the children of Paul Kyba and those of other early settlers whose land bears traces of the early tortuously-shaped lakes which gave the district its early name.

As the two railroad lines were completed to Canora and continued farther north and west, the settlement expanded in the same directions and eventually grew into the largest Ukrainian colony in the province of

Saskatchewan. Canora was already a centre for the large Ukrainian colony before the First Great War and today the district of Canora comprises the following locations:

a) Along the railroad from Kamsack to Humboldt: Veregin, Mikado, Canora, Tiny, Buchanan, Rama, Invermay, Margo, Kuroki, Kylemore, Wadena, Clair, Quill Lake, Wimmer, and Watson.

b) Along the railroad to the north-east: Amsterdam, Tadmore, Sturgis, Preeceville, Hazel Dell, Okla, Lintlaw, Kelvington, Fosston, and Rose Valley.

c) From Sturgis north: Endeavour, Usherville, Reserve, Hudson Bay.

d) From Reserve west: Weekes, Carragana, Porcupine Plain, and Steen.

e) From Sturgis east: Stenen, Hyas, Norquay, Pelly, and Arran.

The last list of railway stations brings the colony close to the Benito settlement in Manitoba. The railroad south-east of Canora through Donwell and Hamton passes close to Calder, Wroxton, and Stornoway which, in turn, border on the Ukrainian settlements around Roblin in Manitoba.

In addition to these closely-connected railway stations, there are more prominent centres of which a partial list follows: Swan Plain, Arabella, Glen Elder, Danbury, Mitchellview, and north of Quill Lake, Ponass Lake.

During the pioneer period every new group of settlers had to endure hardships; settlers had to begin farming without resources, stock, or implements. But state archives do not record any danger of starvation or any request for help from these immigrants; they managed with what they had. As has been mentioned previously, they did not experience any special difficulty because of remoteness from a railway. Although they were forced to travel twenty-five or thirty-five miles to Yorkton, this compared favorably with distances that the first settlers in Alberta had to travel. Furthermore, the immigrants of this area were exceedingly fortunate because railroads were built soon after they had settled.

Very revealing are the memoirs of pioneer life among the first settlers which have been left by Maria Adamowska, whose parents first settled four miles from Canora. She moved with her husband and parents in 1907 to Hyas where they all had to experience pioneer hardships once more.[10] Her account depicts typical pioneer trials and afflictions common to all early settlers who arrived to establish a new colony or to live on the periphery of an old one. In the latter case, they had the advantage of having their own people as neighbours and did not feel that they were separated from them in a foreign land.

As we have already noted, the Crooked Lakes settlement became the nucleus of the largest Ukrainian colony in Saskatchewan. Within this colony the following rural municipalities are almost totally Ukrainian in origin: Sliding Hills #273, Good Lake #274, and Clayton #333. On the other hand, other municipalities in the same area are not as heavily settled by Ukrainians as happens to be the case in northern Alberta, Dauphin, or Stuartburn. This situation can be explained by the fact that this area was not settled exclusively by new immigrants to Canada; many homesteads were acquired by migrants from Manitoba. A large number of these had filed on homesteads, when they first arrived, not because the land was suitable but because they wished to be close to relatives or friends who had arrived earlier and had generally been able to choose more productive land. Sometimes, even these early arrivals were not successful in their choice of homesteads, not only because their judgement was faulty but because they had made up their minds to file on marginal lands just to be near some old country friend or neighbour. When it finally dawned upon them that they could not achieve success on such homesteads, they sold or even abandoned them, depending on circumstances, and moved to areas where there was more productive land.

As an example we can again quote Stashyn, who was one of the first immigrants to settle in Stuartburn in 1896, on a homestead heavily infested with rocks and boulders. He recalls the following:

> Time passed very quickly and imperceptibly when digging rocks out of the ground. The rocks we piled around the field served as a fence which cattle could not cross. Though we had piled stones, the field did not appear different; stones still protruded everywhere. It is not surprising that we cultivated only nine acres of land in eight years.

Finally, continues the author of this memoir, their dreams were fulfilled, and they had their own house. They plastered the walls and ceiling with clay and witewashed the house throughout. They dug a root cellar under the floor and covered the roof of the house with sod. But there came a heavy rain. His story continues:

> Rain penetrated the sod and soaked the ceiling... The wet clay came down. I hid under the table to protect myself from the mud... Water filled the root cellar under the floor, soaking the walls of the root cellar and causing them to slide down in the excavation. Our floor also began to give way. Mother only wrung her hands while I held on to the table to prevent slipping into the root cellar. Everything in the house became soaked and plastered with clay. The labour of years was destroyed.
> This event hastened our decision to leave the colony. Having heard of better land somewhere in Saskatchewan, we resolved to sell everything; farm,

buildings, garden, and grain. Two farmers paid us four hundred dollars for the property. Soon after this we hauled our cattle and equipment to Emerson, loaded a freight car, and set out for Saskatchewan by rail.[11]

The Stashyn (really Stasyshyn) family did not stop in the Canora district but continued to Melfort. Since the railway ended there, they traded their cattle for horses and travelled by wagon to Bonne Madone, St. Julien, and Rosthern to settle finally near present day Krydor, then known as Redberry Lake. Later they moved again to Albertown, still near Krydor, "by a spruce grove" about forty miles north of Radisson, the nearest railway station. It may be argued that this account hardly belongs here because the family did not settle in Canora district. However, it has been chosen because it accurately describes how many settlers, earlier and later, who did not find suitable land from the beginning, moved freely from Manitoba to new locations in Saskatchewan and even in Alberta. To Saskatchewan came many settlers from Stuartburn, Pleasant Home, and also Dauphin. They arrived not only by individual families like the Stashyns but also as individuals, and even in large groups. For instance, Itonia and northern Prelate communities were initiated by small Ukrainian groups of migrants from Gimli, Manitoba, in 1910.[12]

A second account of such a group re-settlement is to be found in the memoirs of Mykhailo Chorneyko entitled *Lest We Forget*.[13] Chorneyko came to Canada with his parents in 1901 to settle around Ethelbert in Manitoba. In 1907 they discovered that better land was available not far away in Saskatchewan, just beyond Benito. This area had been occupied by Doukhobors but because this group insisted on a communal lifestyle and did not want to live on separate homesteads, the government opened the area for homestead entry by others. At that time Benito was the last station on the railroad which had been extended from Swan River. In the spring of 1908 the railroad was continued beyond Benito, a portion of this extension being completed in November. Seven miles beyond Benito, the railroad station of Arran was established and Pelly, another seven miles further. Arran was established among new settlers who had moved from Ethelbert and is thus linked with the settlement of Ukrainians in the Dauphin district.

Obviously, the phenomenon of re-settlement was not confined to the Canora area. There were similar re-settlements in Alberta and Manitoba. The phenomenon of re-settlement takes place whenever people are free to move to seek a better destiny.

Returning to the fifty-one families who settled in Beaver Hills, the colony continued to develop and expand but the rate of expansion was slower than that of the Crooked Lakes district. When Dominion Colonization Agent Speers wrote his report for 1898, the three Yorkton colonies had a population of 275 families,[14] of which 180 were in Crooked Lakes and 45 in

Calder. It would appear that few additional settlers came to the Beaver Hills area at the end of 1898. It is quite possible that immigrants would not settle here at first because of its distance from Yorkton. Homesteads nearer Yorkton had been settled by Anglo-Saxons and others. Expansion of this colony was therefore possible only to the north-west along the proposed, but not yet constructed, railroad—both to the north and south of the proposed route. This was indeed quite a distance from Yorkton.[15]

In time, this colony also spread and the land surrounding the present settlements of Theodore, Insinger, and Sheho was completely occupied. In the south, the colony extended to Parkerview and in a southerly direction from Foam Lake in the west to include West Bend, Bank End, and Wishart.

The expansion of this colony can be attributed to the fact that the original settlers were joined year after year by relatives and fellow villagers so that the area became densely settled by Ukrainians. So concentrated was this population that when a rural municipality was organized later, a majority were Ukrainians. As this municipality is adjacent to Sliding Hills, of which Crooked Lakes is the very centre, it follows that the two colonies have effected a junction with each other though they were once very far removed from one another.

A group of parishioners with Father Kolisnyk in Sheho (South) —1911

Pioneer Teachers from the Canora area of Saskatchewan — 1913

Kolomyia School — St. Julian, Saskatchewan.

15

North-Central Saskatchewan—
Ukrainian Colonies in
the Fish Creek District

Fish Creek Settlement Is Established Against the Wishes of Its Settlers

The number of Ukrainian immigrants increased rapidly with every year. In 1898 the arrival of thousands on a number of transports created problems in locating new settlers on homesteads. It was of no benefit to settlers nor did it meet with government policy to send all new settlers to already existing Ukrainian colonies. It was of no advantage to the immigrants because more productive land near railways had already been occupied. They would either have to settle on marginal land or move to the periphery of existing settlements far removed from any railroad. This was especially true of the Edna territory. It was also objectionable to the government, whose policy it was to avoid too great a concentration of settlers from any one nationality. Especially had this been true with respect to immigrants from Galicia.[1] Although group settlements of one ethnic group had been permitted, if circumstances warranted such action, officials generally attempted to commingle these new arrivals with settlements of Anglo-Saxons, Germans, French, Icelanders, Swedes, Norwegians, Hungarians, or others who were also arriving in Canada in large numbers. Furthermore, the government strove to avoid concentrating settlers in one area and attempted to establish colonies over broad expanses of western Canada wherever there was suitable land for settlement. In furthering this aim, it was government policy to initiate new settlements wherever possible.

The establishment of new areas created certain difficulties and aroused dissatisfaction among immigrants. Ukrainians as a group had more justification than others in objecting to initiating new colonies because of their ignorance of the English language, which made separation from their own kind doubly painful. Accordingly, Ukrainians generally requested that colonization agents allocate them in areas where earlier Ukrainian settlers had already taken up homesteads. This was particularly true of immigrants who already had relatives or friends in Canada and knew where they lived. When the immigration authorities paid no attention to the desires of the immigrants, it often resulted in misunderstandings and unpleasant consequences, as happened in Winnipeg in 1897 when the authorities attempted to force immigrants to initiate settlements in the Yorkton colony in present-day Saskatchewan.

As an example of such disaffection, we will report events which took place with a group of about sixty families of immigrants who left Winnipeg about the middle of May 1898. They understood that they were travelling to Edmonton but the colonization agents were actually transporting them to establish a new colony at Fish Creek near Saskatoon. They reached Saskatoon on May 16. One of the immigrants was aware that Saskatoon was not on the way to Edmonton and guessed that they were being transported elsewhere.[2] When the whole group learned that their destination was Rosthern, where they were to locate homesteads in some unheard of place called Fish Creek, ten to fifteen miles east of Rosthern, they immediately staged a protest. Quite justifiably, they resented the deception; without their knowledge or consent, they were being conveyed to an area to which they had not planned to travel. They refused to leave for Fish Creek and would not board the train.

According to the report of Dominion Colonization Agent Speers in a telegram to the Superintendent of Immigration on May 17, seventy-five men left their families in Saskatoon and set out for Regina on foot, resolving to reach Edmonton. They obstinately persisted in their resolve and threatened to kill the interpreter if they were hindered in any way. Speers reported further that he had never faced such determined resistance and that the situation was out of control. Two days later he informed the Commissioner of Immigration, McCreary, that police had stopped the walking immigrants about thirteen miles out of Saskatoon but he could not convince them to agree to his proposals. He requested that interpreters Genik and Harvey be sent to assist him.

Before the police were able to turn back the angry marchers and even before Genik and Harvey appeared on the scene, Speers had already succeeded in establishing a small colony of twelve families at Fish Creek with some of the immigrants. They had agreed to travel to Rosthern, had surveyed the district, located suitable land, and resolved to settle there. They filed homesteads in Township 41, Range 1, West of the Third Meridian, where Alvena is now located. Among these first settlers were Nykola

Lucyszyn (Lutsyshyn), Franko Rozdolka, Yasko Validuda, Hnat Ganczar (Ganchar), Wasyl Tomyn, Stepan Vawryk, and three Mychalkiws (Mykhalkiws)—Macko (Matsko), Yasko, and Antin.[3]

Accompanied by Commissioner of Immigration McCreary, Genik and Harvey arrived in Saskatoon and Rosthern on May 21. They surveyed the area to satisfy themselves about its suitability for settlement and tried to convince the resentful immigrants that the land was productive and that prospects were bright for settlement. But they would not be persuaded. Thirty families with a total population of 112 left for Edmonton and another seventeen families with a population of sixty-four departed for Sifton in the Dauphin district.[4]

This "revolt" was reported in the Toronto *Globe* on May 21, 1898. The news item reported that trouble with the immigrants arose partially because the officials were conveying them to locations where they did not wish to settle and partially because the immigrant leaders were inclined to fractious behaviour.

Another Group Refuses to Settle because of an Early Frost

No matter what did take place, the officials succeeded in laying the foundations of a new colony, and those who remained were content. A month later Speers conveyed another group of twenty-one families to the same location. After arriving in Duck Lake, they travelled to the site where a government tent had been set up, encamped there, and prepared to seek homesteads in this timbered area. Unfortunately, during the two nights of June 11 and 12, there was an abnormally heavy frost. It coated water with ice to a depth of three-quarters of an inch while foliage on trees and in gardens turned black. In reporting to the Deputy Minister of the Interior, Commissioner McCreary disclosed that the frost was of such unexpected severity that hoar-frost could be gathered by hand like snow. Having arisen in the morning, the immigrants, without discussion or agitation of any kind, prepared to continue their journey. Thirty-five of them set out for Duck Lake to board the train for Regina and thus continue to Edmonton. They concluded that Fish Creek was no place for them to settle.

The officials were again alarmed and attempted to persuade the immigrants that the frost was unusual and brought in former settlers, especially Mennonites, who had been in the area since 1892 and had some experience with weather in this area. All tried to assure the newcomers that such frosts in June had been unknown but the immigrants would not even listen. Finally, Speers arrived from Winnipeg in the company of Father Dmytriw. Assembling the group in the Roman Catholic church in Duck Lake, Father Dmytriw addressed them and tried to persuade them to remain at Fish Creek but also had no success. The immigrants even accused him of being a government informer.[5]

For ten days the officials strove to convince them to file on homesteads but the effort was hopeless, as the immigrants paid no attention to them. However, when they tried to board the train, policemen would not permit them to do so. Finally, Speers, who was unusually understanding and patient, became determined to resort to force in settling the immigrants in this area. On June 22 he advised Commissioner McCreary that he would make one more attempt to persuade them to file on homesteads. If they refused, he reported that he would pull down the tent, deprive them of provisions, and show them in which building they could file on homesteads. They could then act as they wished.

It was not known whether the tents were taken away but the immigrants were deprived of provisions because Speers again reported that they resorted to picking mushrooms to sustain themselves and still refused to settle. Not until the end of June did he inform the Commissioner that twenty-five families had settled on the east side of the Saskatchewan River in Township 41, Range 1, among those who had been settled earlier. Others had settled on the west side of the river in Townships 41 and 42, Range 2, in spite of the very sandy soil in that district.

Although the establishment of the colony was achieved by subterfuge and even some force, it must be admitted that the immigration officials had the future welfare of the newcomers in mind. This colony, especially on the east side, is much more productive than either Stuartburn or Pleasant Home. It is true that this region also had forests and muskegs but these were nowhere as extensive as those in the inter-lake region. Furthermore, there were broad areas covered only with brush which could be cultivated with much less hardship. Those who arrived later in the year, in July and August, settled here wittingly and were grateful they had chanced on such fertile land.[6]

The Colony Grows in Size and Population

Five months after the inception of the colony, Speers again paid it a visit and, as a consequence, reported the names of families who had settled there. In present-day Alvena, east of the river, there were thirty-one families. West of the river nearer Rosthern, there were thirty-two.[7] Moreover, he made an inventory of the possessions of each family and concluded that these people had made more progress in a short time than those in other colonies. Nearly every family owned a cow and almost all of those settled near Alvena had a horse each. Six families possessed a team of horses each. It is also interesting to learn that every member of the Rosthern group, who had less forest land, had prepared one or more acres of land for seeding. Three of them had broken ten acres each while three others had twelve, fifteen, and twenty acres respectively. The Alvena group, with much more forest land, had much less land cultivated.[8]

Fish Creek colony, like other settlements, grew rapidly; it expanded in size and became densely settled. In February 1901 the number of settlers from Galicia reached 1000.[9] But it was impossible for this colony to increase in area to any great extent since large tracts, even before the arrival of Ukrainians, had already been settled by members of other national groups —Mennonites, Germans, French, and Hungarians. Only between ten and twelve townships remained for the Ukrainian immigrants, and these were quickly occupied as Rosthern was a very convenient centre in comparison to others in those times. Rosthern was a shorter distance away from this colony in 1907 than Yorkton from its three colonies, Grenfell from the settlers at Goodeve, Teulon from the colonies at Pleasant Home, or Dominion City from Stuartburn.

With so convenient a centre, Ukrainians continued to arrive in large numbers. In 1899 the following settled: Stephan Kindrachuk with his sons, Mis, Fedko, Dmytro, and Ivan; Nykola and Wasyl Budzhak; Mis Kotelko with his son Yurko; Hryts Pihach; Andrii Bambukh; Dmytro Romanchych; Petro Konovalyk; Karl Navalkowsky with his son Yakiv, Yurko Romanko and others. A year later there followed Ivan Mykhailiuk with his sons, Wasyl, Yurko, Petro, Les, and Ivan; Semen Mykhailiuk, W. Protsiuk, and others. Later arrivals were Les Bodnarchuk and his son Andrii, Ilia Boitsun, Petro Shvydky and others. These were the principal heads of families with children.

The Beginning of New Settlements—Sokal, Wakaw, Bonne Madone and Other Communities

Early in 1901 Speers informed his superiors that some immigrants from Galicia were already squatting without permission in four townships and recommended that these be opened for homestead entry. With the arrival of new immigrants, Fish Creek colony expanded to the east beyond present-day Cudworth and likewise to the south where Laniwtsi was established by newcomers from the village of the same name in the county of Borshchiv. Settlers were also moving north beyond St. Julien. A transport of immigrants in 1902 established the colony of Sokal[10] in Township 43, Range 2. The majority of these arrivals were from the county of Sokal in Galicia but there were also others from the counties of Radekhiv, Borshchiv, and Horodenka.

In a short time the whole territory was populated—east of the river to

Wakaw and Cudworth, south to Laniwtsi, and north to Sokal. Later immigrants who had hoped to settle among their own people had to seek
homesteads still farther away. Many of those who had settled on marginal
lands earlier also joined the search for more productive farms. As a result, a
number of families, who arrived in Rosthern in 1900 and were unable to
locate suitable land at Fish Creek, travelled beyond the Hungarian colony
bordering on present day Wakaw and settled in Bonne Madone district.[11] In
this way originated a new settlement occupying six townships which include
the population centres of Bonne Madone, Reynaud, Tway, Tarnopol,
Crystal Springs, and Yellow Creek. In 1901 twelve families from the province of Bukovyna also crossed the Hungarian colony to settle on both sides
of Lake Wakaw, then known as Crooked Lake.[12] Their settlement linked
the earlier colony of Fish Creek with the newer one of Bonne Madone.

Almost simultaneously, the Fish Creek settlement expanded to the
south where Ukrainian settlers journeyed beyond Vonda and Prud'homme,
inhabited by the French, to file on homesteads at St. Denis, present day
Dana, and still farther south to Meacham.[13]

Colonies "Beyond the Doukhobors"—Krydor, Redberry, Hafford, and Whitkow

Nevertheless, Bonne Madone, Tway, Tarnopol, St. Denis, Dana, and
Meacham were still limited in the number of immigrants that could be accommodated. Together with a number who were dissatisfied with their lot
in Fish Creek, newcomers had to seek land farther away. Good productive
lands, available for homesteading, were to be found "beyond the Doukhobors", according to an expression common among Ukrainians in that area
at that time. The Doukhobors had settled twenty-five miles straight west of
Rosthern, across the Saskatchewan River.[14] Beyond the Doukhobors,
roughly north and north-west of the Saskatchewan River, there was indeed
a vast unpopulated tract extending to Albertown and Lorenzo, which the
Ukrainians knew as "timber" country. New immigrants began to pour into
this country. The first to reach this area, near present day Krydor, arrived in
the spring of 1903 to settle east of Redberry Lake in Township 42, Range 8,
East of the Third Meridian. They were newcomers from the county of Sokal
and included Antin Melnychuk, Dionisy and Wasyl Didych, and Petro and
Tomash Kotelmakh.[15]

Ivan Hawrysh, son of Hryhory Hawrysh, having arrived in Canada in
1903, recalls that his parents came to Canada a year later (1904) and that all
of them settled three miles south of present day Dana, then in the postal
district of Leofeldt. As their homesteads were unsatisfactory, they set out
all together in 1905 for Fish Creek, where Les Hawrysh lived. All of them,

including Hryhor, Ivan, Les Hawrysh and his son Petro then set out for the Redberry Lake district where they filed on homesteads on the south side of the lake. Ivan Hawrysh recalls further that four families had preceded them to this area, Ivan Pridverbetsky, Stepan Nykiforuk, Stepan Dyrbawka, and Yasko Yaremovych. But the earlier settlers were no strangers to them, for they had travelled to Canada in the company of Hryhor Hawrysh in 1904 but he had settled at Redberry Lake from the beginning. Ivan Hawrysh also adds that there were three families further east who had arrived in 1903:[16] Wasyl Pesklevits, Petro Kinash, and Tymniak.

These small groups of settlers soon attracted others, both new immigrants and also migrants from other areas.[17] A number of newcomers from the county of Sokal began in 1905 to occupy homesteads in a compact mass in Townships 42, 43, and 44, Range 8, West of the Third Meridian.[18] Their numbers increased every year. In addition, grown-up sons from many families filed on homesteads for themselves, established residence, and thus expanded the settlement.

The New Railway from Dauphin to Edmonton Aids in the Development of the Colony

In 1905 rapid growth was stimulated by the building of the new railway from Dauphin to the west through Humboldt, North Battleford, Vegreville, and Edmonton. Rosthern then ceased to be a leading railway centre for Ukrainian settlers in this territory as new stations were established on the southern border of this colony. These stations included Dana, previously the post office of Leofeldt; Howell, which became Prud'homme; Vonda and Aberdeen. Vonda became an important gateway for the settlers of Alvena. Further west beyond Saskatoon there also were established the stations of Borden and Radisson. The village of Radisson soon became a convenient trading centre for farmers settled on the south and west side of Redberry Lake.

The new railway not only facilitated travel for new arrivals to Canada but it also paved the way for re-settlement by earlier homesteaders from Fish Creek, Dana, and even parts of Manitoba. As a consequence of the railway reaching Radisson, the Redberry colony was quickly filled to overflowing so that some of the homesteaders, becoming disenchanted with their first choice of land in this district, became ready to explore other areas for re-settlement. A new district was opened for homesteading north-west of present-day Redfield, where a few Ukrainian families moved into Townships 42 to 45, Ranges 9 to 13, West of the Third Meridian. Beginning with the first settlers in 1907, the number of families increased in a short time and established the Ukrainian settlement of Whitkow.[19] The inhabitants of Whitkow district were predominantly from the counties of Horodenka, Borshchiv, Zalishchyky, and Sokal. The name of the settlement came from the name of the village in the county of Sokal from which many had emigrated. As the number of settlers increased, the colony expanded to the north to include Square Hill, Mullingar, and Rabbit Lake.

With the building of a railway from Prince Albert to North Battleford in 1912 along the north side of Redberry Lake and the establishment of the stations of Krydor, Hafford, Speers, and Richard, population in the Redberry Lake colony increased further. Hafford soon became a new centre for the Ukrainians in the district, and Krydor, with its more literate element, also played an important part in its cultural activities. People settled to the north of Hafford, where the rural post office of Albertown was first established, to be followed later by another settlement which was given the name of Alticane.[20]

As an illustration of how many districts developed, we can cite Redberry Municipal District #435 which was organized in 1908. It consisted of twelve townships and, according to the 1941 census, it then had a population of 3330, of which 2342 were of Ukrainian background.

But the early settlement of Fish Creek did not remain far behind. Organized somewhat later than the Redberry Lake Municipal District, it also had twelve townships. According to the 1941 census, this district had a population of 2601, of whom 2045 were Ukrainians, 291 were Poles, and the rest belonged to a variety of other national backgrounds. It is interesting to note that there were already French and Hungarian settlers in this district when Ukrainians first arrived. However, Ukrainians soon outnumbered the others and comprised eighty percent of the population in the 1941 census.

Such was the role played by these early settlers of the Fish Creek region. It was different from others in that it did not keep on expanding like Edna (Star), Stuartburn, Dauphin, Pleasant Home, or the three colonies around Yorkton. Nor did it disappear like Pheasant Forks. It grew by leapfrogging over Doukhobor, Hungarian, and German colonies to create a new, almost independent settlement around Hafford.

16

Manitoba, South of the Riding Mountains—Strathclair, Shoal Lake, and Oakburn

The Last Major Ukrainian Colony

The last large settlement arising out of mass immigration of Ukrainians was in Manitoba, in colonies known in the beginning as Strathclair and Shoal Lake. In reality, these names were used only because they happened to be stations on the railway which ran from Portage la Prairie through Neepawa and Minnedosa to Yorkton.[1] Ukrainian immigrants arrived at the two stations by train before they travelled farther north by wagon beyond a small English-speaking settlement called Oakburn. In 1906, when this district had a large Ukrainian population, another railway was built through this area with the stations of Sandy Lake, Elphinstone, Oakburn, Rossburn, and others. As Oakburn became the centre of this Ukrainian settlement after the building of the railway, the name of Oakburn began to be used in referring to the colony.

It is considered to be the last Ukrainian colony to be established because it had its origin in 1899, which is later than that of other colonies. Pheasant Forks and Edna were established in 1893 and 1894 respectively; Stuartburn and Terebowlia followed in 1896; Pleasant Home and the three Yorkton colonies were located in 1897, and Fish Creek was first settled in 1898. No other mass settlements were initiated in new locations after the Oakburn colony. Ukrainian immigrants who arrived after 1899 were apportioned to augment settlements already established or were settled on the periphery of such settlements where they served to extend their boundaries.

Toward the end of February in 1899, thirty-two immigrants arrived from Galicia, and two shiploads followed very closely upon each other at the end of April to bring 1116 additional newcomers from the same province.[2] But this was only a beginning as others were to follow later. However, the Canadian authorities were not caught unprepared as they had experienced the arrival of 10,000 immigrants from Galicia and Bukovyna during the past two years and information from Oleskiw indicated that there would be no decrease in numbers during 1899. The Canadian immigration authorities began to search for a new unpopulated region early in the new year and had selected a location on the south side of the Riding Mountain National Park, north of Strathclair and Shoal Lake.

On disembarkation, the immigrants were transported west. Quartering one group in Selkirk and another in Winnipeg, Colonization Agent Speers set out to survey this new district in the company of Ivan Bodrug, who acted as interpreter, and four delegates chosen by the immigrants. The delegates concluded that the land was satisfactory and returned to their respective groups in Selkirk and Winnipeg to recommend settlement in the district. Before they left, Speers took the precaution of having the delegates sign a statement that they had inspected the four townships: Range 19, Townships 21, 22, 23, and Range 20, Township 23, and had found the land satisfactory. They were especially attracted to the two townships north of present-day Oakburn, where Olha was the name given to the settlement in later years. In taking this precaution, Speers acted as if he had some premonition of future trouble.[3]

Although the soil conditions were satisfactory to the delegates, the immigrants manifested no desire to establish a new settlement. They preferred to join already established settlers who were relatives, former neighbours, or just acquaintances. Even if none of these were available, they still preferred to be among or not too far removed from their countrymen. To induce the immigrants to settle this new area, immigration officials had to advance various arguments in favor of a new settlement. They claimed that all land in the established colonies was occupied and that no land was available for homestead entry in those colonies. They also asserted that heavy rains had made the roads impassable and it would take a long time before they would be suitable for travel again in those areas. As some of the immigrants had been on the road for six weeks and all were exhausted from travel, they finally agreed on the establishment of the new colony.

The Long Anticipated Departure Meets with Tragedy

On May 8 sixty families in four railway coaches left Selkirk for Winnipeg, where they were joined by twenty families located in the Dufferin School building.[4] As railway coaches were to be prepared to leave Winnipeg between seven and eight that evening, the immigrants left the school very early to be at the station on time. Unfortunately, for some unexplained reason, the coaches were not delivered until very late that night or early next morning. A large number of the passengers with their small children and baggage had to spend a cold night under the open sky because the station was small and could not have accommodated all the people even if it had been kept open. After this delay, two coaches were attached to a train and eighty Ukrainian families, consisting of about four hundred people, left for Strathclair.

To the colonization agents it appeared that this new colony would be established without any difficulty and without any great financial outlay. They were always urged to avoid any excessive expenditure by their superior officers. Of most importance was the fact that the consent of the group for establishing a new colony had been obtained, something which had been a problem with other groups. But they were soon doomed to disappointment. Two children died en route to Portage la Prairie. On the way to Minnedosa, two more died and two others became ill.

On reaching Strathclair in the morning of May 10, the passengers alighted from the train and were taken to two vacant barns which Speers had rented in advance to serve as a temporary immigration hall for the newcomers. He considered that these buildings would be more comfortable than the usual immigration tents. The immigrants were originally expected to remain in the tents for two or three weeks while looking for homesteads and otherwise preparing for settlement. However, even these buildings were not suitable for living quarters as they were unheated and sick people must have warmth.

As soon as he settled the immigrants, Speers summoned the local physician, Dr. Sinclair, who confirmed that there was an epidemic of an infectious disease among the newcomers, probably measles or scarlet fever. Speers informed the Commissioner of Immigration about the tragic situation and the latter immediately dispatched Dr. Patterson of the Provincial Board of Health for a more informed assessment of the situation. It was revealed that the scarlet fever epidemic had erupted suddenly among immigrants in Winnipeg but a cursory inspection of those departing for Shoal Lake had not detected the presence of the disease in this group. It was concluded that the children had been infected while in Winnipeg and that the disease had progressed more rapidly because the people had been waiting for the two additional coaches during the cold May night, when the children needed warmth and medical attention.

As could be expected, the immigrants' resistance to the disease had been weakened because they had been disturbed and alarmed by their departure from their homeland into an unknown world. They were exhausted by the long train journey to the ocean, by their ocean voyage in the bowels of the ship, and by travelling in uncomfortable coaches across Canada. Under these circumstances, sanitary conditions were not always the best. Moreover, resistance to disease had been lowered in children and infants much more than in adults. During the long journey, children were never left in the sun or fresh air which might have hardened them to a degree, enabling them to withstand the trials of the journey.

Once the disease made its appearance, it found favorable conditions for developing rapidly. In one of his reports, Dr. Sinclair related that many a child who appeared healthy and played with other children died two hours later. It is therefore not surprising that the two children who had become ill before their departure to Strathclair died immediately upon arriving there while many others became ill and died in the next three days.

The doctor and the immigration authorities immediately took measures to prevent the disease from spreading, particularly among the local inhabitants. They separated those who were really ill from those who were only suspected of illness. Others were isolated. On the demand of the local population, the able-bodied were transported closer to the location of the proposed settlement on Township 19, Range 23, bordering on Lake Patterson, twenty-six miles north-west of Strathclair. Dr. Patterson, who arranged the transportation of the group to Lake Patterson, returned to Winnipeg, leaving the patients in the care of local physician.[5]

Ten families, consisting of about fifty persons, abandoned the main body to travel to Saskatchewan on their own, while the remainder prepared for the journey to the proposed settlement. The officials obtained tents for the immigrants and themselves, as well as wagons for transportation. After burying twelve child corpses along the railway between Strathclair and Shoal Lake, they set out in a long train consisting of 250 immigrants with fourteen wagons.[6] Obviously, all immigrants could not be accommodated on the wagons, and the men had to walk. This is confirmed by official statements.

They set out on a bright sunny morning on Saturday, May 13. Although the mothers of the buried children were weeping and many of the rest had feelings of foreboding in regard to the fate of their children, others comforted themselves with the thought that their long burdensome journey would soon be over and that they would soon find rest in their own shelter. But they were not destined to be happy for long. That afternoon, clouds gathered and it began to rain. Toward evening it turned cold and the rain turned into snow. This kind of weather accompanied them for the rest of the journey. There was virtually no road, only an overgrown trail, and they had to cross muskegs and creeks; in places they even had to clear trees from the trail. As a result, the wagon train did not reach its destination until midnight; all were tired and soaked to the skin.

Although the immigrants were wet and cold, the setting up of tents required further delay during which the immigrants had to wait. Even after the tents were set up, it was impossible to make their beds as the ground was wet. Furthermore, all of them had to dry their garments and the bed clothes with which they had tried to protect themselves from the rain. To the immigrants, even the barns with their dry hay now appeared luxurious in contrast to their damp and soggy surroundings in the tent.

The spectre of infectious disease still threatened the new settlers. Although records reveal that the authorities were successful in isolating those afflicted with the disease so that the local inhabitants did not suffer, the epidemic exploded with new virulence among the immigrants in their new surroundings, and death continued to claim its victims. On the basis of reports from witnesses of this tragic occurrence, Marunchak writes as follows:

> Nevertheless, the epidemic did not slacken among the children. Late in the evening of the same day, May 14, Antin and Anna Kalyshyn lost their only child, a five-year-old boy.... On the same day Mykola and Ksenia Maidaniuk lost one boy and another the day after. Two children of Mykhailo and Teklia Shvaliuk died soon after ... Kaska and Hrynko Berehulka ... also lost two sons. Two small daughters of Hrynko and Teklia Glushka died.... Andrii and Hanka Voichyshyn lost a small son, and three children of Mykhailo and Anna Holovetsky perished. One died in Strathclair and two in the tent.[7] Zakhary and Anna Dzhumag also lost three children ... All cannot be recalled after sixty-five years. Only the names of friends and fellow-villagers can be remembered; the rest have been effaced from memory. Adults were also afflicted but the harvest of death was not as vengeful among them as among children. During this period the wives of Wasyl Ivanyshyn and Stakh Trach died, as well as an older individual, Voitsikhowsky, according to Mrs. Shvaliuk's information. A large number of children but only a few adults died at this time. Danylo Topolnitsky from the village of Konstantsia in the county of Borshchiv, an Oakburn pioneer who survived this ordeal of death as a fifteen-year-old boy and who reached the age of eighty in 1964, remembers clearly how he with three others of the same age, Filko Kotyk, Ivan Shvaliuk, and Roman Hrynkiv carried the corpses of children daily to the graveyard set up near the camp. Their funeral litter was a stretcher made of cloth attached to two poles. With these they carried the bodies of children from the camp to the graveyard in which the number of burial mounds increased daily.[8]

The local inhabitants kept a watchful eye on proceedings in the immigrant camp, obtaining reports on the group in barns near Strathclair as well as those in the tents. Quite justifiably, they wanted to protect themselves against the epidemic. They demanded that the already quarantined and isolated immigrants be removed somewhere—to the forest or the steppe—they did not care where. Speers acknowledges that he evacuated the barns to accommodate the immigrants in a lumber camp, obviously in the forest.[9] At this point, even the Indians from the Okenesis Reserve, north of present-day Elphinstone, entered the picture by deciding to close roads on both sides of the Minnedosa River to prevent the epidemic from spreading in their direction.[10]

For almost two weeks the weather continued cold, wet, and miserable. After that period there was a change for the better, and the number of deaths decreased. Colonization Commissioner McCreary also provided additional medical services by appointing Dr. Cameron to superintend the colony. Dr. Cameron immediately ordered additional tents to separate those who were ill or suspected of illness from those who were still well. He further provided a stove heater for each tent and also bought cows to provide milk for the invalids.[11]

In spite of these precautions, death among the children continued. When Speers visited the colony on May 31, he reported that twenty children had died in the period before the preceding Sunday. Ten days later, he admitted that twenty-six had already died. On that number the government statistics cease, but the reports of settlers who were witnesses to these events reveal that forty-two persons died before the epidemic was controlled. The victims were generally children below seven years of age.[12] It should be understood that the number quoted above did not include the twelve children who died before the immigrants were sheltered in tents.

The Story of the Burial Ground

As mentioned previously, the dead were buried on crown land in the area close to the tent. At that time no one knew who would be the proprietor of the homestead and its burial ground. On every grave relatives erected a temporary wooden cross and the cluster of crosses served to identify the area as a cemetery. Immediately after these tragic events, the settlers scattered to occupy neighbouring homesteads and all their efforts were directed to their daily needs. They erected buildings and cultivated what land they could for vegetables and grain. As a result, the burial ground, a memorial of their tragic pioneer hardships, gradually became only a faint memory. With the passage of years, the farm with its burial ground passed into the hands of an English pioneer who pastured his cattle along Patterson Lake. The crosses on the graves wasted away and were successively broken so that no traces of the graves remained. The next owner of the farm,[13] unaware of the burial plots, cleared the underbrush on his farm and ploughed not only the cleared land but also the burial ground. When he discovered the existence of the graves, he built a fence around them to separate the burial ground from his farmland.

During the 1920s, many years later, relatives of the dead congregated at this spot to raise one large burial mound on which they erected a large wooden cross. When Ukrainian Canadians were celebrating the fiftieth anniversary of their settlement in Canada in 1941, the relatives once more, together with many visitors and other attentive onlookers, erected a permanent monument in place of the cross with the following inscriptions in English and Ukrainian:

"JUBILEE OF UKRAINIAN SETTLEMENT IN CANADA, 1891-1941"

„ЮВІЛЕЙ НАШОГО ПОСЕЛЕННЯ У КАНАДІ"

On the reverse side of the monument there is another inscription in Ukrainian:

„ТУТ СПОЧИВАЄ 42-ОХ ПІОНЕРІВ. В.Ї.П."

(Here Rest Forty-Two Pioneers; Everlasting Be Their Memory.)[14]

Hardships Fail to Overwhelm the Settlers

The scarlet fever epidemic was a terrible blow to the settlers and also a setback for the government, for whom it was an unexpected and distressing experience. Although all precautions had been taken to establish this colony in the cheapest and most practicable way, all prearrangements had proved useless. Not only did the officials have to abandon the barn shelters to erect a tent, but the necessity for isolation because of the epidemic had demanded more tents, more medical services, and wagons became indispensable for transportation. In spite of the efforts of the officials, expenditures had increased and the establishment of the colony proved more costly than anyone had anticipated. Furthermore, the whole experience had aroused opposition. The government was criticized for bringing in such immigrants as future citizens of this country. Unfortunately for the Ukrainian immigrants, they were in no condition to create a better impression in the minds of the Canadian public of that period.

To the immigrants, the loss of their children was heart-breaking; the parents, and especially the mothers, mourned their loss very bitterly. Many of the mothers lamented the hour in which they agreed to leave their native land to journey to Canada which, even in the beginning, demanded such great and painful sacrifices. Though their native land was poor, it had still provided some security. Almost as great a shock was the attitude of the local inhabitants. They had turned against the newcomers, although they had rejoiced only two months previously about the arrival of the new settlers as they felt that their district would cease to be a wilderness.

However, life went on. The tragic circumstances which accompanied the first settlers[15] did not prevent others from arriving.[16] At the end of May, when officials and medical officers were still struggling with the epidemic, fifty families arrived to settle west of the first encampment. Others settled in the east near Elphinstone. Speers believed that there were productive lands in the area suitable for settlement and stubbornly persisted in carrying out his colonization plan. On June 10 he reported that there were already 160 families settled in the colony and, at the beginning of 1900, he estimated that there was a population of about 1000. He reported further that many of the late arrivals in 1899 had worked on the railway and had earned enough money to live through the winter. He even produced a letter from the railway roadmaster, Robert Waters, who confirmed that about 300 Ukrainians had worked on the railway, that they were good workers, and that some had earned as much as thirty dollars a month. The letter ends as follows:

> They are improving all the time. I would not want better men... Since getting the Galicians I have had no trouble.[17]

Even the Indians, who had protested against the settlers in the beginning, now became more friendly and claimed that these settlers were very industrious and good neighbours. They were also happy that the newcomers cleared out dry trees from the forest and thus minimized danger from fire.[18]

When he visited the colony a year later, Speers reported that still more settlers had arrived in 1900 and that the population was then about 1200.[19] He added further that the settlers had earned enough money to pass the winter and that a storekeeper had informed him that the settlers had purchased 1200 bags of flour, 400 bags of cornmeal, a large quantity of clothes, and other items. They had paid cash for everything. Other merchants also spoke highly of these people. Only one Episcopalian clergyman was opposed to the immigration policy. Speers also mentioned another curious fact. He disclosed that only four families out of a population of between 1100 and 1200 would need state assistance and added, "I am convinced that a larger percentage of needy people can be found among other nationalities."[20]

A year later, on December 18, 1901, Speers sent another report. In his letter he provided the information that the population of the colony had reached 2000 and that every settler now had four or five cows and at least one horse. Furthermore, people had their own mowers, rakes, and wagons. He ended his report by stating that the colony did not need any more settlers since almost all the available land had been occupied. Land which still remained would soon be occupied by young people from among the settlers.[21]

It is clear that Speers paid regular visits to colonies which he had established with immigrants from Galicia because he returned to this colony again in 1903. Following this visit, he noted that the population of the colony had risen to 3000 and that the settlement had now expanded west to Russell and east to Newdale, stretching for a distance of fifty miles. He appeared quite satisfied with the progress of the settlement in the past four years. The domestic animal population of the colony consisted of about 4000 cattle, close to 1000 horses, plenty of hogs, and also poultry (chickens, geese, and ducks). The settlers had also improved their buildings and many had purchased C.P.R. land. His report ends with the following:

> They are very progressive; and, although they commenced life a few years ago poor, they are now very comfortable, and soon will be well fixed. This is seemingly characteristic of the Galician settlers, who are among our very most progressive.[22]

The Growth of the Colony

As already noted by Speers, this colony expanded very rapidly, a common characteristic of Ukrainian settlements at this time. The following seven settlements were brought into existence in the first year, 1899: Olha-Oakburn, Seech, Rossburn,[23] Menzie, Elphinstone, Sandy Lake, and Angusville. In the next year these settlements followed: Ruthenia, Mohyly, north of Rossburn; Marco, north of Olha; Horod, north of Elphinstone; Ozerna, south-east of Sandy Lake; Dolyny, south of Oakburn and Menzie.

Advancing west from Olha along the Riding Mountains, the settlement almost reached the Saskatchewan border and then turned north, forming the two communities of Inglis and Leonard. At this point, in the third decade of the twentieth century, it almost effected a junction with the community of Petlura, (Township 24, Range 26), which was a south-western extension of the Dauphin colony. Extending to the east along the Riding Mountains, it bordered on the Scandinavian colony of ''Scandinavia'' where the railway station of Erickson was later established. This Scandinavian colony originated in 1885 in Townships 17 and 18, Range 17 and 18, but it did not develop very rapidly. Ukrainians quickly absorbed not only all available homesteads but also bought land from the Swedish farmers. As a consequence, Erickson had twenty-four families of Ukrainian origin before 1941[24] and, on the basis of the 1941 census, the municipality of Clanwilliam had a population of 332 Ukrainians. Having penetrated the Scandinavian colony, the Ukrainians thus effected a junction with their countrymen of Mountain Road.

The Mountain Road district was once known as Huns Valley, where Count Esterhazy established a colony in 1885 with almost fifty families, most of whom came from Pennsylvania. The members of the colony were probably not too interested in farming because the population of the colony began to dwindle almost immediately after its establishment, though it had been expected that it would increase. Beginning in 1898, Ukrainians also moved into this district.[25] By 1900 there were already sixty families in this area. The population kept on increasing to such an extent in the course of time that the Greek Catholic parish was able to build one of the largest, if not the largest, churches in a rural area in Canada. In 1941 this church had 150 members while the number of children and other young people bordered on 500.[26]

Advancing to the northwest, the Huns Valley colony almost joined another Ukrainian settlement at Glenella, probably also established in 1899. Although the soil in this area was not as fertile as that in other areas, Ukrainians continued to settle here. The first immigrants to arrive were families who filed on homesteads eight miles north of the village of Glenella from which settlement began to push northward in the direction of Glenhope, east of Alonza station, and west to embrace the village of McCreary.[27] At this point the settlement almost merged with the south-east wing of the Dauphin colony.

However, the Strathclair-Shoal Lake-Oakburn colony did not only spread out east and west in a narrow strip along the Riding Mountains. In 1906 another railway was built through the centre of the colony giving rise to a cluster of new railway stations which included: Clanwilliam, Erickson, Rackham, Sandy Lake, Elphinstone, Glenfors, Menzie, Oakburn, Vista, Rossburn, Birdtail, Silverton, Russel, and Shellmount. As these trading points made it more convenient to sell grain and cattle, the Ukrainian belief in the indispensability of forest land was altered. As a result, they began to advance southward to acquire land which was less wooded and with more open prairie. On such land a farmer could prosper more quickly as land could be brought under cultivation more rapidly. As a consequence of this change of attitude, Ukrainians began to file on homesteads in the direction of those stations (Shoal Lake and Strathclair) from which settlers had travelled originally on their way from Winnipeg to establish the colony. When the supply of homesteads was exhausted, they purchased land from earlier settlers of other nationalities, paying enough to encourage further sale of land. Generally, these earlier settlers left to retire or to invest in some commercial venture. In this way Ukrainians advanced south to Shoal Lake, Strathclair, Newdale, Minnedosa, and Neepawa.

If we include the settlements of Glenella and Mountain Road (Huns Valley) as part of this colony, its extent is comparable to that of Edna colony in Alberta. Though it is narrower in width than the Edna colony, since its width never exceeds twenty-five miles, it still comprises forty-two townships. Excluding railway stations in this colony, there is still an array of farming communities such as Ruthenia, Mears (usually known as Mohyly), Glen Elmo, Marco, Olha, Seech, Dolyny, Ozerna, Mountain Road, and Glenhope. In describing earlier Ukrainian settlements, we called attention to the fact that they were not settled exclusively by Ukrainians. This fact bears repetition in regard to the Strathclair—Shoal Lake—Oakburn colony as there are areas within it where Ukrainians definitely constitute a minority of the settlers. But there is also a number like Olha where Ukrainians are in the majority. The total Ukrainian population in the area extending from Alonza to the Saskatchewan border reached 9000 by 1941.[28]

17

First Steps in the Organization of Social Institutions

Social Composition of Ukrainian Immigrants

Ukrainian immigrants to Canada were predominantly village peasant-farmers. Driven by the misery of their conditions, as already noted, they left their native villages to seek a better destiny in foreign lands. After they had reached Canada and filed on their homesteads, they began farming with almost no resources; the majority did not even have sufficient capital to provide food for themselves and their families for the first year in the new land. After building a shelter, the men usually left their families for a short while to seek work in the cities, on the railways, in the mines, or on the farms of more prosperous neighbours of other nationalities.

Among these early arrivals there were also men without families who came to Canada with the aim of returning to their villages after they had earned enough money to become more prosperous landowners. But the proportion of literate or educated individuals among these immigrants was very small. Generally speaking, the first groups were composed of individuals, the majority of whom were not so much illiterate as they were unconscious of their national origin and heritage. This condition was the result of prolonged occupation by foreign powers who aimed as much as possible to keep the Ukrainian population in abject ignorance. The small number of Ukrainians with an education was only a drop in the ocean in comparison to the large number of newcomers. Unfortunately, this small number of educated Ukrainians did not arrive as an organized group which could have fulfilled the leadership role so essential to these first immigrants. They were primarily political refugees or students who possessed an incomplete educa-

First convention of Ukrainian-Canadian teachers in Manitoba, 1907

First row (from left to right): D. Yakimishak, I. Kotzan, W. Romaniuk, T. D. Ferley, O. Zherebko, P. H. Woycenko.
Second row: W. Kudryk, W. Dedeluk, Y. W. Arsenych, W. P. Hrushowy, P. S. Ogryzlo, M. P. Ostapowych, Y. Holowacky, P. Chaikowsky, A. Nowak.
Third row: W. Mayewsky, Pliatzko, F. T. Hawryliuk. P. Ghigheichuk, W. Saranchuk, W. Chumer, Y. Koltek.
Fourth row: T. H. Petryshyn, W. Smuk, Y. Kuninsky, Baran, O. Hykawy, O. Klymkiw, W. Kohut.
Fifth row: S. Lytwyn, M. Drabyniasty, D. Wowk, T. Stefanyk, Machny, P. Symotiuk, W. Sholdra, Huminilowych.

FIRST BUILDING OF P. MOHYLA INSTITUTE, SASKATOON

tion which they hoped to complete after earning sufficient money in Canada. Nevertheless, this corporal's guard of literate individuals, sometimes against their will, had to adopt a leadership role among Ukrainians scattered throughout the length and breadth of Canada.

Among those who arrived on the first ships from Galicia there were only three individuals who had completed secondary school: Kyrylo Genik, Ivan Bodrug, and Ivan Negrych. Genik was an interpreter and an agent with the immigration authorities for many years, from which position he was able to advise the masses of immigrants who arrived in Canada and aid them in many ways after they had settled. Negrych and Bodrug were the first teachers of Ukrainian origin in Canada and later became important figures in the organization of the Ruthenian Independent Orthodox Church, generally known as the "Seraphimite" Church, organized with the support of the Presbyterian Church. The religious problem was the most burning question among the first Ukrainians in the new world. Upon its solution depended the moral development of Ukrainians in their new environment; a church to a new immigrant was often just as important as his family and daily bread.[1] Therefore, it is not surprising that their first steps in their social organization were directed toward the solution of the religious question, especially to ensure the attainment of spiritual guidance from their own church.

Religious Problems of the Early Immigrants

As we have noted in the chapter on "History of the Ukrainian People", Ukrainians were divided through Polish efforts into two religious groups by what is known as the Berest Union in 1596. A large majority of Ukrainians remained faithful to the Orthodox Church, but those who remained under Polish rule until its partition at the end of the eighteenth century became what were known as Uniates. Austria continued to maintain this union after Galicia became part of its territory in 1772, following the first partition of Poland. Though the two Ukrainian churches differed very little in practice since they shared the same dogma and rites, the hierarchy of the Uniate Church did everything in its power to separate the Uniate Church from the Orthodox. The Austrian government was very favorable to these policies of the Uniate hierarchy and helped them in their activities whenever necessary. One of the acts of the Uniate hierarchy was the surrender of immigrants from Galicia to the guardianship of the Roman Catholic Church in Canada. Rome forbade the immigration of Uniate or Greek Catholic priests into Canada on the pretext that under Uniate Church law, they were permitted to marry. Instructions from the Holy Congregation for the Propagation of the Faith on April 12, 1894, and later on May 10, 1902, openly announced this prohibition. But the Ukrainians were kept in the dark in regard to this policy. Foreign missionaries kept silent on this issue and even sought to win over Greek Catholics by expressing solicitude for "the poor Ruthenians deserted by their own priesthood".

Actually, four Greek Catholic priests, one after another, visited Canada before 1902 but their visits to Ukrainian communities were only for short periods and they quickly returned home.[2] As a result, many immigrants were upset and became hostile to the guardianship of the Roman Catholic Church. The demand of the French hierarchy that all churches be registered in the name of the Roman Catholic Bishop of the diocese aroused further hostility, to the point of rebellion. Leaders in the immigrant communities who were subscribers to *Svoboda* or to the Galician newspaper, *Dilo,* (in both of which Rome's assault on the Greek Catholic Church was openly publicized), supported the struggle of the immigrants against the encroachments of the Roman Catholic Church. But this support was not confined to lay leaders alone. All of the four Greek Catholic priests who had visited Canada had also advised their faithful "not to surrender to the French" and to refuse any aid from them.

Immigrants from Bukovyna and eastern Ukraine also found themselves under the alien guardianship of the Russian Orthodox Mission, which was wealthy, did not require that churches be registered in its name, and had plenty of priests who spoke Ukrainian. In the Russian Orthodox churches, mass was celebrated in Church Slavonic. As this was also the language used in both Orthodox and Greek Catholic churches among Ukrainians, Greek Catholics did not find it difficult to join the Russian Orthodox Church. On the other hand, those who did not wish to join either church sought an alternative in one of the Protestant churches.

Leaders of the day, including Genik, Bodrug, Negrych, and others, quite justifiably came to the conclusion that people, disunited from the beginning and subjected to alien influence, would soon lose their identity. In seeking to rescue their countrymen from this condition, they chose what they considered to be a logical course of action. In 1903 they founded the Ruthenian Independent Orthodox Church, with Winnipeg as its centre.

It should be pointed out that when open and organized opposition to the Latinization of the Church became fully apparent in 1902, the Roman Catholic hierarchy yielded to pressure and brought Ukrainian priests to Canada. However, the newcomers were not members of the lay priesthood, to which most Ukrainians had been accustomed, but were Basilians, a monastic order. It should be remembered that the Basilian Order in Galicia had been reformed by Rome with the aid of the Polish Jesuit Order only a few years previously. As a result, many Ukrainians regarded the Basilians with suspicion and the arrival of three Basilian monks, along with one brother and four nuns,³ did not have much effect on restraining people who had already joined the struggle against the Roman Catholic Church. It rather emphasized the fact that the Roman Catholic hierarchy did not regard lay Greek Catholic priests as members of a true priesthood, and that entry into Canada was forbidden to them.

The founding of the new church was not the creation of a few disgruntled individuals and it was not an unpopular action. That the Independent Orthodox Church appealed to the settlers is witnessed by the fact that in a phenomenally short time, within only a few months, it invaded almost every community in Canada and attracted to its priesthood most of the leading personalities of that period. People welcomed its creation and joined it in large numbers. They hastened to join it because they regarded its creation as their first victory over their age-long enemies in the role of uninvited guardians. Even one of the greatest opponents of the new church, Father Delaere, a Belgian Redemptorist Catholic who arrived in Canada in 1899 and was assigned for service among Greek Catholics in Canada, admitted in his booklet that Ukrainians supported the Independent Orthodox Church very staunchly, and that it enlarged its influence very rapidly.⁴

This movement cannot be explained, as many have striven to do, by labelling its founders as mud-slinging, mercenary, and treacherous apostates. If the mass of people and their leaders participated in it to such an extent, there must have been justifiable reasons for their behaviour. People and their leaders cannot be false to themselves. If they choose to abandon any movement or organization, it is a sign that they are searching for salvation from some intolerable situation. Any other interpretation of this movement is clearly either self-deception or an unjustified smear on the entire group of Ukrainian immigrants who came to Canada during this first decade.

That this enthusiasm for the new church did not last long was the result of other causes. The church chose Bishop Seraphim as its leader, an individual who not only lacked leadership qualities but who also had no intention of heading an independent religious organization among Ukrainians in Canada. Under his leadership, the Independent Orthodox Church declined almost as quickly as it had risen. After misunderstandings with the bishop began to undermine its existence, the church came under the guardianship of the Presbyterian Church and lost its independent status. Ukrainian immigrants, consistent in their adherence to the principle of independence, would not condone this act, and almost no trace of the existence of this church was left after a few years.

Though the church collapsed and still greater confusion in religious affairs arose after its fall, we cannot conceal the fact that the spirit of independence and opposition to alien guardianship was rooted deeply in the souls of the settlers and contributed in no small measure to the growth of national consciousness amongst Ukrainians in Canada. It preserved the identity of the Ukrainian settlers and aided in the development of Ukrainian organizations. Though the movement had religious overtones, it was really a people's movement and was national in its character.

Progress in Education

Coinciding with the dissolution of this church, there emerged another movement on the social scene, one which emphasized the importance of education. It was also to play an important and ineradicable role in the history of Canadian Ukrainians.

Leaders in many communities began to organize public schools on their own, since none existed in the early settlements. Realizing some of the difficulties which would have to be faced, others sought to convince the government that these schools needed teachers who could understand the newcomers and who were willing to teach in the pioneer communities. Since Manitoba had a bilingual system of education which permitted the teaching of Ukrainian to Ukrainian students and because this could not be done by English-speaking teachers, the government of Manitoba instituted in 1905 a special teacher training school which was given the name "Ruthenian Training School". Applications to this school were accepted from young Ukrainians who already had some education. After their training, which extended over several years, they were permitted to accept positions in schools as qualified teachers. The school was first conducted in Winnipeg but was later moved to Brandon, where it remained in operation until 1916. During its existence 150 teachers were trained to teach school among Ukrainian settlers. Following Manitoba, Ukrainians in Saskatchewan and Alberta also persuaded their governments to establish similar institutions. A school was organized in Regina in 1911 and another followed in Vegreville in 1912. These institutions also functioned until 1916 and trained about 100 teachers.

There was some difference in provincial policies toward the teaching of the Ukrainian language. Manitoba teachers taught Ukrainian on an equal basis with the English language. On the other hand, those in Saskatchewan and Alberta could teach Ukrainian for only one hour a day. However, no matter what the regulation, every public school where there was a Ukrainian teacher became a Ukrainian cultural centre. From these schools came thousands of pupils who learned the Ukrainian language. Without those teachers, the children of the first immigrants would have been lost to a premature and unproductive assimilation. Modern Ukrainian life in Canada would have been altogether different.

The early teachers were concerned not only about children; they were also missionaries with broad civic and cultural duties. While daylight hours were reserved for children, evenings were devoted to the instruction of adults. The schools were converted into centres of general culture where the teachers and leading members of the community operated reading rooms, gave lectures, staged concerts, and presented theatrical productions. With those teachers in schools, there came an awakening of national consciousness and support for national-cultural pursuits. The teachers waded on foot through swamps, forests, and snowdrifts to aid other teachers in their education of older citizens.

As teachers and workers in the adult field, they organized a separate teachers' organization and met in annual conventions, which became the forerunners of future national conventions. Leaders in other Ukrainian organizations, who were interested in matters that concerned their people, also participated in these gatherings with the teachers. When they met they considered not only school matters; the conventions became a forum for all matters which concerned the lives of Ukrainian Canadians.

The more active the teachers became in their undertakings, the more they began to attract the distrust of some of the "alien" guardians. As early as 1908, Bishop Langevin, who had complete jurisdiction over Greek Catholics, wrote in his introduction to Father Delaere's book that the Ruthenian Training School in Brandon was a Protestant creation, a political act which would bring disaster to the government which was responsible for its creation. He claimed that the school fostered apostasy. Obviously, priests of the same church mirrored their bishop in relation to the efforts of the Ukrainian teachers. Instead of obtaining aid, the teachers were usually subject to open or covert harassment.

But these obstacles did not discourage the young men. They continued to labour unselfishly for their people and often prevailed on the priesthood to join them in this service. Whoever tries to assess the accomplishments of these teachers and their sacrifice in serving the people must recognize their important contribution to the development of settlements during that difficult pioneering stage. Most of these teachers, overburdened with their daily tasks, did not receive any rewards or important posts but their labour yielded an abundant harvest in thriving cultural achievements. Other teachers furthered their own education and eventually acquired important positions, achieving distinction for themselves and recognition for their people. It will be sufficient to mention these few names: Ferley, Kudryk, Arsenych, Bachynsky, Stechishin, Sawchuk, Czumer, Hawryliuk, Bodnar, Prodan, Bohonos, Martsiniw, Ziubrak, and many others. To talk about the progress of Ukrainians in Canada without including these teachers is like describing a wedding without including the bride and groom.

The Publication of the Ukrainian Voice

According to a decision reached at their 1907 convention, in which other leaders had participated, the first aim of the Ukrainian teachers' association was the publication of a Ukrainian national newspaper which would interpret the aims and guard the interests of the Ukrainian public. This decision was realized only three years later, in 1910, when *Ukrainskyi Holos* (the Ukrainian Voice) was first published.

At that time there were already three Ukrainian language newspapers: *Kanadiiskyi Farmer* (the Canadian Farmer), founded with the support of the Liberal Party in 1903; *Ranok* (Morning), an organ of the Presbyterian Church, first published in 1905; and *Robochyi Narod* (Working People), published by Ukrainian socialists beginning in 1908*. Because of their limited aims, political or religious, it is obvious that none of these newspapers could defend the interests of Ukrainian settlers in every respect. Accordingly, the appearance of a broadly national newspaper which depended entirely on the support of the settlers was no small achievement.

It is difficult to evaluate this achievement today but, in reality, it was a momentous development. For that period it was not only revolutionary but also heroic to label a newspaper with the name Ukrainian when most of the prospective readers still called themselves *"Rusyny"*, *"Ruski"*, and a host of other names. *Ukrainskyi Holos* immediately proclaimed that it was founded by Ukrainian people who were its sole support and whom it was pledged to serve. Though outside financial support would often have solved many of its financial difficulties, the acceptance of this help would have been an encumbrance in its aim to serve the Canadian Ukrainian settler. It attacked the attempts of outside political and religious groups to lead Ukrainians astray and also castigated some Ukrainians for their willingness to abandon their own people to serve others.

The influence of *Ukrainskyi Holos* was felt in the farthest and darkest corners of Ukrainian settlement. It penetrated areas where it was impossible for the Ukrainian teacher to travel. Not only did it receive the support of teachers, but farmers and labourers also welcomed its appearance and, in the main, it became the forum of the more nationally-conscious sector of the Ukrainian community.

Together with the teachers, *Ukrainskyi Holos* literally transformed the attitudes of Ukrainians in about four years. In every district, "National Homes" were built in which libraries were established, reading rooms organized, and various other cultural activities conducted. As a result of this transformation, the ethnic mass of *"Rusyny"* became informed Ukrai-

---

* The first issue of *Robochyi Narod* was published in May 1909. (Ed.)

nians, conscious of their heritage, who dared once more to resist the encroachments of Muscovite, Latin, and Protestant influences. In this effort, the creation of *Ukrainskyi Holos* was a memorable achievement which inaugurated a new and significant period, filled with heroism and sacrifice, in the history of Canadian Ukrainians.

Notes

CHAPTER I

1 The trading route from Scandinavia to Byzantium followed the Neva River from the Baltic Sea to Lake Ladoga, after which it turned south along the Volkhva River to Lake Ilmen. It then followed the Lovat River to its source from where the route crossed over to the Dnieper River and continued south to the Black Sea, Greece, and the Mediterranean.

2 Ivan Krypiakevych, *Ohliad istorii Ukrainy* [A Review of the history of Ukraine] (Kiev-Lviv-Vienna: Vernyhora Press, 1919), p. 10.

3 Mykhailo Hrushevsky, *Ilustrovana istoriia Ukrainy* [An Illustrated history of Ukraine] (Kiev-Lviv: 1912), p. 99.

4 Natalia Polonska-Vasylenko, *Vyznachni zhinky Ukrainy* [Illustrious Women of Ukraine] (Winnipeg-Munich: Ukrainian Women's Association of Canada, 1969), pp. 62-64. The author also reports that Anna, following her husband's death, married a French baron who had deserted his wife. Unfortunately for Anna, a papal decree forced the baron to resume his marriage with his first wife. In describing her royal rival, the first wife pictured Queen Anna as "the most attractive and fascinating of French women" (p. 64).

5 Paul Yuzyk, *Ukrainian Canadians: Their Place and Role in Canadian Life* (Toronto: Ukrainian Business and Professional Federation, 1967), preface. See also Bedwin Sands, *The Ukraine* (London: Francis Griffiths, 1914), p. 25.

6 Natalia Polonska-Vasylenko, *Ukraine-Rus and Western Europe from the Tenth to the Thirteenth Centuries* (London: Association of Ukrainians in Great Britain, 1964).

7 Mykola Chubaty, *Kniazha Rus-Ukraina ta vynyknennia trokh skhidno-slovianskykh natsii* [Principality of Rus-Ukraine and the origin of the three eastern-Slavonic nations] (New York: Organization for the Defence of the Four Freedoms of Ukraine, 1964), p. 48.

8 Krypiakevych, *Ohliad*, p. 18.

9 Mykola Kostomariv, *Istoriia Ukrainy u zhyttiepysakh vyznachnishykh yeyi diyachiw* [History of Ukraine in the lives of its illustrious leaders] (Lviv: Taras Shevchenko Scientific Society, 1918), p. 75.

10 Ibid., p. 75.

11 Krypiakevych, *Ohliad*, p. 18.

12 Dmytro Chyzhevsky, *Istoriia Ukrainskoi literatury* [History of Ukrainian literature] (New York: Ukrainian Free Academy of Sciences, 1956), p. 196.

13 Yar Slavutych, *Conversational Ukrainian* (Winnipeg: Gateway Publishers Ltd., 1960), pp. 446-7.

14 Chyzhevsky, *Istoriia*, pp. 182, 197.

15 Metropolitan Ilarion - Ivan Ohienko, *Slovo pro Ihoriv pokhid*, 2nd ed. [The Tale

of Ihor's Host] (Winnipeg: Society of Volhyn, 1967), pp. 135-6. See also Ivan Kholmsky, *Istoriia Ukrainy* [History of Ukraine] (Munich: Shevchenko Scientific Society, 1949), p. 116.

16 Metropolitan Ilarion, *Slovo,* p. 71.

17 Mykola Arkas, *Istoriia Ukrainy* [History of Ukraine] (3rd ed., Winnipeg: Ukrainian Publishing Company, 1920), p. 129.

18 Omelian Terletsky, *Istoriia Ukrainskoi derzhavy* [History of the Ukrainian state] (Lviv, 1923), p. 134.

19 Kholmsky, *Istoriia Ukrainy,* p. 81.

20 Terletsky, *Istoriia Ukrainskoi derzhavy,* p. 140.

21 Ibid., p. 150.

22 Dmytro Doroshenko, *Narys istorii Ukrainy,* tom 1 [Outline of Ukrainian history, vol. 1] (Warsaw: Ukrainian Scientific Institute, 1932), p. 66.

23 Ibid., p. 67.

24 Chubaty, *Kniazha Rus-Ukraina,* pp. 100-1.

25 Kholmsky, *Istoriia Ukrainy,* p. 131.

26 Ibid.. p. 123.

27 Ibid., pp. 130-2.

28 Edward Likowsky, *Berestiiska Unia, 1596* [Union of Berest, 1596] (Zhovkva, Ukraine: Library of Ukrainian Seminarists of Markiian Shashkevych in Lviv, 1916), p. 3.

29 Ibid., p. 80.

30 Benedict Herbest, ,,Wypisania Drogi", *Yuvileina knyha v 300 litni rokovyny Metropolyta Ipatiia Potia* [Jubilee volume on the 300th anniversary of Metropolitan Ipatiy Potiy] (Lviv: St. Paul Society, 1914), p. 28. As his booklet was published in 1567, this author was probably the first to raise the question of union. He was followed nine years later by another Jesuit, Petro Skarga (Petro Pavedzki), who wrote *Kosciol Bozy pod jednem Pasterzem* [God's Church under One Shepherd], a more detailed attempt, in which he pointed out the "errors" of the Orthodox Church and appealed to its adherents to unite with Rome. In this work he also sought to inform the Polish ruler of the benefits the Polish state might gain from such a union.

31 Likowsky, *Berestiiska unia,* p. 30. The quotation in regard to the bishops reads as follows: "In such circumstances the deciding factor was ordinarily not the merits, virtues, or accomplishments of the priestly candidates for the vacant episcopate but other considerations which had no connection with pastoral merits or justice. The bishops were not chosen from monastic orders as demanded by church tradition and they were not individuals distinguished for their piety or learning. They were sometimes worldly individuals, usually a king's secretary or Lithuanian treasurer, ordinarily the possessor of a large estate in the district.... In a word, he was most likely a member of the Ruthenian gentry who had won favor in the king's court and looked forward toward enriching himself further."

32 Father Ivan Savytsky states this more briefly: "The election of a bishop depended entirely on the king and his court and the bishop's mitre was granted to those who had won favor for services in the king's court- or the queen's 'boudoir'- or in serving the commonwealth." *Yuvileina knyha,* p. 12.

33 The author died before he could review a large part of what he had written. As a result he failed to specify the reference from which this quotation was taken. This circumstance also explains the absence of reference notes for most of the remainder of this chapter.

34 Ivan Vlasovsky, *Narys istorii Ukrainskoi Pravoslavnoi Tserkvy,* tom 1 [An outline of the history of the Ukrainian Orthodox Church, vol. 1] (New York: Ukrainian Orthodox Church of the U.S.A., 1955), p. 266.

35 Ibid., p. 273.

36 Doroshenko, *Narys istorii Ukrainy,* tom I, p. 154.

37 Ibid., p. 192.

CHAPTER II

1 Osyp Oleskiw, *O emigratsii* [About Emigration] (Lviv: Obshchestvo imeny Mykhaila Kachkovskoho, 1895), No. 241.

2 Dionisey Salley, "Spomyny z Kanady: Doroha z New Yorku do Kanady" [Memories of Canada: Journey from New York to Canada]. *Svoboda* (Mount Carmel, Pa., 1895), no. 29-33.

3 Osyp Oleskiw, *Khliborobstvo za okeanom, a pereselencha emigratsiia* [Agriculture beyond the Ocean and Transplanted Emigrants] (Zhovkva: Basilian Press, 1895), p. 48.

4 Nestor Dmytriw, *Kanadiiska Rus* [Canadian Rus] (Mount Carmel, Pa.: Svoboda Publishers, 1897).

5 Pawlo Tymkevych, "Deshcho pro Kanadu" [A Little about Canada] *Svoboda* (1898), no. 29.

6 *Svoboda* (1906), no. 43. Mykhailo Marunchak is probably in error when he claims Bachynsky was in Canada for two months. See Marunchak, *Istoriia Ukraintsiv u Kanadi* [History of Ukrainians in Canada], 2 vols. (Winnipeg: UVAN, 1968), vol. 1, p. 333-4.

7 Julian Bachynsky, *Ukrainska Immigratsiia u Zyedynenykh Derzhavakh Ameryky,* tom 1 [Ukrainian Immigration in the United States of America, vol. 1] (Lviv: vol. 1, Shevchenko Scientific Society, 1914). This book has seventy-five illustrations and two maps.

8 "Z diyalnosty oo. Vasilianiv v Kanadi" [From the activities of the Basilians in Canada] *Svoboda* (1907), no. 10.

9 Julian Bachynsky, *Yak ya vydavaw "Ukrainsku Emigratsiiu"* [How I published "Ukrainian Emigration"] (Lviv: Rada Publ., 1930), p. 32.

10 *Pro Kanadu — yaka tse zemlia i yak u nii zhyvut ludy* [About Canada — the country and its people] (Kiev: Prosvita Society, 1908), no. 27, p. 47.

11 J. S. Woodsworth, "Ukrainian Rural Communities," Report of Investigation by Bureau of Social Research, Winnipeg, 1917 (Mimeographed folio).

12 Julian Stechishin, *Twenty-five Years of the Petro Mohyla Ukrainian Institute in Saskatoon* (Winnipeg: Ukrainian Publishing Co., 1945), p. 132.

13 Osyp Nazaruk, *V lisakh Alberty i Skalystykh Horakh* [In Alberta forests and the Rocky Mountains] and *V naibilshim parku Skalystykh Hir* [In the largest park of the Rocky Mountains] (Chicago: Sich Organization of the U.S.A., 1924). *Vchasna vesna v pivnichnii Alberti* [Early spring in northern Alberta] (Lviv: Ukrainska Khrystiyanska Orh., 1929), p. 32.

14 P. Bozhyk, *Istoriia ukrainskoi emigratsii v Kanadi za chas vid 1890 do 1930 roku* [History of Ukrainian Emigration in Canada from 1890 to 1930] (Winnipeg: National Publ. Co., 1930). Also see his earlier *Tserkov Ukraintsiv v Kanadi: prychynky do istorii ukrainskoho tserkovnoho zhyttia v Brytiiskii Dominii Kanadi, za chas vid 1890-1927* [Ukrainian Churches in Canada: Studies in the History of Ukrainian Religious Life in the British Dominion of Canada from 1890 to 1927] (Winnipeg: Canadian Ukrainian Publishers, 1927).

15 L. Yasenchuk, *Za okeanom* [Beyond the Ocean] (Lviv: Ridna Shkola, 1930).

16 Ch. H. Young, *The Ukrainian Canadians* (Toronto: Thomas Nelson and Sons, 1931).

17 Zygmunt Bychynsky, *Istoriia Kanady* [History of Canada] (Winnipeg, 1928), with an introduction by Dr. Charles W. Gordon (Ralph Connor).

CHAPTER III

1 The Canadian census figures for 1961 were as follows: Anglo-Saxons (British) 7,998,669; French 5,540,346; Germans 1,049,559; Ukrainians 473,337. The figures for western Canada were as follows: Anglo-Saxons 1,371,682; Germans 434,369; Ukrainians 290,146; French 227,079.

2 For more on Pylypiw and Eleniak see chapter 4.

3 Dr. Mykhailo Huculak, "Ukrainets-spivtvorets kordoniv Kanady i Alasky" [A Ukrainian who collaborated in the creation of a boundary between Canada and Alaska], *Biblioteka ukrainoznavstva,* XXIV [Library of Ukrainian Studies, XXIV] (Vancouver and Toronto: Shevchenko Scientific Society, 1967), p. 21.

4 Hence, the strait between the Chukotsk peninsula and Alaska was named the Bering Strait, and the sea surrounding the peninsula — the Bering Sea.

5 *Encyclopedia Britannica,* 1963 ed., vol. 1, p. 497.

6 Ibid.

7 The plenipotentiary who negotiated the treaty on behalf of the Russian government was Petro Poletyka (1778-1849) (Pierre de Poletica), a Ukrainian in the Russian service. Mt. Poletica (7620 ft. in altitude), on the border between Alaska and British Columbia, was named after him. J.B. Rudnyckyj, *Z podorozhi po Italii* [From the Italian journey] (Winnipeg: *Novy Shliakh,* 1965), p. 50.

   In "Mt. Poletica", *Eighteenth Report of the Geographical Board of Canada* (Ottawa, 1924), p. 226, the mountain was named "after M. Pierre de Poletica, former Russian Minister to the U.S. and plenipotentiary in Russian negotiation with the U.S. in 1824 regarding the Alaskan boundary." See also Huculak, "Ukrainets-spivtvorets", in its second footnote.

8 W. Luciw, *Ahapius Honcharenko* (Toronto: Slavia Library, 1963), p. 52.

9 "Se tsikave" [This is interesting], *Svoboda,* no. 11, 1894.

10 *Propamiatna Knyha vydana z nahody soroklitnoho iubileiu Ukrainskoho Narodnoho Soyuzu* [Commemorative Volume published on the fortieth anniversary of the Ukrainian National Association]. (Jersey City, N.J.: Ukrainskyi Narodniy Soyuz, 1936), pp. 28-9; Luciw, *Ahapius Honcharenko,* p. 68.

11 *Propamiatna Knyha.... Ukrainskoho Narodnoho Soyuzu,* p. 30.

12 Myroslaw Stechishin, "Ukrainske Bratstvo v Kalifornii" [The Ukrainian Brotherhood in California], *Kalendar "Ukrainskoho Holosu" na perestupniy rik 1940* (Winnipeg: Vydannya Ukrainskoi Vydavnychoi Spilky v Kanadi, 1940), pp. 111-21. (An original calling card, together with an original letter from Honcharenko to Myroslaw Stechishin, was passed on to the author of this work and he has placed it in his own archives — Ju. S.).

13 I. Telman, *U dalekiy storoni* [In far-away lands] (Kiev: Radianskiy Pysmennyk, 1956), p. 106.

14 A. M. Shlepakov, *Ukrainska trudova emihratsiia v S.Sh.A. i Kanadi* [Emigration of Ukrainian labor in U.S.A. and Canada] (Kiev: Akademiia Nauk, 1960), p. 114.

15 P. Krawchuk, *Na novii zemli* [In a new land] (Toronto: Tov. Obyed. Ukrainskykh Kanadtsiv, 1958), pp. 78-9.

16 S. Matsiyevych, "Ukraintsi v Kanade" [Ukrainians in Canada], *Slaviane* (Moscow), no. 6, 1953. (Matsiyevych was at one time an editor of *Ukrainske Zhyttia,* a newspaper published in Toronto by Ukrainian Canadians affiliated with the Communist Party of Canada. His article was written in the Russian language — translated by the author of this work — and was highly propagandistic, full of historical errors and lacking objectivity).

17 Yu. O. Zhluktenko, *Ukrainsko-anhliiski mizhmowni vidnosyny* [Ukrainian-English interlingual relations] (Kiev: Vydavnytstvo Kyivskoho universytetu, 1964), p. 18.

18 Matsiyevych, "Ukraintsi v Kanade," pp. 23-8.

19 A. Vihornyi, "Podorozh dovkola svitu" [A voyage around the world], in *Ukrainskomu kalendari na 1967 rik* [Ukrainian almanack for 1967] (Warsaw: Ukrainsko-suspilno-kulturne tovarystvo, 1967), pp. 323-5; Yuri Semyonov, *Siberia, Its Conquest and Development* (Montreal: International Publishers' Representatives (Canada), 1963), pp. 215-19.

20 Urey Lysiansky, *A Voyage Around the World in the Years 1803-1806* (London: J. Booth, 1814). This book has 388 pages.

21 *Forum: A Ukrainian Review* (Scranton, Pa.), (Winter 1967), vol. I, no. 1, p. 26.

22 Ibid.

23 G. Okulevich, *Ruskie v Kanade* [Russians in Canada] (Toronto: Izdania Holovnoho Pravlennia Federatsii Ruskykh Kanadtsev, 1952), pp. 13-14.

24 Dr. Mykhailo Huculak of Vancouver was engaged in research on Ukrainians in British Columbia at the time this work was being written.

25 W. L. Morton, *Manitoba: A History,* 2nd. ed. (Toronto: University of Toronto Press, 1967), p. 145.

26 Charles G. D. Roberts, *A History of Canada* (Toronto: George A. Morang and Co., 1902), p. 63; J. W. Dafoe, *Clifford Sifton in Relation to His Times* (Toronto, 1931), p. 104.

27 A. Royick, "Roman Bachynsky—pershyi ukrainets u Kanadi?" [Roman Bachynsky—first Ukrainian in Canada?], *Northern Light* (Edmonton: Slavuta Publishers, 1965), p. 183.

28 J. M. Kirschbaum, *Slovaks in Canada* (Toronto: Canadian Ethnic Press Association of Ontario, 1967), p. 49.

29 Ibid., pp. 250-1.

30 Ibid., p. 249; *Propamiatna knyha poselennia ukrainskoho narodu v Kanadi* [Memorial volume on the settlement of Ukrainians in Canada] (Yorkton, Sask.: The Voice of the Redeemer, 1941), p. 266.

31 Kirschbaum, *Slovaks in Canada,* p. 54. Here Kirschbaum errs when he states that Huns Valley was located 18 miles west of Minnedosa.

32 A. A. Marchbin, "Early Immigration from Hungary to Canada," *The Slavonic (and East European) Review* (vol. 13, 1934-1935), pp. 127-38. See also J. B. Hedges, *Building the Canadian West* (New York, 1939), p. 118.

33 Kirschbaum, *Slovaks in Canada,* p. 56.

34 John Gellner and John Smerek, *The Czechs and Slovaks in Canada* (Toronto: University of Toronto Press, 1968), p. 64.

35 Kirschbaum, *Slovaks in Canada,* p. 57.

36 M. H. Marunchak, *Studii do istorii ukraintsiv Kanady* [Studies in the history of Ukrainians in Canada] 4 vols. (Winnipeg: UVAN, Series Ukrainica Occidentalia, 1964-71), vol. 1, pp. 57-8.

37 More will be said about these "fathers" of immigration to Canada in later chapters.

38 W. B. Makowski, *History and Integration of Poles in Canada* (Lindsay, Ont.: Canadian Polish Congress, 1967), pp. 47-69.

39 Ibid.

40 Wasyl Burianyk, "Do istorii ukrainskykh uchyteliv-pioneriv u Kanadi" [In relation to the history of Ukrainian pioneer-teachers in Canada], *The New Chronicle,* July-September, 1962, pp. 68-9.

41 A. Royick, "Roman Bachynsky," pp. 181-4.

42 Kaye also stated that he could find no trace of Bachynsky's name in the acts of naturalization nor in the government census of 1871 in the Renfrew district. This lends support to Burianyk's claim that Backensky (Bachynsky) and Wozny were only temporarily in Canada on their way to settling in the United States.
    It should be added that we have no proof that Backensky (Bachynsky) or Wozny, even if they stayed in Canada, were actually Ukrainians.

43 M. Haiman, *Slady polskie w Ameryce* [Polish traces in America] (Chicago: Dziennik Zjednoczenia, 1938), p. 46. Haiman gained access to the records of the Ministry of War in London, where he obtained the lists of Polish soldiers in these regiments, and states clearly that there were a number of *"Rusyniv"* from eastern Galicia and even Russians from Korsakow's corps among both the De Watteville and the De Meuron regiments. See also Zenon Pohorecky, "Ukrainians in Canada in the War of 1812 by Alexander Royick." *Forum: A Ukrainian Review* (Scranton, Pa.), vol. 1, no. 2 (Spring 1967), p. 29.

44 W. B. Makowski, *History and Integration...,* p. 11.

45 Following the end of the American-Canadian War of 1812, Lord Selkirk arrived in Montreal in 1815, on his way to the settlement he had founded on the Red River. Selkirk's journey was in support of the settlers, who were threatened by the hostile

supporters of the North-West Company, who were mainly French and French-Indian mixed-bloods (Metis). The Metis did not want to allow Anglo-Saxons to settle in Western Canada. Selkirk organized this new group of settlers from the De Watteville regiment to consolidate the claims to this territory which had been established by the preceding group of Scottish settlers.

46   R. L. Reid, "Who Were the De Meurons?" *The Beaver* (Winnipeg: Hudson's Bay Company, 1942), pp. 28-9.

47   Ibid.

48   G. Bryce, "The Old Settlers of Red River," *Transactions of the Manitoba Historical and Scientific Society*, no. 19 (1885-1886).

49   *Winnipeg Free Press,* October 16, 1909.

50   *Gazeta Katolicka,* November 2, 1909.

51   V. Turek, "Poles Among the De Meuron Soldiers," *Transactions of the Manitoba Historical and Scientific Society,* Series III, no. 9 (1954), pp. 53-68.

52   *Slavica Canadiana* (Winnipeg: UVAN Series Slavistica, no. 24, 1955), p. 15.

53   Lord Selkirk Papers, vol. 15, pp. 5237-8.

54   Marunchak, *Studii,* vol. 1, p. 15.

55   Haiman, *Slady polskie,* pp. 46, 61, 65.

56   A. Royick, from unpublished study of the national origins of these three men (in the author's possession).

57   S. P. H. (Stefan P. Hrebak), "Pro pershoho ukraintsia na kanadiiskii zemli" [Concerning the first Ukrainian on Canadian soil], *Kanadiiskyi Farmer,* no. 7, 1965.

58   Mykhailo Bryk-Deviatnytsky, "Sotnyk Ivan Strilbytsky", *Shliakh Peremohy* (Munich), 1967, nos. 6-8; D. Buchynsky, "Ukrainians in Spain," *Almanack of the Ukrainian National Association* (1954), p. 254; A. Royick, "Sotnyk Ivan Strilbytsky pershyi ukrainets u Kanadi" [Captain John Strilbytsky, first Ukrainian in Canada], *Novyi Shliakh* (Winnipeg), 1967, nos. 26-8.

59   Letter from Gwen Metcalfe, curator of Dundurn Castle, to A. Royick, 9 Jan. 1966, in Royick's archives.

60   W. L. Morton, *Manitoba: A History,* p. 160.

61   Roberts, *A History of Canada,* p. 385.

62   The island of Khortytsia or Chortitza in the Dnieper River was once a fortified establishment of the Zaporozhian kozaks and was known as the Sich. After its destruction by Czarina Catherine the Great, herself a German, the lands were granted to Mennonites for settlement with the guarantee that Mennonites would never be conscripted into the Russian army. When the Russian government invalidated this agreement, the Mennonites began to emigrate to other lands.

63   J. Rudnyckyj, Materialy do ukrainsko-kanadiiskoi folklorystyky i dialektolohii" [Materials dealing with Ukrainian-Canadian folklore and dialectology], *Zbirnyk zakhodoznavstva,* tom 3 [Western Collection, vol. 3] (Winnipeg: UVAN, 1956), p. 273.

64   O. Woycenko, *Litopys Ukrainskoho Zhyttia v Kanadi* (The Annals of Ukrainian Life in Canada), vol. 1 (Winnipeg: Trident Press, 1961), p. 4.

65   J. Rudnyckyj, "Do pochatkiv ukrainskoho poselennia v Kanadi" [The beginning of Ukrainian settlement in Canada] *Canadian Farmer Jubilee Almanack, 1963,* p. 137.

66   M. H. Marunchak, *V zustrichi z ukrainskymy pioneramy Alberty* [Among Ukrainian pioneers of Alberta] (Winnipeg: Zahalna Biblioteka, U.K.T., 1964), pp. 16-17.

67   Marunchak, *Istoriia ukraintsiv Kanady,* vol. 1, p. 27.

68   *Svoboda,* nos. 35, 40, 44, 45, 1897; no. 2, 1898.

69   Wasyl Romaniuk, "Spomyny," *Ukrainski Visti* [Ukrainian News] (Edmonton), no. 51, 1955.

70   Letter from V. J. Kaye (Kysilewsky) to A. Royick, 9 August 1966, A. Royick's archives.

71 Ibid., 3 March 1967.
72 Vera Lysenko, *Men in Sheepskin Coats* (Toronto: Ryerson Press, 1947), p. 6.
73 W. Czumer, *Spomyny pro perezhyvannia pershykh ukrainskykh pereselentsiv u Kanadi* [Reminiscences of the first Ukrainian immigrants in Canada] (Edmonton: The Author, 1942), p. 28.
74 Lysenko, *Men in Sheepskin Coats,* p. 6.
75 T. Tomashewsky, "Bilshe svitla na zatemnenu spravu" [More light on an obscure matter] *Ukrainskyi Pioner* [The Ukrainian Pioneer], no. 1(5), 1956.
76 V. J. Kaye to A. Royick, 14 December 1968, A. Royick archives.
77 J. G. MacGregor, *Vilni Zemli* (Toronto: McClelland and Stewart, 1969), p. 14.
78 Hilda Mohr, "Josephburg Heritage," (Fort Saskatchewan, Alberta, 1967) (mimeographed); I. Goresky, "Stefan Koroluk," *Ukrainians in Alberta* (Edmonton: Ukrainian Pioneers' Association of Alberta, 1975), pp. 249-53. This reference has been added by the translator because of additional information which it contains about Stefan Koroluk.
79 But see Goresky, "Stefan Koroluk", pp. 249-53, in which he indicates that Nykola Koroluk came from Bukovyna.
     No proof of his arrival in Canada in 1888 is available, but his application for title to his homestead indicates that he filed in February 1892. According to his nephews and nieces, it would appear that his brother-in-law, Jacob Hennig, wrote to Stefan Koroluk about Canada after arriving in Canada. It would appear that Stefan Koroluk came to Canada in 1891, but no record of his arrival has been found in the steamship records in Ottawa. In all probability, he came to western Canada via the United States.
80 *Ukrainian Canadian Review* (Winnipeg), vol. 7, no. 3-4, 1942, p. 49.
81 See Tomashewsky, "Bilshe svitla."
82 See Royick, "Roman Bachynsky."
83 Letter from Mrs. Matthews and her daughter in Royick's possession, A. Royick's archives.
84 A. Royick, "Horetzky's Contribution to Canadian History", *Slavs in Canada,* vol. 2 (Toronto: Inter-University Committee on Canadian Slavs, 1968), p. 280.
85 "Chy ukraintsi zhyvut u Kanadi diisno lyshe 60 rokiv?" [Have Ukrainians lived in Canada for only sixty years?] *Novyi Shliakh,* no. 56-7, 1951.
86 L. Biletsky, *Ukrainian Pioneers in Canada, 1891-1951* (Winnipeg: Canadian Ukrainian Committee, 1951), p. 17.
87 Royick, "Roman Bachynsky - pershyi ukrainets u Kanadi."
88 Letter from Dr. D. W. Matheson to A. Royick, 20 January 1970. Efforts to verify all births from 1885 to 1890 brought no results.
89 Letter from O. Woycenko to A. Royick, 6 November 1966, A. Royick's archives.
90 Letter from V. J. Kaye (Kysilewsky) to A. Royick, 18 December 1967, A. Royick's archives.
91 Goresky, "Stefan Koroluk", pp. 249-50.

CHAPTER IV

1 Oleskiw, *O emigratsii. Pro Vilni Zemli* [About Free Lands] (Lviv: Naukove Tovarystvo Shevchenka, 1895).
2 Dmytriw, *Kanadiiska Rus.*
3 Between 1896 and 1906, *Svoboda* printed letters and articles from about one hundred Canadian contributors. Some of these contributed only once but a number of them can be considered regular correspondents.
4 I. Bobersky, "Pryiikhav u rotsi 1891" (He arrived in the year 1891], *Providnyk Almanack* (Winnipeg: St. Raphael's Association, 1933).
5 Czumer, *Spomyny,* pp. 17-27.
6 Ibid., p. 25. Czumer quotes Bobersky.

7 Marunchak, *Z Ukrainskymy pioneramy Alberty*, p. 15.

8 "Pershyi Ukrainskyi Kanadets" [The first Ukrainian Canadian], *In commemoration of the Sixtieth Anniversary of the Lives and Achievements of Ukrainians in Canada* (Winnipeg: Ukrainske Slovo, 1950), p. 8. The author, who is not cited in the publication, claims that Pylypiw studied for some time in the *gymnasium* in Stanislaviv (now Ivano-Frankivsk).

9 Ibid.

10 Lysenko, *Men in Sheepskin Coats*, p. 8.

11 "Pershyi Ukrainskyi Kanadets", p. 8. The author claims that Pylypiw travelled to the Kuban province of Russia to study possibilities of settlement. Though he did not find the fertile land or favorable conditions which he sought, he found German settlers from Galicia from whom he discovered more about Canada and obtained the address of a former schoolmate, Johann Krebs, who had already emigrated to Canada.

12 Wasyl Eleniak, "Pershi Ukrainski imigranty v Kanadi" [The first Ukrainian immigrants in Canada], [in] *Yuvileinim Kalendari Ukrainskoi Rodyny na rik 1941* [Jubilee Almanack of the Ukrainian Family] (Mundare, Alberta: Basilian Fathers, 1941), pp. 81-3.

13 Professor Bobersky was very accurate and precise in his records. Being unable to visit Pylypiw a second time to verify his written account of the interview, he obtained a copy of the court proceedings in Stanislaviv (#468/36 for 1892), in the district court where action had been taken against Pylypiw and Ziniak for inciting people to emigrate to America and enticing them to make advance payments on their fares. As a result, a discrepancy was uncovered between Pylypiw's statement to Bobersky in 1932 and that which he reported at the trial. To Bobersky he related that the third member of the group which had started for Canada was Yurko Panishchak but his own statement, according to court records indicates that the third member was Tyt Ziniak. As further proof of this fact, his statement in court reveals that Ziniak was not permitted to continue the journey because he possessed only 120 *rynsky*. Furthermore, as Ziniak did not need the money immediately, Pylypiw also reported that he had borrowed twenty *rynsky* from him for contingencies. In this statement there was no mention of Panischak. On this account the author has chosen to adhere to this statement contrary to versions accepted by many others because it was made under oath and because Pylypiw's memory of events in 1892 was certainly better than it was forty years later, when he was already 73 years old. Czumer, *Spomyny*, p. 25.

14 Ibid. Czumer follows Bobersky in claiming that St. Raphael's Ukrainian Immigrant Welfare Organization had verified that the ship *Oregon*, with Pylypiw and Eleniak on board, left Liverpool on August 28, 1891, and reached Montreal on September 7, 1891.

15 The railway to Langenburg had been completed in 1886. It is in present day Saskatchewan, about fifteen miles west of Russel, Manitoba.

16 A homestead was a free grant of one hundred sixty acres given to a settler for his own in return for certain cultivation and residential requirements.

17 Reading Pylypiw's account to Bobersky, the reader is left with the impression that they left for some "Greenfield" in Alberta. Actually, they were passing through Grenfell in present day Saskatchewan on their return to Manitoba.

18 A township is a square block of land six miles to a side, consisting of thirty-six sections. Since each section had four quarters of land, and each quarter contained one hundred sixty acres, this would mean a settlement of one hundred forty four persons.

19 Czumer, *Spomyny*, p. 26. The letter from the Wolff agency quotes fares as follows: adults, 86 *rynsky;* children 5-12, half fare; children 1-5, 29 *rynsky;* children under 1, 6½ *rynsky*. A *rynsky* or *gulden* was approximately fifty cents in Canadian money.

20 Ibid., pp. 25-7. From the court records we have the following information: the gendarme who arrested Pylypiw and Ziniak was Karl Shchepansky; the persecuting attorney was Agrasinsky and the defence attorney was Majeranowsky;

the trial judges who composed the tribunal were Shankowsky, Shymanovich, Starosolsky, and Piskozub.

21 I. Romaniuk, "Deshcho z zhyttia pershoi Ukrainskoi oseli v Kanadi" [A few things about the life of the first Ukrainian settlement in Canada], *Kalendar "Ukrainskoho Holosu" na rik 1939* [Illustrated Almanack of the "Ukrainian Voice", 1939], p. 60.

22 Unpublished records of Dr. George Dragan of Saskatoon who was married to a granddaughter of Mykola Tychkowsky.

23 Marunchak, *Z Ukrainskymy pioneramy Alberty,* p. 15.

24 I. Romaniuk, "Pochatky nebylivskykh rodyn u Kanadi" [The beginnings of the Nebyliv families in Canada], *Kalendar "Ukrainskoho Holosu" na rik 1942* [Almanack of the "Ukrainian Voice" for 1942], pp. 81-5.

25 See above, pt. 1, ch. 3, pp. 31-3. If we omit Stefan Koroluk they are the first Ukrainians to file on homesteads in Canada.

26 Czumer, *Spomyny,* p. 22.

27 Ibid. Bobersky's information was that Pylypiw died at a wedding in the home of a relative in North Bank, Alberta. Leaning too far out of a window to cool himself on a hot day, Pylypiw lost his balance and fell out of the window, killing himself instantly.

  Also see "Pershyi Ukrainskyi Kanadets", p. 12. This account states that the occasion was a wedding at the home of Pylypiw's cousin, Wasyl Kulka of North Bank. Pylypiw had been drinking and was helped to one of the bedrooms upstairs to rest. During the night, mistaking the large window for a door, he walked through and fell to the ground, killing himself instantly. The doctor who was called affirmed the cause of death as a broken neck.

28 Eleniak, "Pershi Ukrainski imigranty," pp. 81-8.

  Also see I. Bobersky, "Yak pershykh dvokh Ukraintsiv zayikhalo do Kanady" [How the first two Ukrainians reached Canada], *Kalendar "Kanadiiskoho Farmera" na rik 1937]* ["Canadian Farmer" Almanack for 1937], republished in Czumer, *Spomyny,* pp. 17-27.

28 Romaniuk, "Deshcho z zhyttia...", pp. 60-5.

30 Marunchak, *Z Ukrainskymy pioneramy Alberty,* p. 16.

31 Further research will be necessary to discover which families arrived with Eleniak and which came later. However, it seems reasonable to assume that Eleniak was accompanied by his two brothers and that the Melnyks arrived later.

32 Marunchak, *Z Ukrainskymy pioneramy Alberty,* pp. 19-20.

33 A. Royick, "Ukrainian Settlements in Alberta," *Canadian Slavonic Papers,* X, No. 3, (1968), pp. 278-97. Royick does not mention the number of children, confining himself to the number of grandchildren and great-grandchildren.

  Also see P. Yuzyk, "The First Ukrainians in Manitoba," *Historical and Scientific Society of Manitoba,* Series III, No. 8, (1953), p. 35. Yuzyk gives the number of Eleniak's children as eight.

CHAPTER V

1 *Propamiatna Knyha... Ukrainskoho Narodnoho Soiuzu,* p. 9.

2 V. J. Kaye, *Early Ukrainian Settlements in Canada, 1895-1900* (Toronto: University of Toronto Press, 1964).

3 Kaye, *Early Ukrainian Settlements,* pp. 3-4.

4 The High Commissioner at that time was Sir Charles Tupper.

5 Oleskiw, *Pro Vilni Zemli,* p. 9.

6 Through treachery, the Russian general, Tekely, was able to move his artillery close to the Sich, the Zaporozhian stronghold, forcing the *kozaky* to surrender. Before arrangements could be made to move them, more than half of them escaped to Turkish territory around the Black Sea at Ochakiv. Though the *kozaky* were quite happy here, the Turkish authorities moved them to territory around the estuary of the Danube.

7   Kaye, *Early Ukrainian Settlements*, pp. 34-8. All information regarding Oleskiw's journey to western Canada follows Carsten's report.

8   Kirschbaum, *Slovaks in Canada*, p. 56.

CHAPTER VI

1   The following were present at the conference: Lonhyn Rozhankiwsky, a lawyer from Zolochiv; Pavlo Dumka, a peasant poet, later a member of parliament, and Stefan Harmatiy, both from Kupchyntsi; Kyrylo Genik-Berezowsky, a teacher from Bereziv; Ivan Raduliak from Hlushkiv; Ivan Hoshovaniuk, Mykhailo Lawryshko, and Teofil Okunewsky, a lawyer, all from Horodenka; Father I. Maschak from Poputory, Petro Rybitsky from Nezhvysk, and Dr. Chaykowsky, a lawyer and author from Berezhan. From Lviv itself there were: Ivan Franko, an author; Viacheslaw Budzynowsky, an author and the editor of *Hromadskyi Holos*, Dr. Andriy Kos, who later became a member of parliament; and Dr. Mykola Shukhevych. *Svoboda*, no. 40, December 12, 1895.

2   *Svoboda*, no. 18, April 30, 1896. News quoted from *Halychanyn* (Lviv), no. 54, 1896.

3   Oleskiw, *O emigratsii*. This brochure was published by the Kachkovsky Society, a group which had a pro-Russian orientation. This resulted in some Russification of the author's language. The above information is confirmed by Oleskiw's daughter, Sophia Fedorchak, in her memoirs. S. Fedorchak, *Preria* [The Prairie] (Winnipeg: The Society of St. Raphael, 1928).

4   Oleskiw, *O emigratsii*, p. 62.

5   More will be written about this settlement later.

6   *Svoboda*, no. 4, February 15, 1894.

7   Ibid., no. 6, 1894.

8   Letter from V. J. Kaye to A. Royick, 13 November 1969, Royick's archives.

9   *Svoboda*, no. 39, 1896.

10 Kaye, *Early Ukrainian Settlements*, pp. 60-1. The following immigrants are listed: Lucian Keryk (Kyryk); Josef, Daria, Leon, and Eva Procinsky (Protsinsky); Ivan, son of Andriy Lakusta, his wife Katharine, and two children, Anna and Ivas; Ivan, son of Todyr Lakusta; Ivan and Anna Halkiw with four children; Antin and Maria Tesluk with seven children; Nykola and Maria Stecyk with two children; the Nemirskys consisting of Konstantine, Theodore, Basil, two women, Maria and Magdalena, with two younger children; Josef and Magdalena Dziwenka; Tetiana Danyluk; Gregor Samograd; Antin and Rosalia Savka with their daughter; Ignatz Samborsky; Pawlo Kobersky; Wasyl and Pelagia Pisklivets with two children; Demko and Adelphine Maceloski with six children, Ivan and Anna Hawrylenko with five children; Teodor Fuhr.

11 Ibid., p. 183.

12 Ibid., p. 61.

13 A. Hospodyn, "Spomyny Sofii Fedorchakovoi, dochky Osypa Oleskowa" [Memoirs of Sofia Fedorchak, daughter of Osyp Oleskiw], *Kanadiiskyi Farmer*, no. 49, 1965.

14 Kaye, *Early Ukrainian Settlements*, p. 65.

15 Oleskiw uses the term "Austrian Greek Catholics" instead of Ukrainian or Ruthenian to allay any suspicion on the part of both Canadian and Austrian authorities that his interests lay specifically with Ukrainians. Such a suspicion would have hindered his immigration projects.

16 Kaye, *Early Ukrainian Settlements*, p. 70. Reply of the Minister of the Interior, dated June 22, 1891.

17 Ibid., p. 78. Letter of Oleskiw to the Commissioner of Dominion Lands in Winnipeg.

18 Ibid., p. 137. Kyrylo Genik arrived with his wife and children on July 22, 1896.

19 Ibid., pp. 81-4. Letter was written September 7, 1896.

20 Ibid., p. 84.
21 Ibid., p. 281. Letter was written May 15, 1897.
22 Though Empress Elizabeth, Franz Joseph's consort, had been assassinated, the legend that she was still alive persisted among people in the Austrian empire.
23 Kaye, *Early Ukrainian Settlements,* p. 285. Letter written to the Minister of the Interior, May 29, 1897.
24 *Winnipeg Tribune,* Thursday, May 27, 1897.

CHAPTER VII

1 Kaye, *Early Ukrainian Settlements,* p. 102.
2 Ibid., p. 73. R. A. Ruttan to the Commissioner of Dominion Lands, Winnipeg, June 6, 1896.
3 Ibid., p. 96. Sir Donald A. Smith to Sir Clifford Sifton, 24 April 1897.
4 Ibid., pp. 326-8. S. W. Sutter, Agent Dominion Lands Office in Edmonton, to W. F. McCreary, Winnipeg, 27 September 1897.
5 Ibid., p. 295. Telegram from E. Schultze, Austro-Hungarian Consul to W. F. McCreary, Winnipeg, from the *Argus* (Stonewall, Manitoba), 16 September 1897.
6 Ibid., pp. 170-1. Ignatius Roth to James Thom of the Hamburg-America Packet Company, 5 September 1897.
7 Ibid., pp. 97-8. James A. Smart, Ottawa, to Sir Donald A. Smith, London, 30 October 1897.
8 Ibid., p. 98. Telegram from W.F. McCreary, Winnipeg, to James A. Smart, Ottawa, 27 November 1897. Also a telegram from James A. Smart, Deputy Minister of Immigration, to the High Commissioner for Canada in London. Note that the name "Galicia" was applied to the whole area of western Ukraine by Canadian Government officials.
9 Ibid., pp. 108-9.
10 Ibid., p. 131. Memo re Oleskiw by Charles H. Beddoe, Accountant, Department of Interior, Ottawa, for the Deputy Minister.
11 Ibid., p. 85.

CHAPTER VIII

1 It should be noted that geographical meridians, running north to the North Pole, come closer to one another as they move north. If the same distance is to be kept between them, then some of the range meridians must disappear. Furthermore, because meridians are numbered from the east, they are eliminated in the west as necessary. On account of the narrowing distance between meridians, not only do range lines disappear, but not all townships have third-six sections, not all sections have 640 acres, and not all quarter sections have 160 acres.

   Each province issues its own maps on which the location of its lands are indicated by meridians, townships, and ranges. On examining a map, we note that the centre of Winnipeg lies in township 11 and range 3 east of the first meridian; Dauphin is in township 25 and range 19 west of the first meridian; Saskatoon is in township 35 and range 5 west of the third meridian; and Edmonton is in township 53 and range 24 west of the fourth meridian.

   In the same way, a person can quickly and accurately identify the location of a farm. Let us suppose someone has settled or is still living on the north-west quarter of section 2, township 2, and range 6 east of the first meridian (NW2-2-6 El). We can easily see that this quarter is found in one of the earliest Ukrainian settlements in Canada, Stuartburn (it is actually the quarter of Wasyl Zahara who arrived in Canada in 1896). Or again let us suppose we are looking for someone who settled on the north-east quarter of section 19, township 26, range 20 west of the first meridian (NE19-26-20 W1). We can immediately ascertain that this quarter is in present day Valley River in Dauphin district (it is actually the quarter of Wasyl Ksionzhyk who also arrived in Canada in 1896). If anyone settled on the south-east quarter of section 12, township 55, range 22 west of the fourth meridian (SE12-55-22 W4), we find that this quarter is close to Edmonton, and actually the quarter on which Mykhailo Romaniuk is reported to have filed on June 26, 1892.

CHAPTER IX

1 There were large numbers of prairie chickens in this valley but they were regarded as pheasants by the first settlers — hence the name.

2 The location of this building was approximately the centre of the settlement. It was on SE22-21-9 W2.

3 Angelina H. Campbell, *Man! Man! Just Look At This Land* (Ellisboro Old-Timers' Association, 1966).

4 Ibid.

5 Hopkins Moorhouse, *Deep Furrows* (Toronto and Winnipeg: George McLeod, 1918), p. 63. Rat Portage was renamed Kenora and is in Ontario.

6 A. S. Morton, *History of Prairie Settlement* (Toronto: McMillan and Company, 1938).

7 Oleskiw, *O emigratsii*, pp. 49-53.

8 Dmytriw, *Kanadiiska Rus*, p. 9

9 *Svoboda*, no. 38, 1897.

10 This information was given by Yurko Pylypiw of Saskatoon who arrived in Canada with his parents in 1893 and grew up in Pheasant Forks. Andrun and Mikhas are diminutives for Andrew and Michael, commonly applied to children, but the names may persist into adulthood.

11 Oleskiw, *O emigratsii*, p. 52. Dorundiak relates an interesting story about Shymko. Prior to his departure for Canada, it appears that Shymko informed a local Ukrainian magnate in Kalush, Korytowsky, that he planned to emigrate to Canada where he could eat bread from white flour which was only used for baking buns and pastry in Austria. Korytowsky is supposed to have replied, "Look Pavlo! You have bread here; respect it! Don't go looking for buns in America or you will hunger for bread." But this caution did not prevent Pavlo's departure. Having arrived in Canada, Pavlo built a prosperous home with a kitchen, a guest room, and porch. He also built a storehouse, a granary, and a barn. He bought two yoke of oxen, a team of horses, a cow, and was really on the way to becoming a very prosperous farmer. When he sat down at the table to a meal, he would often boast, "Here I am with white bread which looks like a bun. Squire Korytowsky's threat was empty." It was unfortunate, however, that Pavlo did not enjoy his white bread for long. While driving a team of spirited horses, he lost control when they were frightened, fell off the wagon, and broke his backbone and one of his ribs. He died the next day and was buried on St. Demetrius' day (November 8).

12 Kaye, "Liudy z rannoi nashoi istorii, novi materialy do istorii ukrainskoho poselennia" [People of our early history, new materials about Ukrainian settlement], *Ukrainski Visti* [Ukrainian News], (Edmonton), no. 1, 1964.

13 The name of Yurko or George was apparently omitted in Kaye's account either through a printing error or because of inaccurate records in the immigration archives. He was five years old at the time of the family's arrival. Yurko gave the author a good deal of information about his family and the Pheasant Forks colony. Yurko claimed that their family did not come from Kalush but from the village of Ulychne in the county of Drohobych and were not related to the Pylypiws of Nebyliv.

14 Dorundiak did not err entirely in calling Senkiw by the name of Shymko. George or Yurko Pylypiw related that he had always been known as Shymko in Pheasant Forks. Dr. Michael Boykovich, who's father was Shymko's neighbour both in Kalush and in Neudorf which was near Pheasant Forks, confirms that Senkiw and later his widow were both known as Shymko or Simko.

15 Kaye's research is valuable not only because of the discovery of Pylypiw and

Shymko but also because it reveals how much time and effort have to be spent in seeking information on Ukrainian pioneers in Canada. To discover the official record of Pylypiw's arrival in Canada in 1893, he was compelled to examine closely the manifests of one hundred fifty ships which arrived in that year, bringing 42,999 passengers to Canada through Quebec. When this brought no results, he repeated his efforts with sixty-one ships which had arrived in Halifax with their thousands of passengers. Finally, on the manifest of the thirty-fifth ship, *Pickhuben,* he came across the family of Pylypiw but the name was listed as Filipow.

His research activities on Shymko were also as arduous as in the case of Pylypiw. Dorundiak had reported that Pylypiw arrived in 1891. Kaye went through the lists of eighty-two ships which had arrived in Quebec with 15,955 passengers in that year without finding any trace of Shymko. The Halifax lists for that year also brought no result. Thinking that Shymko might have arrived in 1890, he again examined the lists from both ports with no better success. Returning to the task, he began to go through the 1892 lists. He found the Nebyliv immigrants very early in the process but Shymko finally appeared on the manifest of the twenty-third ship, Mongolian, which arrived in Halifax on April 16, 1892. On this list was passenger 4164 with the name of Pawlo Seynkiw and the names of his family followed. But Kaye still had to ascertain that this was the Shymko of Dorundiak's account, and that Andrun and Mikhas Umoroslavych were Andrun and Mykhailo Huminolovych. To determine the latter he had to review 36,000 names of immigrants who were naturalized in the years 1893-1903.

16 Oleskiw, *O emigratsii,* p. 52.

17 The date of arrival of the Kulchitskys has not been confirmed but they lived in Pheasant Forks for some time before they dispersed to different parts of Canada. Though they did not achieve prominence as national or provincial leaders, they nevertheless played an important part in the communities in which they lived.

18 Leon Boykovich became a Canadian citizen and the owner of his land on October 2, 1900. Though he felt at home with German settlers whose language he knew quite well, he still felt a nostalgia for life among his fellow-countrymen. Accordingly, he rented his own farm and moved first to Brandon and then to Winnipeg where he opened his own store. His oldest son Nicolas was the first Ukrainian to become a policeman in Canada. As life in Winnipeg did not appeal to him, we find him moving to Goodeve where he bought a hotel and continued to live here until his death. He was an active member in his community and a leader in his district. His daughter, Petrunia, who married a Korchinsky, was one of the first teachers of Ukrainian origin in Saskatchewan. Michael, the youngest son, became a teacher and a leading member of his community. He is now a dentist in Saskatoon. Leon Boykovich's granddaughter, Olga Niles, is married to Rev. Dr. S. W. Sawchuk.

19 According to the personal memoirs of Maria (Slipchenko) Bozhok, the daughter of Fedir Dumka, she arrived with her parents in the port of Halifax on the *Bulgaria* in April 1902.

20 From the personal memoirs of Mykhailo Davydiuk who arrived in Halifax on the *Arcadia* in 1903.

21 The name of Lemberg would suggest that the German settlers came from Galicia as Lemberg is the capital of that province.

22 Campbell, *Man! Man! Just Look At This Land!* p. 79. The actual town plan is included.

23 The Chernecki (Chernetsky) family arrived in Halifax on April 3, 1903, on the *Armenia* and settled on SW22-23-9 W2.

24 *Propamiatna knyha poselennia ukrainskoho narodu v Kanadi* [Memorial volume of the settlement of Ukrainians in Canada] (Yorkton, Sask.: The Voice of the Redeemer, 1941), p. 266.

25 From an interview with Yurko Pylypiw and confirmation by other immigrants who found refuge with Pylypiw on arrival in Canada before settling on their homesteads.

26 A. S. Morton, *History of Prairie Settlements,* p. 123. The author does not give the number of the townships but it is understood that they include the areas toward Birmingham, Fenwood, Goodeve, and Hubbard.

CHAPTER X

1 Oleskiw, *O emigratsii,* p. 62. The following twelve families are listed: Andriy
Paish, Stepan Chichak, Mykhailo, Mykola, and Fedir Melnyk, Ivan Pylypiw,
Wasyl Feniak, Petro and Matiy Melnyk from Perehinske, Mykola Tychkowsky,
Mykhailo(?) from near Sambir, and Ivan Dombrowsky from near Zolochiv.
  J. G. McGregor claims that five Ukrainian families arrived in the fall of 1894
and suggests that among them were two brothers of Antin Paish, Mykhailo and
Yosef (Joseph), their father Andrew, and, probably, the Staciuk (Statsiuk) family.
McGregor, *Vilni Zemli,* p. 62.
2 Both Nemirskys were Russophiles, but it is not known whether they arrived as
members of this group from their homeland or whether they became so in opposition to the French Roman Catholic attempts to establish its guardianship over the
Ukrainian (then Greek) Catholic Church. Whatever the reason, they joined the
Russian Orthodox Church and remained its adherents until their death. This is
probably the reason that they did not play an important role in the later years of
Ukrainian settlement.
3 Nebyliv was then in the county of Kalush and not the county of Stryi. It is now in
Ruzhnytivsky *rayon* (district).
4 Dmytriw, *Kanadiiska Rus,* pp. 36-40, 46. The author records detailed and interesting information about five settlers: Wasyl Feniak, Ivan Dombrowsky, Ivan
Lakusta, Mykola Tychkowsky, and Kost Nemirsky. He describes the settlers' progress with some information on farming conditions, including the cost of farm
animals and farm machinery. He also contrasts the condition of settlers who had
arrived under Oleskiw's care and guidance with that of other settlers. As Oleskiw
had been selective in his choice, the comparison definitely favored Oleskiw's
group.
5 Kaye, *Early Ukrainian Settlements,* pp. 324-6. The above statistics were compiled
from the report of Corporal G. D. Buttler.
6 These are the names in the report: Wasyl Marian, Dm. Balan, G. Klapatiuk,
Wasyl Hunka, Gregori Wasylenchuk, Tanasko Skintey, Michael, Nykola,
Hryhory, and Achtemy Hrehirchak, Hawrylo Andriets, Georgi Melnyk, Danylo
Kutzengavich, Wasyl Stetsko, Ivan and Nykola Topolnitsky, Phillip Woitas, Ivan
Makowitsky, Antin Gurba, Pawlo Gudzan, Ivan Farion, Ivan Bucza, Yasko
Kalanchuk, Yasko Melenka, Ivan Slywka, Wasyl Gluchie, Michael Babiak, Wasyl
Zaharia, Petro Palahniuk(?), Wasyl Hrynkiw, Ivan Kuryski(?), Wasyl Strashok,
Fedir Sokhatsky, Michael Kakhupski, H. Babych, Ivan Scraba, Nykola Verenka,
Dmytro Chilko, Ilia Soloniuk, Andriy Polinsky, Maksym and Dmytro Zakharko,
Fedir Lakusta, Wasyl Kryz, Panko Onuchko, Ivan and Antin Tancowny, Nastia
Zakharko, Ivan Matsko, Ivan Strochynski, Ivan Polovy, Franko Vozniak, Yosef
Vyspansky, Ivan Lupul, Ivan Talpash, Rosalia Sawka, Ivan Kucy, Antin
Svoboda, Pawlo Hrycak, Ivan Yurkiw, Sobko Andrukhiw, Leon Procinsky, and
others. See ibid., pp. 324-42.
7 Ibid., pp. 357-8.
8 Czumer, *Spomyny,* pp. 50-1.
9 Ibid., pp. 51-2.
10 Ibid., pp. 52-3.
11 Ibid., pp. 54-5.
  Czumer obtained his information under difficult conditions and was unable
to confirm his information because of the difficulties and expense of travel. The
memory of most pioneers is not always clear in regard to dates and there are errors
in both Zahariychuk's and Maria Yureychuk's accounts. The translator interviewed Kost Zahariychuk's son Peter, whom Kost mentions in his account, and
discovered that the Zahariychuks arrived with the second group of immigrants
from Toporivtsi in 1900. The first group had arrived in Canada in 1899. The
biography written on that occasion is in the translator's possession. He also interviewed relatives of Mrs. Yureychuk, especially her son-in-law, Petro Luchak, who
was still alive in 1974. According to his information, the Yureychuks arrived from
the village of Ispas in Bukovyna in 1901 and not from Halychyna as she seems to

imply. The date is further corroborated by her own statement when she relates that Ratsoy had arrived two years earlier because Ratsoy was with the first group of immigrants from the village of Toporivtsi. There is also another error. It was not Pasichney who lived in Wasel but Pasichnyk.

CHAPTER XI

1 Kaye, *Early Ukrainian Settlements,* pp. 141-2. The names of these settlers and their land locations are listed as well as most of the villages from which they arrived. The majority came from villages in the county of Zalischyky, especially from the village of Synkiw (Senkiw). These include Nykolai Kohut, Josef Bzowy (Yosef Bzovy), Onufry Smuk (Smook), Ivan Storoszczuk (Storoshchuk), Semen Salamandyk, Wasyl Salamandyk, Ivan Salamandyk, Wasyl Stefura, Josef Szelep (Yosef Shelep), Fedor (Fedir) Pidhirny, and Fedor (Fedir) Dymianyk. From other villages in the same county came Maksym Stasyszyn (Stasyshyn) from the village of Solone, Fedor Horobec (Fedir Horobets) and Ivan Tomaszewski (Tomashewsky) from the village of Blyszczanka (Blyshchanka), and Petro Strumbicki (Strumbitsky) from the village of Dobrivliany. There were also a number from the county of Kolomyia which is partly within the Carpathian Mountains. From the village of Bereziw came Ivan Negrycz (Negrych), Cyril Genik (Genyk), also Ivan, Michael, Hryhory, and Nykola Prygrocki (Prygrotsky). Petro Majkiwski (Maykiwsky) and his brother Nykola were from the village of Hvozdets in the same county. Two of the immigrants were from the county of Borszcziw (Borshchiv) east of the county of Zalischyky, Ilasz (Ilash) Prokopczuk (Prokopchuk) from the village of Ustie and Vasyl Perun (Peroon) from Bilcze (Bilche) Zolote. Nykola Wysoczynski's native village is unknown. Wasyl Zahara arrived from the village of Bridok, county of Zastavna, in the province of Bukovyna. Information on a number of names, on which information was not available from Kaye's notes, was obtained from Mrs. John Paley of Dominion City, Manitoba, daughter of Vasyl Bzovy.

2 Sometimes the reader is confused by the fact that the two provinces of Bukovyna and Galicia are so sharply differentiated by many in Canada. Distances are so vast in Canada that we tend to believe they are the same in Europe. Actually Bridok, which means a ford, is just across the Dniester River from Synkiw. In the Austrian Empire people travelled freely from one village to the other. After Poland annexed Halychyna and Roumania occupied Bukovyna after the First War, communication became much more difficult, which might have been the reason for the overemphasis in differentiation. Church differences might also have had their effect.

3 Kaye, *Early Ukrainian Settlements,* pp. 150-2. Among those mentioned the following are more widely known: Wasyl Hawryluk (Vasyl Hawryliuk), Andriy Glowatsky (Glovatsky), Ivan Sandul, Ivan and Mykhailo Mukanyk, Mykhailo Sokolowsky, O. Kuchinsky, Wasyl (Vasyl) and Mykhailo Zahara, Mykhailo Cesmystruk (Tsesmystruk), I. Sokolyk, Mat. (Matiy) Probizhansky, Kost Dydyk (Didukh), Ozarko Niwransky, Maksym Stasyshyn, and Josef (Yosef) Bzowy (Bzovy). See also Michael Stashyn, "Moi spomyny" [My Reminiscences], *"Ukrainian Voice" Almanack,* 1938. Stashyn also mentions Nykola Genik.

4 Michael Stashyn, "Moi spomyny".

5 Kaye, *Early Ukrainian Settlements,* pp. 159.

6 Ibid., p. 172. Report by Leon Roy.

7 Ibid., p. 148.

8 Ibid.

9 Ibid., p. 154.

10 Ibid., p. 166.

11 Stashyn, "Moi spomyny", p. 75. Stashyn regarded them as C.P.R. lands, but he was wrong.

12 Kaye, *Early Ukrainian Settlements,* pp. 175-8. Kaye lists all the settlers and also the land on which they are located. Among these names, excluding those which have already been listed, we find the following (families): Wiwchar (Viwchar) —

Ivan and Jarema (Yarema); Zaporozan (Zaporozhan) — Ivan and Ilia; Danylejko
— Andrij (Danyleyko Andriy); Wiwsianyk (Viwsianyk) — Stefan, Andrij (An-
driy), and Michalo (Mykhailo); Jaremij (Yaremiy) — Michal (Mykhailo), Oleksa,
and Fedor (Fedir); Tkaczyk (Tkachyk) — Ivan, Wasyl (Vasyl), Matij (Matiy), and
Dmytro; Rekrut, Onufry; Kossowan (Kossovan) — Andrij (Andriy), Wasyl
(Vasyl), Gregoire (Hryhory), Dmytro, Iwan (Ivan), Nykolaj (Nykolai), Kirylo
(Kyrylo), Kost, Oleksa, Petro, Elash (Ilash), and Aksenia (widow); Zahara —
Jakob (Yakub) and Iwan (Ivan); Rozka (Rozhka) — Wasyl (Vasyl) and Nikolaj
(Nykolai); Zyha (Zhyha) — Michal (Mikhal or Mykhailo), Iwan (Ivan), Petro, and
Arkadij (Arkadiy); Onysko, Michajlo (Mykhailo); Nazarewicz (Nazarevich), Iwan
(Ivan); Solomon — Nykola, Joseph (Yosef) and Petro; Maksymchuk — Semen
and Todor; Niwranski — Jakiw (Yakiw) and Dmytro; Kulaczkowski
(Kulachkowsky), Jan (Ivan); Bugera — Hryc (Hryts) and Dmytro; Panchuk,
Nazarko; Wachna (Vakhna) — Theodosy and Dmytro, Podolski (Podolsky) —
Iwan (Ivan), Phylyp, Wasyl (Vasyl), and Hrynko; Bodnarchuk, Andrij (Andriy);
Tanchak, Wasyl (Vasyl); Smuk (Smook) Wasyl (Vasyl); Paskaruk — Timko
(Tymko) and Hryc (Hryts); Machnij (Makhniy) — Iwan (Ivan) and Kost; Kolisnyk
Semen; Cysmystruk (Tsysmistruk), Nykola; Woroniuk (Voroniuk) Iwan (Ivan);
and many others. There is no mention of Vasyl Drul on whose farm the village of
Vita was later located and Ivan Mihaychuk who also arrived from the village of
Bridok to settle in what was later known as Arbakka.

13 *Svoboda* (Philadelphia), no. 24, June 16, 1898.
14 John Panchuk, *Bukovinian Settlements in Southern Manitoba* (Battle Creek,
Mich.; The author, 1971).
15 Ibid., p. 4. Panchuk claims that this was the location of the post office which was
given the name of Overstone during the years 1898-1905. In 1905 it was changed to
Oleskiw in memory of the father of Ukrainian immigration to Canada. The
change in name came as a result of pressure from the community influenced by a
local teacher, Theodore Kochan (Kokhan). Some years later, when he was influenced by the Russophile movement and became interested in Tolstoi's literary
works, he again influenced the community to change the name to Tolstoi.
16 Originally this district was known as Shevchenko but the railway station was given
the name of Vita.
17 Paul Yuzyk, *The Ukrainians in Manitoba: A Social History* (Toronto: University
of Toronto Press, 1953), p. 39.

CHAPTER XII

1 *Svoboda,* no. 16, April 15, 1897.
2 Dmytriw, *Kanadiiska Rus,* pp. 14-17, 19.
3 The author is probably exaggerating his difficulties in the last six miles of travel. It
is difficult to believe that, after travelling with horses for three days, one hour of
walking, and again travelling with horse, he had travelled only four and a half
miles and was still "a farm and a half" or three quarters of a mile away from his
destination.
4 Dmytriw, *Kanadiiska Rus,* pp. 13-17, 19. Father Dmytriw did not record the date
of his visit in Terebovlia. Kaye thought, *Early Ukrainian Settlements,* p. 185, that
Dmytriw's visit took place after he had been in Stuartburn on Palm Sunday and
Edna on Easter Sunday (Easter being on April 18 in 1897). See Kaye, *Early Ukrainian Settlements,* p. 185. However, Father Dmytriw writes as follows: "I will
record my observations in order since that arrangement will be most convenient
for me to (record) my journey." This would imply that he described events in the
order that they took place, and the visits were arranged in the order that suited him
best. Therefore, if he describes the journey to Terebovlia first, it is clear that this
must have been his first visit. If he had visited it after returning from Alberta,
from which he returned on May 9, there would not have been drifts of snow in
Terebovlia as he states in his book. Furthermore, Kaye corrected his first version
in a later article, that Father Dmytriw celebrated his first mass during his visit on

April 12, which was before his visits to Stuartburn and Edna. *Ukrainski Visti* [Ukrainian News] (Edmonton), no. 14, 1964.

5 Kaye, *Early Ukrainian Settlements*, p. 187. Also see Kaye, *Dictionary of Ukrainian Canadian Biography, Pioneer Settlers of Manitoba* (Toronto: Ukrainian Canadian Research Foundation, 1975), p. 72. Complete information on John Niplanski can be found in item 277 of this second source. (Translator's note).

6 M. Marunchak, *Kanadiiska Terebovlia* [Canadian Terebovlia] (Winnipeg: General Library, U.K.T., 1964), p. 11.

7 Dmytriw, *Kanadiiska Rus,* p. 186. Kaye raised doubts about the claim of Father Dmytriw that there were fifteen families in Terebovlia at the time of his visit because this claim was not supported by immigration and naturalization records, which indicate the presence of only eight families. Nevertheless, Marunchak, basing his facts on his interview with W. Nimets, writes that seven additional families arrived in Terebovlia on December 25, 1896, which would confirm Father Dmytriw's account of the presence of fifteen families. *Kanadiiska Terebovlia,* p. 11. It is curious and perplexing to note why Father Dmytriw, who was so careful to record so many names of Stuartburn and Edna immigrants, did not give us a single name of any settler in Terebovlia. He did not even give the name of "that man" whom he found so difficult to reach, at whose home he was quartered, and who was a subscriber to *Svoboda.*

8 N. Hryhorchuk, "Ukrainska koloniia Ethelbert" [Ukrainian Colony of Ethelbert], *Propamiatna knyha Ukrainskoho Narodnoho Domu u Winnipegu* [The Memorial Book of the Ukrainian National Home in Winnipeg] (Winnipeg: Narodnyi Dim, 1949), p. 489.
   Hryhorchuk states that Yurko Syrotiuk selected a homestead in the present day settlement of Ethelbert in 1896 and wrote to his village inviting his relatives to follow him as there were prospects for a great future in Canada.

9 Dmytro Romanchych, "Ukrainski Kolonii v okruzi Davfyn" [Ukrainian Colonies in the Dauphin District], in ibid., p. 515.

10 Ibid., p. 516. The thirteen families who settled here are: Antin, Ivan, and Nykola Genik, Stepan Urbanovych, Vasyl Symchych, Teodor Sklepovych, Yosef and Dmytro Romanchych, Antin Milowsky, Semen Fitsych, Ivan Slyzhuk, Mykhailo Ilnytsky, and Dmytro Malkovych.

11 On the basis of the records of Semen Leskiw the following came from the village of Hleshava: Vasyl Smylsky, Petro and Vasyl Pidodvorny, Mykhailo Leskiw and his son Semen; Matiy and Stepan Kumka, Petro and Mykhailo Matlashewsky, Mykhailo and Stepan Koshowsky, Mykhailo Chorney, Semen Magalas, Tomko and Blazhko Tabaka, Stepan Samets, and Mykhailo Duda. From other villages came Yosef, Ivan, Nykola, Mykhailo, and Tomko Pukhalsky, Ivan and Fedko Bosiak, Mykhailo Myk, Mykola Boyko, Fedko and Lazar Shkvarok, and Pawlo Trach.

12 Philemon Leskiw, *Pionerske zhyttia v Kanadi* [Pioneer life in Canada] (Winnipeg: Christian Press, 1953), pp. 23-4.

13 Marunchak, *Kanadiiska Terebovlia.* Marunchak has written a complete account of this settlement.

CHAPTER XIII

1 Dmytro Drohomorecki (Drohomoretsky) settled in this district in the spring of 1898 and was one of its pioneers. His unpublished memoirs, excerpts from which are included in this chapter, were written especially for this history at the urging of Mykola Zalozetsky of Winnipeg.

2 Kaye, *Early Ukrainian Settlements,* pp. 243-4.

3 Dmytro Drohomoretsky listed the following families and individuals: Drohomorecki (Drohomoretsky) — Hryhor, Mykhailo, Petro, Mykhailo (Ivan's son), Hryhor, and Dmytro; Urbanovycz (Urbanovych) — Petro, Vasyl, and Ivan; Oleksa Lazarovycz (Lazarovych); Symczycz (Symchych) — Hryhor, Vasyl, Petro,

and Ivan; Hawrylo Suliatycki (Suliatytsky); Percowycz (Pertsovych) — Dmytro, Ilko, and Petro; Jakiw Jakymiszczak (Yakiw Yakymishchak); Jakiw Wacyk (Yakiw Vatsyk); Mykola Szybinski (Shybinsky); Prokip Pakuliak; Mychajluk (Mykhailiuk) — Ivan and Tanas; Wasyl (Vasyl) Kyryliuk; Wasyl Malitczyn (Vasyl Malitchyn); Doroszczuk (Doroshchuk) — Ilarion, Jakim (Yakim), Martian, and Karlo; Wasyl (Vasyl) Porayko; Ivan Roha; Antin Wolczuk (Volchuk); Smere- czanski (Smerechansky) — Jakiw (Yakiw) and Antos; Chymczak (Khymchak) — Jas (Yas), Fed and Stach (Stakh); Mykhailo Hawryliuk; Hiliarko Jakymiw (Yakymiw); Wasyl (Vasyl) Dutchak; Prokip Antoniuk.

4 A cord was 128 cubic feet. The cordwood was cut in four foot lengths. The cord would be four feet high, four feet wide, and eight feet long.

5 *Svoboda,* no. 47, (1897).

6 Ibid., no. 8, (1903).

7 Yuzyk, *The Ukrainians in Manitoba,* p. 39.

8 Ivan Pawlychyn, "Z zhyttia ukrainskykh poselentsiv na homstedakh u pivnichniy Manitobi" [From the lives of Ukrainian settlers on homesteads in northern Manitoba], *Ukrainske Slovo* (Winnipeg), no. 8, (1965). This letter was written by Mykhailo Kovaliw who settled in Chatfield about 1901 and is quoted in the above article.

9 Colonia was a Jewish colony of about thirty families. It was planned like a Ukrai- nian village with two rows of houses and a well in the centre of the village. Before 1910 there were two stores in the village, a convenience for Ukrainian settlers because they did not have to travel all the way to Teulon for provisions. When the inhabitants discovered during 1911 and 1912 that the railroad would by-pass them two miles to the west and that new villages were being planned around established stations, they abandoned the village. Nothing now remains of Colonia and poplars again grow on the site of the old settlement.

10 Pawlychyn, "Z zhyttia ukrainskykh poselentsiv." Information about this journey was obtained by I. Pawlychyn from Ivan Deley of Winnipeg.

11 Ibid.

CHAPTER XIV

1 They were as follows: Ivan and Petro Haliuk, Pylyp Fedorchuk, Matey and Pawlo Viwsianyk, Yusep and Ivan Nykolayiw, and Yusep Dribnenky. Among those who arrived later, between 1898 and 1900, were Matey Dac (Dats), Vasyl Pyndus, Ivan Snihur, Vasyl Boytsun, Simon Kovalchuk, Mykhailo Sprynchynatyk, Mykhailo Cibulsky (Tsibulsky), Stepan and Dmytro Tymofiy.

2 The following families are known: Teodor Fedusiak, Vasyl Budzinsky, Hryc (Hryts) Poberezhnyk, Ivan Hudymka, Stepan Gryvul, Dora Hnatiuk, Oleksa Baziuk, Kost and Diordiy Mesenchuk, Semen Gara, Hryhory Radysh, and Simon Babiychuk. To the later group which arrived between 1898 and 1902, the following belong: Vasyl Minken, Mykola Chornopysky, Parteniy Ostapovych, Yosef, Vasyl, and Dmytro Kyrstiuk, Georgiy Choropita, Vasyl Koshman, Kost Lysak, Georgiy Kozak, Stepan Dumansky, Mykola and Kost Parteniy, Vasyl Kuprowsky, Vasyl Koropatnitsky, Vasyl and Ilko Ostapovych, M. Kereliuk, S. Fostiy, Georgiy Nykolaychuk, Yakiw Feniuk, Dmytro and Ilko Polovyk and others.

3 J. Hawkes, *The Story of Saskatchewan and Its People* (Chicago and Regina: S. J. Clarke Publishing Company, 1924), vol. 2, p. 718.

4 Ibid., pp. 731-2.

5 Ibid., p. 733.

6 Kaye, *Early Ukrainian Settlements,* p. 300.

7 Varkholiak and Khakholiak were educated and conscious of their heritage. Khakholiak was generally regarded as a "well-read" person. Varkholiak arrived in the United States in 1889 and became an American citizen three years later. Both were well known to the author.

8 *Svoboda,* no. 38, (1897).

9 Among those who belonged to the first group of immigrants the following names are noted: Vasyl Krypiakevych, Petro Jaholnicki (Yaholnytsky), Vasyl Oystryk, Ivan Tymryk, Vasyl Stefaniuk, Stepan Graba, Hawrylo Yurkiw, Semen Kushnir, Yosef Korchynsky, Franko Bandura, Antin Brezinsky, Antin Akhtymiychuk, Vasyl Naduriak, Tanas Haras, Vasyl Chorney, Andriy, Vasyl, and Mihay Anak.
The following were part of a group who arrived later: Pawlo Kyba, Fedir and Dmytro Stratiychuk, Dmytro and Vasyl Oliynyk, Mykhailo and Pawlo Okhitva, Milko Cymbalisty (Tsymbalisty), Pawlo Denys, Vasyl Gabora, and Yakiw Kuziak.

10 M. Adamowska, "Pionerski harazdy v Kanadi" [Pioneer hardships in Canada], *Propamiatna knyha Ukrainskoho Narodnoho Domu u Vinnipegu]*, pp. 449-58.

11 Mykhailo Stashyn, "Moi spomyny."

12 The following were part of this group: Yurko Babicki (Babitsky), the originator of this colony, Prokip Skorobohach with his son Fedir, Stepan Filyk, Mykhailo and Ivan Raychyba, Ivan, Mykola, and Dmytro Charnecki (Charnetsky), Antin Kanasevych, Maksym and Yakiw Boychuk, Vasyl Humenny, Yosef and Stepan Palamar, Kyrylo Krym, Hryc (Hryts) Boyarchuk, Mykhailo Bohachyk, and Fedir Gizen.

13 M. Chorneyko, *Shchob ne zabuty i denni podii* [Lest we forget and daily events] (Saskatoon: Globe Printers, 1964), pp. 32-4.

14 See Kaye, *Early Ukrainian Settlements,* p. 296.

15 Stepan Dumansky, a pioneer who filed on a homestead four miles south of present day Sheho soon after the settlement was established, often related to the author how he and his neighbours had walked fifty miles to Yorkton for their purchases and carted them home on their backs. Such hardships did not attract settlers very readily.

CHAPTER XV

1 Kaye, *Early Ukrainian Settlements,* p. 251. Letter of General Colonization Agent C. W. Speers to Frank Pedley, Superintendent of Immigration, Ottawa, 4 April 1899.

2 In 1898 there was one main railway route running from Winnipeg through Regina and Calgary to Vancouver. From the main route there were two branch lines running north, one built in 1890 from Regina through Saskatoon and Rosthern to Prince Albert, and the other completed in 1892 from Calgary to Edmonton. There was no direct rail connection between Saskatoon and Edmonton until 1905.

3 Kaye, *Early Ukrainian Settlements,* p. 306.

4 Ibid., pp. 304-6. The author reports the names of those who travelled to both Edmonton and Sifton.

5 Ibid., p. 307.

6 Andrew Turta, who arrived in Canada with his parents at the age of seventeen in May 1898 and settled in Fish Creek, informed the author that his father had exhorted his children for many years to pray for the health of Kyrylo Genik who had convinced them to settle at Fish Creek.

7 Kaye, *Early Ukrainian Settlements,* pp. 311-6. The author lists the names of settlers who arrived in 1898. Omitting the ten names already reported, the following were on the east side of the river (Alvena): Ivan Yurashyk, Ilko Bukurak, Vasyl Romanchych, Frank Holiuk, Yosef Hrytsak, Ivan Barchynsky, Oleksa Chryk (Khryk), Yakiw Matkowsky, Mykhailo Turta, Kaz. Biletsky, Kost Shymeliuk, Andriy Hawryshchak, Nykola Vyshynsky, Yosef Bilinsky, Toma Kozak, Martsin Oleskiw, Semen Bunka, Kost Shcherbaniuk, Ivan Zayachkowsky, Mykhailo Zaleschuk, Nykola Chyzhyk, Yakym Trach. The following were on the other side of the river: Petro Ryhorchuk, Nykola Zhulkowsky, I. Tvarynsky, F. Srayko, Les Hawrysh, Petro Bilyk, Safat Kaminsky, Yakiw Huchkowsky, Yakiw Manyk, Hryh. Vizniuk, Aleksander Rypchynsky, Antin and Nykola Ternowsky, Kyrylo Klepak, Stepan Rogozinsky, Vasyl Mukanyk, Mykhailo Cherepakha, Stepan Chorney, Vasyl Chepurda, Ivan Rachynsky, Tomko Prokopiw, I. Zhuravynsky, Nykola Pustey, Oleksander Tanaska, Zakhar Vozniak, Ivan Hladiy, Ivan Rawlyk,

Ivan Lazarovych, Dmytro Bytskalo, Ivan Huzan, Hawrylo Orlitsky(?), Mykhailo Mykhalkiw.

8 Ibid., pp. 311-316.

9 Ibid., p. 317.

10 The following were early settlers in Sokal: Hryhory Vashchuk, Ivan Sarchuk, Roman Shewchuk, Pylyp and Ivan Mamchur, Stepan Makohon, Fedir Bodnarchuk, Panko Sheremata, Vasyl Shewchuk, Voytko Vilkhovy, Makar Ostapchuk, Ivan and Antin Vawryk, Dmytro Kulyk, Vasyl Hrynevych, Prokip Mamchur, Ivan Vintonyk, Pawlo Zarytsky, Fedir Skopyk, Paraskevia Sheremata, Mykhailo Zholinsky, Hryhory and Andriy Vorobets, and others.

11 V. I. Borsa, who was born and raised in Bonne Madone, reported that four of the original five families in Bonne Madone were as follows: I. Voitsikhowsky, I. Tomashewsky, I. Borsa, and Emil Bilinsky, the last becoming a priest with Bishop Seraphim. He related further that the following four families from Bukovyna also settled there: Petro Tomniak, Yurko Budnyk, Kostyniuk, and Penteliuk. In 1903 they were joined by immigrants from the village of Stoianiv in the county of Radekhiv. These were I. Stelmashchuk, Marko Hawryliuk, Petro Karasiuk, Ilko Matviychuk, Goliansky, and others.

12 Some of these settlers were as follows: Dm. Cherniawsky, Hr. Holinaty, Y. Lutsiuk, Todor and Yurko Hnid, I. Kvasnytsia, Yurko, Nykola, and Mykhailo Balion, Vasyl, Ivan, and Dmytro Oleksyn, Todor and Andriy Burekhailo, Vasyl and Ivan Chopiuk, Oleksa Mykytiuk, Vasyl Sydoriuk, Ivan Danchuk, Vasyl Berezowsky, Nykola Komeniuk, Stefan Kushneryk, Rudiychuk, Shchitka, and Shcherbyn. Somewhat later came Mykh. and Vasyl Kokhan.

13 It appears as if the colony of Meacham was first settled by Izydor Novosad who arrived in 1903 to live on a homestead in Bonne Madone but moved to Meacham two years later. He was followed by Ivan Lazarovych, who moved to Wakaw later, Petro Ivasiuk, and Ivan Vasylyk. In 1906 the following came to Meacham: Vasyl Romanchych, Antin and Yosef Markowsky, Pawlo Bodnarchuk, and A. Kliukevych. They were followed later by Oleksa Kozak, Fedir and Mykhailo Trischuk, Ivan Soroka, F. Konovalyk, Kost Tokarchuk, Yustyn Tomashchuk, Nykola Metropolyt, Vasyl Hawrysh, Yurko Troyan, I. Vasyltsiw, and others.

14 The Doukhobors called their village Petrowka. They established their villages on homesteads where they lived a communal life. In time, individuals dissociated themselves from the group, abandoned the villages, and lived independently on homesteads like other settlers. The village of Petrowka disappeared and no trace of it or the other Doukhobor villages remains. The inhabitants of these early villages can now be found in the districts of Blaine Lake, Marcelin, and Leask. Ukrainians recall gratefully the kindness of the Doukhobors who were very hospitable to early Ukrainian settlers travelling from Rosthern through Petrowka where they stayed overnight. Peter Makaroff, a lawyer in Saskatoon, often related how these early settlers were accommodated in the home of Hryshka Makaroff, his father. There were often so many guests in their house that there was no place for the family to sleep.

15 This information was furnished by Yosef Bazarkevych who was secretary-treasurer of the village of Krydor for many yeras and had the opportunity to learn much about its early settlers. To the early group also belong Hryts and Roman Zherebetsky from the county of Sokal and Stepan Tesliuk from the county of Horodenka.

16 Pysklyvets, Temniak, and Kinash arrived in Canada with the first transport of Ukrainians sent by Oleskiw to Edna in Alberta. They were persuaded by an Orthodox priest, Rev. Yakiw Korchinsky, to emigrate to Russia with the assurance that they could obtain land for settlement. When they could not obtain land as had been promised, they returned to Canada and settled in Saskatchewan.

17 In addition to the Hawryshes who moved to the Redberry colony in 1905, the following also settled with their families: Petro Bilyk, Nykola Gramiak, Ilko Bilyk and his son Yurko, Mykhailenko with his son Matiy, Matiy Lazorko, F. Andrushko, Petro Babchuk, Dmytro Mukanyk with his son Mykhailo, Vasyl Katerynych, and others. In 1906 Ivan Yurashyk moved here from Fish Creek and was followed by Nykola Lazarovych with his sons, Vasyl, Dmytro, and Hryhory.

In 1907 these former residents of the village of Bereziv were joined by their countrymen Vasyl and Dmytro Suliatysky, and also by Mykhailo and Dmytro Symchych.

18   From the village of Ninovychi, county of Sokal, there came in 1905 Yurko Kharko with his sons, Petro, Vasyl, and Antin, also Petro Tsiura with his sons Ivan and Demko. They all settled south of Krydor. On the invitation of Yurko Kharko, his brother Petro Kharko with his sons, Mykhailo and Ivan, came a year later and also settled at Krydor. Two weeks later Hryhory Sagansky followed with his sons, Pylyp and Pawlo, and his son-in-law, Stepan Romaniuk. Yustyn Worobec recalls that he arrived in Canada in the company of Petro Kharko in 1906 but remained behind to obtain work in Winnipeg and did not reach Krydor until 1907. When he arrived in Krydor, he found two other settlers there, Teodor Lutsyk and Anton Chekhnita. Some of the settlers who arrived later are Parkhom, Krysak, Voytovych, Harakh, Bashuk, and Borytsky.

19   The following belong to the early group with families in Whitkow: Emil Sokhatsky, who came from Manitoba in 1907; Stepan Nykyforuk, with his sons, Dmytro, Mykhailo, Andriy, and Pawlo, all of whom moved here from Radisson in 1910; Mykyta Napasniuk, Voytko and Mykhailo Kozlowsky, also Vasyl and Stepan Kovalchuk, all of whom arrived in 1911. About the same time also came Ivan Kindrachuk, Dmytro Kotyk with his son Petro, Onufry, Matiy, and Fedir Tokaryk, Ivan Dmytruk, Mykhailo Tuchak, Dmytro Pidverbetsky, Mykola Nykyforuk, Ivan Kovalsky and his sons, Mykola and Mykhailo, Ivan Pokhodzilo, Mykhailo Holiak, the Buziak brothers — Yasko, Stepan, Petro, Leon, and Mykola. Later arrivals were Prokip Swystun with his son Sylvester, Filemon Andrushchak, and Maksym Stashyn with his son Mykhailo.

20   To the pioneers of Alticane belong the following settlers who arrived there in 1913: Ivan Keyko, Hryts Khmelnyk, and Ksenia Vudkevych. Other known pioneers are Fedir Tsalyn, Mykhailo Bilash with his sons, Stepan, Mykola, and Dmytro, Ivan Verezhak, Fedir Kossak, Yuriy Bytskal, Ivan Moskalyk, Vasyl Kovalchuk, Mykyta Tsukh, Ivan Karpiuk, and P. Nykyforuk.

CHAPTER XVI

1   A. S. Morton, *History of Prairie Settlement,* pp. 99. Morton states that the railway was started from Portage la Prairie in 1881 and reached Gladstone in the same year. In 1883 it was continued through Neepawa to Minnedosa, and in 1886 through Russel to Langenburg and Saltcoats. By 1890, it was completed as far as Yorkton.

2   Kaye, *Early Ukrainian Settlements,* p. 249. The author reports that 353 adults and 194 children arrived on the *Armenia* while another 398 adults and 171 children arrived on the *Palatia,* a total of 1116 people.

3   Ibid., p. 254. The delegates who inspected the land and signed the statement were Ivan Bukatchuk, Fedir Burtnyk, Sylvester Vasylyniuk, and Vasyl Kostyniuk.

4   The immigration hall in Winnipeg could not accommodate all the immigrants from the two vessels. Additional space for lodging was found in the vacant Dufferin school on the corner of Logan and Salter.

5   Marunchak, *Studii do istorii ukraintsiv Kanady,* vol. 2, p. 290. Proutt's assertion that Strathclair was the last railway station is not correct. As mentioned earlier in this chapter, the railway had been extended to Yorkton nine years previously.

6   Kaye, *Early Ukrainian Settlements,* p. 256. Kaye quotes Speers' letter which definitely states that the immigrants were transported on fourteen wagons. Relying on Proutt's information (Proutt was one of the guides on the wagon train), Marunchak claims in *Studii,* vol. 2, p. 291 that there were twenty wagons. Speers' claim would appear to be more authentic as his report was written when the events were fresh in his mind. On the other hand it may be that fourteen wagons were for the immigrants alone and the others could have been used to transport officials and supplies.

7   Eudokiya Anderson, the daughter of Fedir Tokaryk, a girl of nineteen when these

tragic events took place, recalls that the Holovetskys did not have any more children in Canada and experienced only sorrow and tragedy in their new home. Holovetsky's wife could not endure the loss of her children and died three years later. She was followed by her husband not long after. Mrs. Anderson claims that no one died in her family because "we had a stove which mother insisted on buying before we left Winnipeg. This stove benefited not only our own family but others as well."

8   Marunchak, *Studii,* vol. 2, pp. 282-3.

9   Kaye, *Early Ukrainian Settlements,* p. 262.

10 Ibid., pp. 261-2.

11 Ibid., p. 259. On the basis of Proutt's statement Marunchak confirms that nine cows were bought but claims that none of them supplied any milk. Marunchak, *Studii,* vol. 2, p. 291.

12 There are few official records about the experiences of the immigrants in the first two weeks. Those that are available reveal that no medical services were provided, and that the officials were wholly involved in settling immigrants on the land as early as possible. It is probably on this account that James Proutt, in his conversation with Marunchak exclaimed, "It was dreadful and a shame!" Marunchak continued Proutt's story in Ukrainian. In it Proutt claims that people were treated like cattle and, after two weeks in the tent, only a few children below the age of ten were left. Marunchak then resumes Proutt's own story, "These were the most tragic moments of my life. I still hear the lament of the mothers." Ibid., pp. 283, 291, 293.

13 The second owner was Yakiw Maydanyk, known for his creation of the comic character of "Shtif Tabachniuk". Yakiw arrived to teach Olha school in 1915 and knew nothing of the tragic beginnings of this colony and its burial ground.

14 Marunchak, *Studii,* vol. 2, pp. 284-5. The author includes many interesting reminiscences from the period of Ukrainian settlement in this colony.

15 No one has collected or published an exact list of the first group of settlers. In addition to those quoted by Marunchak, we list the following whose names are remembered by those who still remain alive: Kindrat Shvaliuk, Yurko Ivanyshyn, Antin Danyliuk, Fedko Tokaryk, Dmytro Nychyk, Dmytro Lazorko, Petro Dyrbawka, Dmytro Verezhak, Ivan Boklashchuk, Pylyp Rusyn, Dmytro Maksymchuk, Yuzko Kotys, Demian Tsiura, Sylvak Sawchuk, Ivan Yavorsky, Semko and Ivan Yanyk, Yuzko Kuzniak, Adam Sitsinsky, Matsko Bewza, Mykyta Ivasiuk, Mykhailo Antonyshyn, Yasko Tverdokhlib, Mykola Kuzyk, Harasym Osadets, Vasyl Svystun, Andriy and Ivan Antonyshyn, Hryhory Madiuk, Ivan and Petro Koltutsky, Teodor Stebelsky, Panko Luhovy, M. Matiyeshyn, Hr. Berehulka, Yasko Kovaliuk, Kotyk, and Hrynkiw.

16 Among those who arrived later in the same year only the following are known: Roman and Hryhory Oleniuk, and Antin Krynitsky. There were others but they settled at Rossburn, Sandy Lake, and neighbouring districts.

17 Kaye, *Early Ukrainian Settlements,* p. 268.

18 Ibid.

19 The following are known of the group arriving in 1900: Fedko Barabash, Wasyl Kits, Stepan Derkach, P. Tverdun, P. Matsiyowsky, and St. Hnatiw.

20 Kaye, *Early Ukrainian Settlements,* p. 271.

21 Ibid. The following are among those arriving in 1901: Fedko Karasevych, M. Mykhailyshyn, Klymko Kaskiw, M. Kaskiw, Ivan Stadnyk, Vasyl and Yosef Dunets, Gresko Skavinsky, M. Danyliuk, and Ivan Bodnartsiw.

22 Ibid., p. 276.

23 Marunchak, *Studii,* vol. 2, pp. 304, 306, 308, and 322. The settlement around Olha, near Oakburn, was the largest. In this area the following eighteen families from the first transport settled in 1899: Andriy and Ivan Antonyshyn, Ivan Boklashchuk, Antin Danyliuk, Zakhar Dzhumaga, Yurko Ivanyshyn, Antin Kalyshyn, Ivan and Petro Koltutsky, Mykola Kuzyk, Panko Luhovy, Hryhory Madiuk, Mykola Maydaniuk, Dmytro Nychyk, Harasym Osadtsiw, Vasyl Svystun, Fedir Stebeletsky, and Fedko Tokaryk. They were later joined by Ivan

Hirchak, Ivan Golets, Mykyta Krysovaty, Vasyl Luhovy, Mykola Manuliak, Antin Pawchuk, Ivan Svyryda, and M. Chegus.

These were the first pioneers in Seech district: Fedir Barabash, Yosef, Stepan, and Maksym Gerelus, Stepan Derkach, Vasyl and Kost Kuts, Stepan and Yurko Karasevych, Petro and Stepan Matsiyowsky, Mykhailo Mykolayishyn, Franko Rudniak, Ivan Stadnyk, Vasyl Tverdun, and Pawlo Yaryshewsky.

The following are known to have been the first pioneers in Rossburn district: Hryhor and Mykhailo Hrankiwsky, Ivan Danyleyko, Ivan Klym, Damian Lazaruk, Mykhailo Leshchyshyn, S. Panas, Mykola Sidliar, Vasyl Shmyr, Andriy Shust, Dmytro Yaremiy, and Vasyl Yaskiw.

24 *Propamiatna knyha Ukrainskoho Narodnoho Domu u Vinnipegu,* p. 161.

25 Ibid., p. 157. This account indicates that Ukrainians arrived in this district at the beginning of 1900. However, Andrew Sawchuk of Sheho, Saskatchewan, affirms that he arrived in Huns Valley with his parents in 1899 and that they already found the following settlers there: Ilia Zakhidniak, who had arrived in 1896; Petro Haliarevych, who arrived in 1897; also Mykola Adamek, Ilia, Matey, and Mykhailo Baraniuk, Yosef Zakhidniak, Vasyl Ivasiuk, Andriy and Matey Labiuk, Matey Pasovysty, and D. Sverbyvus, all of them arriving in 1898. In 1899 there followed Stakh Balkowsky, Ivan Baryla, Mykhailo Bogora, Petro Bonsak, Mykola Vyshniowsky, Vasyl Volotsky, Vasyl Hrubey, Mykola Kostanchuk, Yurko Kostanchuk, Ivan Kryvetsky, Petro Owsianyk, Yurko Polishchuk, Yurko Rawliuk, Stepan Rebachok, Ivan Sloboda, Ivan Soroka, Aksentiy Todoruk, four Sawchuk brothers—Ilia, Matey, Safron, and Vasyl, and three Yakiwchuk—Ivan, Safron, and Yurko.

26 Ibid., p. 157. In this account we find that the church was built between 1923 and 1925 and that it was designed by Father Rue. It is 129 feet long and 90 feet wide. In the centre there is a large dome whose top is 150 feet above ground. The church has 10 doors, 135 windows, five altars, a number of vestries, and a number of choir elevations.

27 Ivan Vakhniak arrived in the Glenella district with his parents in 1907 and reports that Ukrainian settlement in this district began in 1899. He reports that the first settlers were Hrynko and Yatsko Glova. They were followed by the Turko brothers, Ivan, Fedir, and Danko; the Zhdany brothers, Stepan, Hrynko, Andriy, Petro, and Mykhailo; the Suly brothers, Ivan and Dmytro; the Kuzyk brothers, Semko and Stepan; the Kravets—Mykhailo and Ivan, M. Babinsky, Panko Stravonts, Bachevychs, Kopytkos and others.

28 Yuzyk, *The Ukrainians in Manitoba,* p. 39; N. J. Hunchak, *Canadians of Ukrainian Origin* (Winnipeg: Ukrainian Canadian Committee, 1945), pp. 109-13.

CHAPTER XVII

1 This recalls the story of an immigrant who was so overcome with nostalgia at leaving his homeland that he left his wife and children in an earth shelter in Saskatchewan in 1903 to return to his village. When his fellow villagers inquired why he had returned, he replied, "It is impossible to live where there is no God." A good deal of persuasion was required to convince him to return to his family in Canada. *Propamiatna knyha Ukrainskoho Narodnoho Domu u Vinnipegu],* p. 87.

2 These priests were fathers N. Dmytriw, P. Tymkevych, I. Zaklynsky, and V. Zholdak.

3 Fathers Filias, Dydyk, and Strotsky.

4 *Memoire sur les Tentatives de Schisme et d'Heresie au milieu des Ruthenes,* (Quebec, 1908). Father Delaere prepared two memoirs, the one quoted above and another in 1909. *Propamiatna knyha ukrainskoho narodu u Kanadi,* p. 40.

Bibliography

A. Sources in Ukrainian

Adamowska, Maria. "Pionerski harazdy v Kanadi" [Pioneer hardships in Canada], *Propamiatna knyha Ukrainskoho Narodnoho Domu v Vinnipegu* [Memorial volume of Ukrainian National Home in Winnipeg]. Winnipeg: Trident Press, 1949.

Arkas, Mykola. *Istoriia Ukrainy* [History of Ukraine]. Winnipeg: Ukrainian Publishing Company, 1920.

Author Unknown. "Pershyi ukrainskyi kanadets: Ivan Pylypiw z Nebylova" [The first Ukrainian Canadian: Ivan Pylypiw from Nebyliv], *In commemoration of the sixtieth anniversary of Ukrainians in Canada*. Winnipeg: Ukrainske Slovo, 1950.

Bachynsky, Julian. *Ukrainska immigratsiia v Zyednenykh Derzhavakh Ameryky* [Ukrainian immigration in the United States of America]. Lviv: Naukove Tovarystvo im. Shevchenka, 1914.

————. *Yak ya vydavaw "Ukrainsku emigratsiiu"* [How I published "Ukrainian Immigration"]. Lviv: Naklad Rady, 1930.

Bobersky, Ivan. "Pryiikhav u rotsi 1891" [He arrived in 1891], *Providnyk Almanack, 1933*. Winnipeg: St. Raphael's Society, 1933.

Bozhyk, Panteleymon. *Istoriia Ukrainskoi Emigratsii v Kanadi za chas vid 1890 do 1930* [History of Ukrainian Emigration]. Winnipeg: National Publishing Co., 1930.

————. *Tserkov Ukraintsiv v Kanadi* [The Ukrainian Church in Canada]. Winnipeg: Canadian Ukrainian Publishing Co., 1927.

Bryk-Deviatnytsky, Mykhailo. "Sotnyk Strilbytsky" [Captain Strilbytsky]. *Shliakh Peremohy* (Munich), nos. 6, 7, & 8, 1967.

Buchynsky, Dmytro. "Ukraintsi v Espanii" [Ukrainians in Spain], *Almanack of the Ukrainian National Association*. New Jersey: Svoboda Press, 1954.

Burianyk, Vasyl. "Do istorii ukrainskykh uchyteliv-pioneriv v Kanadi" [In relation to the history of Ukrainian pioneer-teachers in Canada]. *The New Chronicle* (Winnipeg), July-September, 1962.

Bychynsky, Zigmunt. *Istoriia Kanady* [History of Canada]. Winnipeg, 1928.

Chyzhevsky, Dmytro. *Istoriia ukrainskoi literatury* [History of Ukrainian literature]. New York: UVAN, 1956.

Chorneyko, Mykhailo. *Shchob ne zabuty* [Lest We Forget]. Saskatoon, Sask.: By the Author, 1942.

Chubaty, Mykola. *Kniazha Rus-Ukraina a vynyknennia trokh skhidnoslovianskykh natsii* [Principality of Rus-Ukraine and the origin of the three eastern-Slavonic nations]. New York: Organization for the Defence of the Four Freedoms of Ukraine, 1964.

Czumer, Wasyl. *Spomyny pro perezhyvannia pershykh pereselentsiv v Kanadi* [Reminiscences of the experiences of the first Ukrainian immigrants in Canada]. Edmonton, Alberta: By the Author, 1942.

Doroshenko, Dmytro. *Narys istorii Ukrainy,* tom 1 [Outline of Ukrainian history, vol. 1]. Warsaw: Ukrainskyi Naukovyi Instytut, 1932.

Dmytriw, Nestor. *Kanadiiska Rus* [Canadian Rus]. Mount Carmel, Pa.: Svoboda Press, 1897; reprinted ed., Winnipeg, Man.: Ukrainian Free Academy of Sciences, 1972.

Eleniak, Wasyl. "Pershi ukrainski imihranty v Kanadi" [The first Ukrainian immigrants in Canada], *Yuvileinyi kalendar ukrainskoi rodyny* [Jubilee almanack of the Ukrainian family]. Mundare, Alberta: Basilian Fathers, 1941.

Fedorchak, Sofia. "Spomyny pro Osypa Oleskova" [Reminiscences about Osyp Oleskiw], *The Prairie* [St. Raphael's Society Almanack, Winnipeg, 1928).

Herbest, Benedict. "Wypisania Drogi" [Charting the road], *Yuvileina knyha v 300 litni rokovyny Metropolyta Ipatiia Potiia* [Jubilee volume on the 300th anniversary of Metropolitan Ipatiy Potiy]. Lviv: Tovarystvo sv. Pavla, 1914.

Hrushevsky, Mykhailo. *Ilustrovana istoriia Ukrainy* [Illustrated history of Ukraine]. Kiev-Lviv: 1913.

Huculak, Mykhailo. "Ukrainets-spivtvorets kordoniv Kanady i Alasky" [A Ukrainian collaborator in the creation of the boundary between Canada and Alaska], *Biblioteka ukrainoznavstva,* XXIV [Library of Ukrainian studies, XXIV]. Toronto: Shevchenko Scientific Society, 1967.

Kholmsky, Ivan. *Istoriia Ukrainy* [History of Ukraine]. Munich: Shevchenko Scientific Society, 1949.

Kostomariv, Mykola. *Istoriia Ukrainy v zhyttiepysakh vyznachnishykh yeyi diyachiv* [History of Ukraine in the lives of its illustrious leaders]. Lviv: Naukove Tovarystvo im. Shevchenka, 1918.

Krawchuk, Petro. *Na novii zemli* [In a new land]. Toronto: Kraiovyi Vykonavchyi Komitet Tovarystva Obyednanykh Kanadtsiv, 1958.

Krypiakevych, Ivan. *Ohliad istorii Ukrainy* [Review of the history of Ukraine]. Kiev-Lviv-Vienna: Vydavnytstvo Vernyhora, 1919.

Kysilewsky, V. J. "Liudy z rannoi nashoi istorii, novi materialy do istorii ukrainskoho poselennia" [People of our early history, new information regarding Ukrainian settlement]. *Ukrainian News* (Edmonton), no. 1, 1964.

Leskiw, Philemon. *Pionerske zhyttia v Kanadi* [Pioneer life in Canada]. Winnipeg: Christian Press, 1953.

Likowsky, Edward. *Berestiiska Unia, 1596* [Union of Berest, 1596]. Lviv: Nakladom Chytalni im. M. Shashkevycha, 1916.

Marunchak, Mykhailo. *Studies in the History of Ukrainians in Canada,* vols. 1 & 2. Winnipeg: Trident Press, 1966-1967.

————. *Among Ukrainian Pioneers in Alberta.* Winnipeg: General Library UKT, 1964.

————. *Canadian Terebowlia.* Winnipeg: General Library UKT, 1964.

Metropolitan, Ilarion (Ivan Ohienko). *Slovo pro Ihoriv pokhid,* 2nd ed. [The tale of Ihor's Host]. Winnipeg: Society of Volyn, 1967.

Nazaruk, Osyp. *V lisakh Alberty i Skalystykh Horakh* [In Alberta forests and the Rocky Mountains]. Chicago: Sich Organization of the U.S.A., 1924.

————. *V naibilshim parku Skalystykh Hir* [In the largest park of the Rocky Mountains]. Chicago: Sich Organization of the U.S.A., 1924.

————. *Vchasna vesna v pivnichnii Alberti* [Early spring in northern Alberta]. Lviv: Ukrainska Khrystiyanska Orh., 1929.

Okulevich, H. *Ruskiye v Kanadie* [Russians in Canada]. Toronto: Izdania Hlavnoho Pravlenia Federatsii Ruskykh Kanadtsev, 1952.

Oleskiw, Osyp. *O emigratsii* [About emigration]. Lviv: Kachkovsky Society, 1895.

————. *Pro vilni zemli* [About free lands]. Lviv: Prosvita Society, 1895.

————. *Khliborobstvo za okeanom i pereselencha emigratsiia* [Agriculture beyond the ocean and transplanted emigrants]. Zhovkva, Halychyna: Z drukarni oo. Vasylian, 1896.

Pawlychyn, Ivan. "Z zhyttia ukrainskykh poselentsiv u pivnichnii Manitobi" [From the lives of Ukrainian settlers in northern Manitoba]. *Ukrainske Slovo* (Winnipeg), no. 8, 1965.

Polonska-Vasylenko, Natalia. *Vyznachni zhinky Ukrainy* [Illustrious women of Ukraine]. Winnipeg: Ukrainian Women's Association of Canada, 1969.

Romanchych, Dmytro. "Ukrainski kolonii v okruzi Davfyn" [Ukrainian colonies in Dauphin district], *Propamiatna knyha Ukrainskoho Narodnoho Domu v Vinnipegu* [Memorial volume of the Ukrainian National Home in Winnipeg]. Winnipeg: Narodny Dim [National Home], 1949.

Romaniuk, Ivan. "Pochatky nebylivskykh rodyn u Kanadi" [The beginnings of the Nebyliv families in Canada]. *Almanack of the "Ukrainian Voice"*, Winnipeg, 1942.

———. "Deshcho z zhyttia pershoi ukrainskoi oseli v Kanadi" [Something of the life in the first Ukrainian settlement in Canada]. *Illustrated Almanack of the "Ukrainian Voice"*, Winnipeg, 1939.

Romaniuk, Wasyl. "Spomyny" [Reminiscences]. *Ukrainian News* (Edmonton), no. 51, 1955.

Rudnyckyj, Jaroslaw. "Do pochatkiv ukrainskoho poselennia v Kanadi" [About the beginnings of Ukrainian settlement in Canada]. *Almanack of the "Canadian Farmer"*, Winnipeg, 1963.

———. "Materialy do ukrainsko-kanadyiskoi folklorystyky i dialektolohii" [Materials dealing with Ukrainian-Canadian folklore and dialectology. *Zbirnyk zakhodoznavstva*, tom 3 [A compilation of research on the west, vol. 3], Winnipeg: UVAN, 1956.

Salley, Dionisy. "Spomyny z Kanady: Doroha z Niu Yorku do Kanady" [Memories of Canada: journey from New York to Canada]. *Svoboda* (Mount Carmel, Pa.), nos. 29-33, 1896.

Savytsky, Ivan. *Yuvileina knyha v 300 litni rokovyny Metropolyta Ipatiia Potiia* [Jubilee volume on the 300th anniversary of Metropolitan Ipatiy Potiy]. Lviv: Tovarystvo sv. Pavla, 1914.

Shlepakov, A. M. *Ukrainska trudova emihratsiia v S.Sh.A. i Kanadi* [Emigration of Ukrainian labor in the U.S.A. and Canada]. Kiev: Akademiya Nauk, 1960.

S. P. H. "Pro pershoho ukraintsia na kanadiiskii zemli" [About the first Ukrainian on Canadian soil]. *Canadian Farmer* (Winnipeg), no. 7, 1965.

Stashyn, Mykhailo.	"Moi spomyny" [My reminiscences]. *Almanack of the "Ukrainian Voice"*, Winnipeg, 1938.
Stechishin, Julian.	*Twenty-five Years of the Petro Mohyla Ukrainian Institute in Saskatoon.* Winnipeg: P. Mohyla Institute, 1945.
Svoboda, Mount Carmel, Pa.	Nos. 18 & 39, 1896; nos. 16, 35, 38, 40, 44, & 45, 1897; nos. 2, 24, & 29, 1898.
Telman, I.	*U dalekii storoni* [In far-away lands]. Kiev: Radiansky Pysmennyk, 1956.
Terletsky, Omelian.	*Istoriia Ukrainskoi derzhavy* [History of the Ukrainian state]. Lviv: Uchitesia Braty Moi, 1923.
Tomashewsky, T.	"Bilshe svitla na zatemnenu spravu" [More light on an obscure matter]. *The Ukrainian Pioneer* (Edmonton), no. 1, 1956.
Tymkevych, Pavlo.	"Deshcho pro Kanadu" [A little about Canada]. *Svoboda* (Mount Carmel, Pa.), no. 29, 1898.
Ukrainian National Association.	*Propamiatna knyha* [Commemorative volume]. Jersey City: Ukrainian National Association, 1936.
Ukrainian Catholic Church.	*Propamiatna knyha poselennia ukrainskoho narodu v Kanadi* [Commemorative volume of the settlement of Ukrainians in Canada]. Yorkton, Sask.: The Voice of the Redeemer, 1941.
Ukrainian News (Edmonton).	No. 51, 1955.
Vihorney, A.	"Podorozh dovkola svitu" [A voyage around the world]. *Ukrainskyi kalendar na 1967 rik* [Ukrainian almanack for 1967]. Warsaw: Ukrainske suspilno-kulturne tovarystvo, 1967.
Vlasowsky, Ivan.	*Narys istorii Ukrainskoi Pravoslavnoi Tserkvy,* tom 1 [An outline of the history of the Ukrainian Orthodox Church, vol. 1]. New York: Ukrainian Orthodox Church of the U.S.A., 1955.
Woycenko, O.	*The Annals of Ukrainian Life in Canada.* Winnipeg: Trident Press, Ltd., 1961.
Yasenchuk, Lew.	*Za okeanom* [Beyond the Ocean]. Lviv: Ridna Shkola, 1930.
Zhluktenko, Y. O.	*Ukrainsko-anhliiski mizhmowni vidnosyny* [Ukrainian-English interlingual relations]. Kiev: Vydavnytstvo Kyivskoho Universytetu, 1964.

B. Sources in English and Other Languages

Bryce, G.	*The Old Settlers of the Red River.* Winnipeg: Manitoba Historical and Scientific Society, Transaction 19, Season 1885-1886.

Campbell, *Man! Man! Just Look At This Land!* Ellisboro Old-
Angelina Timers' Association, 1966.
Hughan. Census Reports, 1941.

Dafoe, J. W. *Clifford Sifton in Relation to His Times.* Toronto, 1931.

. *Encyclopedia Britannica,* Vol. 1, 1963 ed.

Forum: A Ukrainian Review. Scranton, Pa., vol. 1, winter 1967.

Free Press (Winnipeg), Oct. 16, 1909.

Gazeta Katolicka (Winnipeg), Nov. 2, 1909.

Gelner, John, and *The Czechs and Slovaks in Canada.* Toronto: University
Smerek, John. of Toronto Press, 1968.

Haiman, *Slady polskie w Ameryce* [Polish traces in America].
Mieczyslaw. Chicago: Dziennik Zjednoczenia, 1938.

Hawkes, John. *Saskatchewan and Its People,* vol. 2. Chicago-Regina: S. J. Clarke Publishing Company, 1924.

Hedges, J. B. *Building the Canadian West.* New York: McMillan and Co., 1939.

Hunchak, N. J. *Canadians of Ukrainian Origin.* Winnipeg: Ukrainian Canadian Committee, 1945.

Kaye, *Early Ukrainian Settlements in Canada 1895-1900.*
Vladimir, J. Toronto: University of Toronto Press, 1964.

Kirschbaum, *Slovaks in Canada.* Toronto: Canadian Ethnic Press
J. M. Association of Ontario, 1967.

Lisiansky, Urey. *A Voyage Around the World in the Years 1803-1806.* London: J. Booth, 1814.

Lord Selkirk Papers, vol. 15.

Luciw, W. *Ahapius Honcharenko.* Toronto: Slavia Library, 1963.

Lysenko, Vera. *Men in Sheepskin Coats.* Toronto: Ryerson Press, 1947.

McGregor, J. G. *Vilni Zemli.* Toronto: McClelland and Stewart, Ltd., 1969.

Makowski, *History and Integration of Poles in Canada.* Lindsay,
William Ont.: Canadian Polish Congress of Niagara Peninsula,
Boleslaus. 1967.

Marchbin, *Early Immigration from Hungary to Canada.* Slavonic
Andrew A. (and East European) Review, vol. 13, 1934-1935.

Mohr, Hilda. Josephburg Heritage, 1967. (Mimeographed).

Moorhouse, *Deep Furrows.* Toronto and Winnipeg: George J.
Hopkins. McLeod Publishers, 1918.

Morton, A. S. *History of Prairie Settlement.* Toronto: McMillan Company of Canada, 1938.

. *Manitoba. A history.* Toronto: University Press, 1967.

Pohorecky, "Ukrainians in Canada in the War of 1812 by Alexander
Zenon. Royick". *Forum: A Ukrainian Review,* vol. 1, no. 2, 1967.

Panchuk, John.	*Bukowinian Settlements in Southern Manitoba.* Battle Creek, Mich.: By the Author, 1971.
Reid, Robie L.	"Who Were the De Meurons?" *The Beaver. A Magazine of the North.* Winnipeg: Hudson's Bay Co., December, 1942.
Roberts, Charles G. D.	*A History of Canada.* Toronto: G. A. Morang Educational Co., Ltd., 1909.
Royick, Alexander.	"Horetzky's Contribution to Canadian History", *Slavs in Canada,* vol. 2, 1968. Toronto: Homin Ukrayiny, 1968.
————.	*Ukrainian Settlements in Alberta.* Canadian Slavonic Papers, vol. 10, no. 3, 1968.
Rudnickyj, J.	*Slavica Canadiana, Series Slavistika* no. 24. Winnipeg: UVAN, 1955, p. 15.
Semyonov, Yuri.	*Siberia, Its Conquest and Development.* Montreal: International Publishers' Representatives (Canada) Ltd., 1963.
	Slavistica, no. 24. Winnipeg: UVAN, 1955.
Slavutych, Yar.	*Conversational Ukrainian.* Winnipeg: Trident Press, 1960.
	The Canadian Magazine, Nov. 8, 1969.
Turek, Victor.	"Poles Among the De Meuron Soldiers". Papers read before the Historical and Scientific Society of Manitoba, Series III, no. 9, Winnipeg, 1954.
	Ukrainian Canadian Review (Winnipeg), vol. 8, nos. 3 & 4, 1942.
Woodsworth, J. S.	*Report of Investigation by Bureau of Social Research.* Winnipeg: Governments of Manitoba, Saskatchewan, and Alberta, 1917.
	Winnipeg Tribune: May 27, 1897.
Young, Charles H.	*The Ukrainian Canadians.* Toronto: Thomas Nelson and Sons, Ltd., 1931.
Yuzyk, Paul.	"The First Ukrainians in Manitoba." Paper read before the Historical and Scientific Society of Manitoba, Series III, no. 9, Winnipeg, 1954.
————.	*Ukrainian Canadians: Their Place and Role in Canadian Life.* Toronto: Ukrainian Canadian Business and Professional Organization, 1967.

Name Index

Names of Localities of Ukrainian Settlement

Glenella 182, 214
Glenfors 182
Glenhope 182-3
Grandview 147
Gretna 65, 75, 78-80, 90

Halycz 146-8
Hammerlick 153
Hodgson 151-3
Horod 181
Huns Valley 58-9, 71, 83, 96,
    181-2, 196, 214

Inglis 181
Inwood 151

Jaroslaw (Yaroslaw) 151, 160

Kaliento 134
Keld 145
Komarno 151
Koroliwka 140
Kossiw 145-6, 148
Kupchenko 140

Leonard 181
Lukiwtsi 140

Malonton 151
Marco 181, 183
Meleb 151
Menzie 181-2
Merridale 147
Minnedosa 58, 173, 175, 182, 196,
    212
Minnetonas 147
Mohyly 181, 183
Mountain Road district 58, 181-3

Neepawa 143, 156, 173, 182, 212
Newdale 181-2

Oakburn 173-4, 177, 181-3, 213
Obertal 65
Okno 151
Oleskiw 207
Olha 174, 181, 183, 213
Overstone 207

Ozerna 181, 183

Pearl Bank 140
Petlura 146, 181
Pine River 147
Pleasant Home 149-51, 155, 163,
    168-9, 172-3
Poplarfield 151-3
Postup 147

Rackham 182
Rembrandt 151
Ridgeville 140
Riding Mountain National Park
    174
Riding Mountain Reserve 145
Riding Mountains 141, 145-6, 173,
    181-2
Rigby 144, 147
Riverton 151
Roblin 147, 161
Rosa 140
Rossburn 173, 181-2, 213-14
Rus 134
Russell 159, 181-2, 199, 212
Ruthenia 181

St. Norbert 100
St. Rose 146
Sandiland 140
Sandy Lake 173, 181-2, 213
Sarto 140
Scandinavia 181
Seech 181, 183, 214
Selkirk 62-3, 71, 174
Shellmount 182
Shevchenko 140
Shoal Lake 156, 173-6, 182-3
Shorncliffe 151
Shortdale 147
Sifton 144-7, 167, 210
Silverton 182
Sky Lake 151
Slater 147
Steinbach 65
Stonewall 149

Jasmin 119-20

Kamsack 161
Kelliher 120
Kelvington 161
Krydor 163, 170, 172, 211-12
Kuroki 161
Kylemore 161

Langenburg 68, 75, 198, 212
Laniwtsi 169-70
Lemberg 98, 118-19, 204
Leofeldt 170-1
Lintlaw 161
Lorenzo 170

MacNutt 159
Margo 161
Mazepa 156, 160
Meacham 170, 211
Melfort 163
Melville 95, 120
Mikado 161
Mitchellview 161
Mullingar 172

Neudorf 43, 95, 98, 114-19, 203
    (see also Pheasant Forks)
New Jaroslaw (Yaroslaw) 160
Norquay 161
North Battleford 171-2

Okla 161

Parkerview 164
Pelly 161, 163
Pheasant Forks 95, 113-14, 116-21,
    124, 128, 133, 172-3, 203-4
Ponass Lake 161
Porcupine Plain 161
Preeceville 161
Prelate 163
Prince Albert 172, 210
Prud'homme 170-1

Quill Lake 161

Rabbit Lake 172
Radisson 163, 171, 212

Rama 161
Rat Portage 114
Redberry 162-4, 211
Redberry Lake 163, 170-2
Redfield 171
Regina 125, 166-7, 188, 210
Reserve 161
Reynaud 170
Rhein 160
Richard 172
Rose Valley 161
Rosthern 163, 166-71, 210-11

St. Denis 170 (see also Dana)
St. Julien 163, 169
Saltcoats 101, 104-5, 149, 156-8,
    212
Saskatoon xiv-xv, 110, 120, 166-7,
    171, 200, 202-4, 210-11
Sheho 120, 156-7, 164, 210, 214
Sliding Hills 162, 164
Sokal 169-70, 211
Speers 172
Square Hill 172
Stanislawtsi (see Bedfordville)
Steen 161
Stenen 161
Stornoway 157, 159, 161
Sturgis 161
Swan Plain 161

Tiny 161
Tarnopol 170
Tadmore 161
Theodore 156-7, 164
Tway 170

Usherville 161

Veregin 161
Vonda 170-1

Wadena 161
Wakaw 169-70, 211
Watrous 120
Watson 161